Patterns, Programming and Everything

Karin K. Breitman • R. Nigel Horspool
Editors

Patterns, Programming and Everything

Springer

Editors
Karin K. Breitman
Informatics Department
PUC-Rio
Rio de Janeiro, RJ, Brazil

R. Nigel Horspool
Department of Computer Science
University of Victoria
Victoria, BC, Canada

ISBN 978-1-4471-2349-1 ISBN 978-1-4471-2350-7 (eBook)
DOI 10.1007/978-1-4471-2350-7
Springer London Heidelberg New York Dordrecht

Library of Congress Control Number: 2012938227

Printed on acid-free paper

Springer is part of Springer Science+Business Media (www.springer.com)

Foreword

I was absolutely delighted to be asked to write the forward to this book, which is a tribute to a friend, a colleague and a great computer scientist.

I have known Judith since we did our PhDs together at the University of Southampton. We both graduated in 1977 from the Department of Mathematics. I was studying Pure Mathematics, Judith was one of the minority in the Department studying the new subject of Computer Science and she has been a pioneer of the subject ever since.

She came to Southampton from South Africa to work with David Barron. In those days they were breaking new ground by developing new compiler techniques to overcome the disastrous performance issues of the computers of that era. The significance of the work was demonstrated through its take up by industry. After her PhD was finished, Judith quickly grasped the significance of the newly emerging Ada programming language for distributed programming—a topic which few were ready to recognise or grapple with at the time—and became an international expert in the development of the language in no time at all. Her book writing career started around this time with her monograph on Data Abstraction in Programming Languages.

She continued to develop her ideas about distributed programming and parallel computing throughout the 1980's during which time we both found ourselves back at Southampton working in the Department of Computer Science. Judith was a tremendous help to me at the time because of her wealth of experience in research and teaching computer science. I was a new comer to the field and found her books on programming, particularly Pascal which was the standard teaching language of the time, both easy to read and incredibly rich in practical examples. She managed to bring the language alive to her readers, which is something that seems to elude most authors of computer science texts.

Always ahead of the crowd, she spotted the importance of Java in the post-Web era, and wrote the first Java text-book. Her work on Java web-frameworks was taken up by industry and put her and her team at Pretoria firmly on the international map. She then moved onto the world of .NET and C#. Her work in this area was very highly valued by Microsoft, and she was frequently asked to speak at meetings organised by the company—a portent of things to come.

Through her books, her frequent appearance at conferences and her work on international committees such as IFIP, Judith became very well known on the international stage. Her books have been translated into five other languages and sold around the world. She is always one of the first to spot new trends in computer science and to both apply them in her research and introduce them to her students and the wider world through her books.

As one would expect from reading her textbooks, Judith is a wonderful teacher. She really cares about her students and works to instil in them the love for computer science she has herself. She is also a very experienced research supervisor and her students can now be found in any number of research laboratories around the world. Over the years, her work has been taken up and used by industry and she was a valued industrial consultant. Building on this and ever ready for a challenge, Judith moved both continents and career paths to join Microsoft Research as Director of Computer Science in 2009. She has thrown herself into this new role with her usual mix of enthusiasm and professionalism and has made the role very much her own.

Having talked so much about her career and the impact she has had on the international computer science community, I must also add that Judith is one of the kindest most generous people it has been my privilege to work with and I am proud to be able to call her one of my closest friends. She gives far more than she takes from her interactions with everyone she meets.

The list of authors of the papers in this book is testament to the fact that so many leading computer scientists around the world feel the same way as I do.

Southampton, UK Wendy Hall

Preface

This volume contains contributions written by authors who have all worked in some capacity with Judith Bishop during her distinguished career. When Judith reached a certain milestone in her age (and we will leave the reader to figure out which one), we had the idea of putting together this book in recognition of her career and her accomplishments. We contacted various researchers and industry professionals who have worked with Judith and asked them if they would be willing to contribute material for this book. Their responses were overwhelmingly positive. Please note that we made a deliberate decision not to invite any colleagues from her current employer, Microsoft Research, to contribute material as this might have led to conflict of interest issues. However we made an exception for Tony Hey who is Judith's superior at Microsoft Research; he graciously agreed to provide an Afterword for this volume. Since Tony represents the last place where Judith has worked, we thought that it would be symmetric to have a Foreword from someone at the first place where she worked. That someone is Wendy Hall from the University of Southampton. We are grateful to her too.

The material in this book spans a wide variety of research areas. The variety reflects the many research interests of Judith and her collaborators, and also reflects her transitions from one important research area to another over the course of her career. We have also included two contributions which are anything but Patterns (or Programming). We leave it to the reader to discover which ones these are. We hope you will find them to be as amusing as we did.

We thank every author for contributing their time and energy into helping this book come to fruition. We also thank Springer for publishing this volume and for providing their help.

Victoria, Canada — R. Nigel Horspool
Rio de Janeiro, Brazil — Karin Breitman

Contents

Contributors

Marco Autili Dipartimento di Informatica, Università degli Studi di L'Aquila, L'Aquila, Italy

John Aycock Department of Computer Science, University of Calgary, Calgary, Alberta, Canada

Róbert Béládi Department of Software Engineering, University of Szeged, Szeged, Hungary

Vilmos Bilicki FrontEndART Software Ltd, Szeged, Hungary

K. John Gough School of Computer Science, Queensland University of Technology, Brisbane, Australia

Thomas Gschwind Zurich Research Laboratory, IBM, Rüschlikon, Switzerland

Tibor Gyimóthy Department of Software Engineering, University of Szeged, Szeged, Hungary

Mathias Hedenborg School of Computer Science, Mathematics, and Physics, Linnaeus University, Växjö, Sweden

Mike Hinchey Lero–the Irish Software Engineering Research Centre, University of Limerick, Limerick, Ireland

Paola Inverardi Dipartimento di Informatica, Università degli Studi di L'Aquila, L'Aquila, Italy

Miklós Kasza Department of Software Engineering, University of Szeged, Szeged, Hungary

Derrick G. Kourie Fastar Research Groups, Department of Computer Science, University of Pretoria, Pretoria, South Africa

Welf Löwe School of Computer Science, Mathematics, and Physics, Linnaeus University, Växjö, Sweden

Jonas Lundberg School of Computer Science, Mathematics, and Physics, Linnaeus University, Växjö, Sweden

Bertrand Meyer ITMO & Eiffel Software, ETH Zurich, Zürich, Switzerland

Zoltán Rak FrontEndART Software Ltd, Szeged, Hungary

Massimo Tivoli Dipartimento di Informatica, Università degli Studi di L'Aquila, L'Aquila, Italy

Emil Vassev Lero–the Irish Software Engineering Research Centre, University of Limerick, Limerick, Ireland

Ádám Végh Department of Software Engineering, University of Szeged, Szeged, Hungary

Jan Vitek Computer Science Faculty, Purdue University, West Lafayette, USA

Bruce W. Watson FASTAR Research Group, Center for Knowledge Dynamics and Decision-Making, Stellenbosch University, Stellenbosch, Republic of South Africa

Assessing Dependability for Mobile and Ubiquitous Systems: Is There a Role for Software Architectures?

Marco Autili, Paola Inverardi, and Massimo Tivoli

Abstract A traditional research direction in Software Architecture (SA) and dependability is to deduce system dependability properties from the knowledge of the system SA. This well reflects the fact that traditional systems are built by using the closed world assumption. In mobile and ubiquitous systems this line of reasoning becomes too restrictive to apply due to the inherent dynamicity and heterogeneity of the systems under consideration. Indeed, these systems need to relax the closed world assumption and to consider an open world where the system context is not fixed. In other words, the assumption that the system SA is known and fixed at an early stage of the system development might be a limitation. On the contrary, the ubiquitous scenario promotes the view that systems are built by dynamically assembling available components. System dependability can then at most be assessed in terms of components' assumptions on the system context. This requires the SA to be dynamically induced by taking into consideration the specified dependability and the context conditions. This paper will illustrate this challenge and, by means of an illustrative scenario, will discuss a possible research direction.

1 Introduction

A traditional research direction in Software Architecture (SA) and dependability is to deduce system dependability properties from the knowledge of the system SA. Taking into account characteristics and properties (e.g., failure rate, performance in-

This work is supported by the European Community's Seventh Framework Programme FP7/2007-2013 under grant agreement number 231167 (project CONNECT—http://connect-forever.eu/).

M. Autili (✉) · P. Inverardi · M. Tivoli
Dipartimento di Informatica, Università degli Studi di L'Aquila, L'Aquila, Italy
e-mail: marco.autili@di.univaq.it

P. Inverardi
e-mail: paola.inverardi@di.univaq.it

M. Tivoli
e-mail: massimo.tivoli@di.univaq.it

K.K. Breitman, R.N. Horspool (eds.), *Patterns, Programming and Everything*,
DOI 10.1007/978-1-4471-2350-7_1, © Springer-Verlag London 2012

dexes, responsiveness, etc.) of the components constituting the system and how they are assembled together, the goal of the dependability analysis is to predict the values of dependability attributes. Following this line of research, architects, designers and developers usually realize dependable systems by adopting a software development process where models for dependability analysis are generated by considering the *a priori specified* systems SA. This well reflects the fact that traditional systems are built by using the closed world assumption which says that (at least part of) the system context is a priori known and the information concerning the overall structure of the system can be taken into account early at design time [8]. In Mobile And Ubiquitous Systems (MAUS) [10, 11] this line of reasoning becomes too restrictive to apply due to the inherent dynamicity and heterogeneity of the systems under consideration.

During the last few years, the distribution of communicating mobile devices is accelerating, and the ever growing ubiquity of software is fostering the possibility for the dynamic connection to "almost everything", anywhere, anytime. This means that heterogeneous components (everything) can be put together in unknown contexts (anywhere) at an unforeseen point in time (anytime). That is, MAUS need to relax the closed world assumption and to consider an open world where the system context is not fixed. In other words, the assumption that the SA is known and fixed at an early stage of the system development might be a limitation. On the contrary, mobility and ubiquity shift the focus of systems development from coding and statically assembling components (according to a preestablished SA) to dynamically composing systems out of available components. System dependability can then at most be assessed in terms of components' assumptions on the system context. This requires the SA to be dynamically induced by taking into consideration the specified dependability and the context conditions. Furthermore, the assembling process of MAUS can be no longer assumed to be handled by IT experts only. Rather, end users play a crucial role prior to and after the composition process, and changes to their needs, as much as in context of use, should be adequately handled. Note that, in principle, it might be possible to build self-contained applications that embed the adaptation logic as a part of the application itself. Therefore, while conforming to a fixed SA, these applications are a-priori instructed on how to handle dynamic changes in the context and user needs, hence reacting to them at run time. However, because of the open nature of MAUS, it is not feasible to predict all the possible changes in the context and user needs, which are unforeseen by their very nature. This paper discusses the above challenges and, by means of an illustrative scenario, shows how the role of SA is inverted in the context of MAUS.

The paper is organized as follows: Sect. 2 introduces the terminology and briefly provides background notions concerning MAUS. Section 3 discusses the challenge of assessing dependability for MAUS. Section 4 illustrates this challenge by means of a sample scenario in the e-learning domain. Section 5 gives concluding remarks discussing possible future research directions.

2 MAUS: Mobile And Ubiquitous Systems

When building a traditional closed system the system's context is determined and the (non-functional) requirements (operational, social, organizational constraints) take the context into account. On the contrary, MAUS [10, 11] are *open systems* in the sense that they have to deal with both possible changes in the *context* and *user needs*. Examples of context can be the network context conditions and the execution environment offered by the mobile devices. User needs can be expressed in terms of *dependability* requirements (i.e., availability, reliability, safety, and security requirements). For example, availability can be expressed in terms of performance indexes such as responsiveness, throughput, service utilization. If the context and user needs change, then the system requirements change and, hence, the system itself needs to change accordingly. Thus changes in the context and user needs might imply system evolution, e.g., architectural configuration changes (e.g., addition/arrival, replacement, removal/departure of system components). The system needs to change at run-time, while it is operating. This can be achieved through (self-) adaptiveness. For instance, Sect. 4 gives an example on how the throughput, considered as a dependability attribute, can affect the way available software components should be assembled in order to make a system up while fitting the dependability requirements according to the user preferences and context of use.

Different kinds of changes at different levels of granularity, from SA to code, can occur. In this paper we focus on architectural configuration changes. We will show that, by considering context changes in conjunction with the user needs, it is unfeasible to fix/choose a specific architectural configuration at an early stage in order to fulfill the dependability requirements and retain the configuration during the system execution. On the contrary, the ubiquitous scenario promotes the view that systems can be dynamically composed out of available components possibly accounting for dependability requirements. This view is promoted because dependability can at most be assessed in terms of components' assumptions on the system context and the "best" (w.r.t. dependability requirements) architectural configuration can only be dynamically induced by taking into consideration the respective assumptions of the system components'. That is, for MAUS, it can be unfeasible to fix a priori the SA and, then, deduce dependability since, e.g., due to changes in the context, the experienced dependability might be not the wished one. A scenario in which this phenomenon can occur is discussed in Sect. 4. Then our thesis is that for MAUS the role of the SA is to provide the *dynamic* composition rules that dictate how to compose (resp., reconfigure) the system in order to achieve (resp., keep) the wished dependability, despite the context changes. That is, the SA is induced by a high-level specification of the wished dependability degree. As discussed in more detail in the following section, this introduces a new challenge concerning how to assess dependability for MAUS by the dynamic induction of the SA that fulfills as best as possible the specified dependability.

3 The Challenge of Assessing Dependability for Mobile and Ubiquitous Systems

MAUS are supposed to execute in an ubiquitous, heterogeneous infrastructure with no mobility constraints. This means that the software must be able to carry on operations while changing different execution environments or contexts. Execution contexts offer a variability of resources that can affect the software operation. *Context awareness* refers to the ability of an application to *sense* the context in which it is executing and therefore it is the base to consider (self-)adaptive applications, i.e., software systems that have the ability to change their *behavior* in response to external changes.

It is worthwhile stressing that although a change of context is measured in quantitative terms, an application can only be adapted by changing its behavior, i.e., its functional/qualitative specification. Section 4 shows an example indicating how context changes can lead to changes in the system's functionalities when trying to bind quantitative aspects of the system. For instance, (physical) mobility allows a user to move out of his proper context, traveling across different contexts and, to our purposes, the difference among contexts is determined in terms of available resources like connectivity, energy, software, etc. (see Sect. 4). However, other dimensions of contexts can exist relevant to the user, system and physical domains, which are the main context domains identified in the literature [9]. In standard software systems the pace at which context changes is slow and the changes are usually taken into account as evolutionary requirements. As already mentioned in Sect. 2, for MAUS, context changes occur due to physical mobility while the system is in operation. This means that if the system needs to change this should happen dynamically.

MAUS need also to be dependable. *Dependability* is an orthogonal issue that depends on QoS attributes, like performance and all other *-bilities*. Dependability impacts all the software life cycle. In general dependability is an attribute for software systems that operate in specific application domains. For MAUS, we consider dependability in its original meaning as defined in [7], that is *the trustworthiness of a computing system which allows reliance to be justifiably placed on the service it delivers… Dependability includes such attributes as reliability, availability, safety, security*. MAUS encompass any kind of software system that can operate in the future ubiquitous infrastructure. The dependability requirement is therefore extended also to applications that traditionally have not this requirement. Dependability in this case represents the user requirement that states that the application must operate in the unknown world (i.e., out of a confined execution environment) with the same level of reliance it has when operating at home. At home means in the controlled execution environment where there is complete knowledge of the system behavior and the context is fixed. In the unknown world, the knowledge of the system is undermined by the absence of knowledge about contexts, thus the dependability requirement arises also for conventional applications. Traditionally, dependability is achieved with a comprehensive approach all along the software life cycle from requirements to operation to maintenance by analyzing models, testing code, monitor and repair execution. Traditionally, SA is considered as the *earliest* comprehensive system model along the software lifecycle built from requirements specification. It is increasingly part of standardized software development processes because it represents a system abstraction in which design choices relevant to the correctness of the final system are taken. This is particularly evident for dependability requirements like security and reliability, and quantitative ones like performance. As already said, for MAUS, the assumption that the system SA is known and fixed at an early stage of the system development might imply that, in given contexts, it is not possible to obtain a dependable application without changing the SA. Thus, the overall challenge, in assessing dependability for MAUS, concerns the problem of making systems up by assembling available components whose dependability can at most be assessed in terms of their assumptions on the system context. In this setting, it is crucial to dynamically and efficiently induce the SA by taking into consideration the respective assumptions of the system components. The following section illustrates this challenge by means of an example concerning the development of MAUS for the e-learning domain.

4 An e-Learning Scenario

In the scenario of MAUS, service mash-up and widget User Interfaces (UIs) represent technologies attempting to shift system composition activities, out of a set of ready-to-use components and underlying composition mechanisms, from static time to run time, and from the developer level to the end-user level. Thus, they might be considered promising technologies to ease the consideration of user-level dependability requirements during system composition. However, the current limitation of these technologies is that, even though they provide higher-level composition mechanisms (e.g., widget drag-and-drop), they do not allow one to deduce the "best possible" architectural configuration from dependability requirements. On the contrary, what currently happens is that the user chooses the architectural configuration (i.e., the set of widgets and the way they have to be connected) and then experiences the resulting "offered dependability". Thus, service mash-up and widget UIs are technologies still conceived to be used by deducing system dependability properties from the system architectural configuration chosen/fixed a priori. Indeed, while keeping a high-level composition mechanism, those technologies should (i) allow the user to specify the dependability requirements, and (ii) propose the composition that fulfills, as best as possible, dependability and keep it despite possible context changes.

In the following, by considering widget UIs in an e-learning application context, we sketch two possible scenarios illustrating: (a) how an architectural configuration fixed a priori can imply a, possibly unexpected, problem and (b) how, instead, a dependability requirement can induce the "best possible" architectural configuration.

Marco is a student traveling from Italy to Canada. While on the train to the airport, he wants to start an e-learning session through his stand-alone e-learning client, as deployed upon registration to the e-learning service.

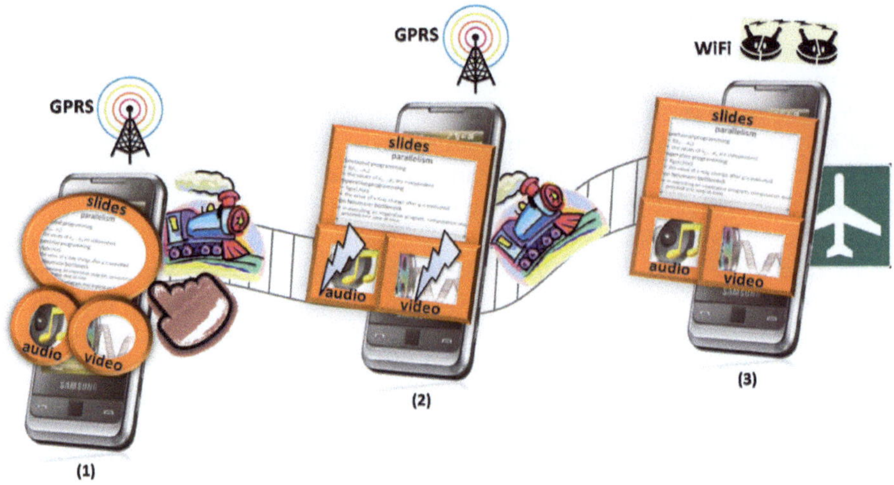

Fig. 1 e-learning scenario (a)

► **Scenario (a)**: The e-learning client allows Marco to directly mash up widgets to create lesson structure and add powerful online-test widgets, communication widgets (chat, forum and personal messages), content scheduling widgets, and activity tracking, announcements, content flows, cooperative content building widgets.

Foreground: Marco takes up his smartphone and connects, through his e-learning client, to the e-learning service to get the latest available lesson of the Computer Science course. Marco wishes to directly mash-up widgets to experience a fully featured lesson. Thus, acting with his smartphone, Marco drags from the widget repository and drops into the e-learning client UI all the widgets needed for providing video, audio and other multimedia content (Fig. 1(1)). Unfortunately, while in the train, Marco realizes that slides are correctly shown (by the slide displaying widget), but video and audio are stuttered and not synchronized with the current slide (Fig. 1(2)). Upon reaching the airport Marco recharges his smartphone and he tries again to use the previously built widget mash-up and he is surprised to be able to enjoy video, audio and other multimedia content of the fully featured version (Fig. 1(3)). As a result, Marco does not trust the e-learning service and judges it as non-dependable since it is not as trustworthy as wished.

Behind the scenes: The system configuration (i.e., the widget components mash-up) that Marco has directly built, requires a high level battery state-of-charge and a fast connection speed to properly work. Unfortunately, considering the current network condition, only a (low-speed) GPRS connection can be established and, hence, the built system is able to only display slides with stuttered audio and video, and not synchronized video and audio. Upon reaching the airport, the system Marco is using relies on the same architectural configuration but, since now the battery is fully charged and a fast WiFi network is in range, the configuration is able to properly show video, reproduce audio and show other multimedia content. This highlights that an architectural configuration chosen a priori might ensure a certain degree of

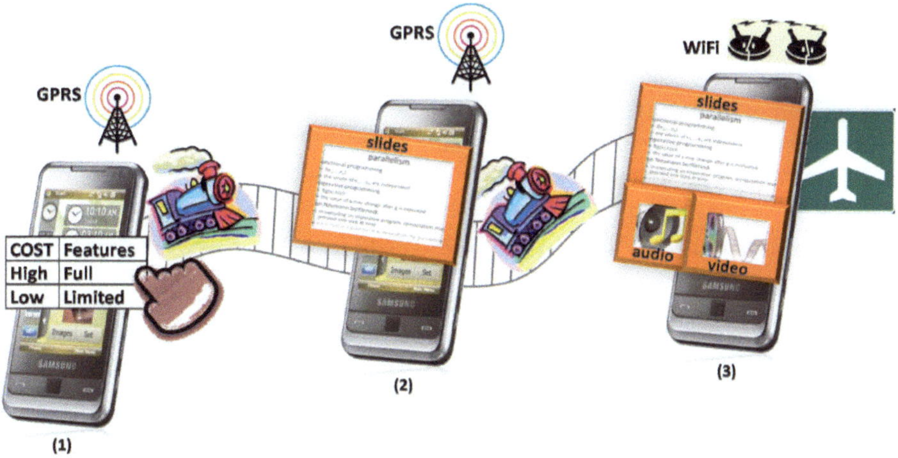

Fig. 2 e-learning scenario (b)

dependability only under specific context conditions and, hence, it is not suitable for an open environment.

► **Scenario (b)**: The e-learning client allows Marco to specify dependability requirements in terms of a notion of cost of the chosen solution depending on both the network connection speed, i.e., **throughput**, and lesson content, i.e., **size**. We recall that availability, as dependability attribute, can be expressed in terms of performance indexed such as throughput. The client lets the e-learning service propose the widget components and their composition that represent the "best possible" mash-up with respect to the specified cost, the current network context (e.g., type of network in reach), and the execution environment context (e.g., battery state-of-charge). This scenario is inspired by the scenario presented in [1] where we use the CHAMELEON framework [1, 2] for implementing the e-learning client and server components. This framework is fully implemented in Java [4, 5] and allows for developing context-aware applications that are adaptable to the resources offered by the execution environment and network, and to some (a priori specified) dependability requirements of the user.

Foreground: Marco takes up his smartphone and connects, through his e-learning client, to the e-learning service to get the latest available lesson of the Computer Science course. Since Marco wants to obtain a fully featured lesson, he is willing to invest considerably in the process. When the e-learning client asks for the cost by displaying a multiple-choice control with both high and low cost options, he will opt for a high cost solution delivering the fully featured version (Fig. 2(1)). After processing the choice, the e-learning service will inform Marco, via a pop-up message, that the fully featured lesson is not obtainable since a high-speed connection cannot be established and his battery state-of-charge is insufficient to support the energy demands for the duration of the fully featured solution. As an alternative, the e-learning service proposes a low-cost version of the lessons in which only slides will be provided. The system also informs Marco that as soon the conditions exist, it will automatically switch to the fully featured version. Marco accepts and, while in the train, only slides are shown (Fig. 2(2)). Upon reaching the airport Marco recharges his smartphone and, after awhile, he is able to enjoy video, audio and other multimedia content of the fully featured version (Fig. 2(3)).

Behind the scenes: Initially, the e-learning client can only establish a (low-speed) GPRS connection and, hence, gets (from the widget repository) the widget that is able only to display slides, i.e., the low-size lesson. In other words, this widget guarantees slide displaying having a low speed connection as assumption. Indeed, the current architectural configuration of the e-learning client also comprises a hidden (to Marco) widget that monitors the battery state-of-charge and WiFi connection availability. Upon reaching the airport, the widget monitor detects that the battery is fully charged and a WiFi network is in range. Thus, additional widgets (that have an high speed connection as assumption) are selected (from the widget repository) and added to the current architectural configuration for providing video, audio and other multimedia contents. This allows Marco to enjoy a widget mash-up representing the fully featured lesson. This means that the architectural configuration, initially proposed, evolved to fully satisfy the specified dependability.

In order to give a more concrete flavour to the scenario it might be useful to briefly introduce the CHAMELEON framework and to see how it can be regarded as a possible approach to be exploited for solving the issue of dynamically inducing the "best" possible architectural configuration from user-specified dependability requirements.

Roughly, the approach offers a programming model [3] for adaptable applications. The programming model provides developers with a set of agile and user-friendly extensions to Java for easily specifying *generic code* in a flexible and declarative way, while being close to the Java programming language. The generic code consists of two parts, the *core code* and the *adaptable code*, and allows for specifying both the invariant semantics and the degree of variability of the application, respectively. Concretely, the adaptable code provides developers with extended Java constructs to specify variability in terms of *adaptable class*es that define *adaptable methods*, and *alternative class*es that define them (see Fig. 4). Then, an ad-hoc preprocessor resolves variability by generating standard Java methods within standard Java classes that, opportunely combined, make-up different *application alternatives*, i.e., different ways of implementing an adaptable application specification.

In the setting of the widget-based e-learning scenario here presented, the e-learning client can be implemented as an adaptable midlet and different alternatives, i.e., different architectural configurations using/assembling different widgets, are declaratively (i.e., implicitly without having the full knowledge of all the possible architectural configurations) specified for it in terms of generic code. Each alternative guarantees some dependability requirements according to the specific context of use (i.e., the resources offered by the execution environment provided by the Marco's device and the network condition). Furthermore, each alternative represents a possible architectural configuration (different from the others) given in terms of the widgets that are assembled and made interoperable in order to implement the client application's SA. For instance, as it is shown in Fig. 3, at a higher

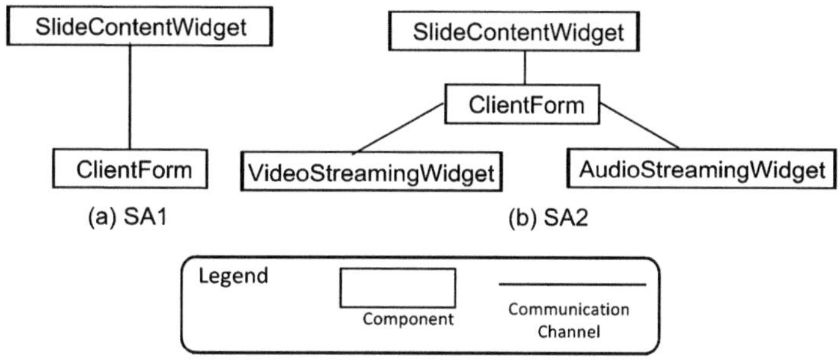

Fig. 3 Two different SAs for the e-learning scenario's client application

level, i.e., at the SA level, the client application can be described by two different architectural configurations. One configuration, see Fig. 3(a), is related to the SA that properly works with a slow network connection, e.g., GPRS. The other configuration, see Fig. 3(b), concerns the SA that properly works for a faster network connection, e.g., WiFi, and a good battery state-of-charge. As it is shown in Fig. 4, the adaptable e-learningMidlet has two alternatives to accommodate this at a lower level (i.e., code level). Each alternative provides implementation for all the adaptable methods. The GPRS alternative connects via GPRS and, considering the limited speed of this connection, allows for streaming (via the getLesson method) the lesson slides only, i.e., only the slides' content given into a textual format by means of the `SlideContentWidget`. The WiFi alternative connects via WiFi and, exploiting the higher connection speed, allows for streaming the high-quality video lesson with all its multimedia content (slides plus other interactive multimedia objects) by means of an assembly of the three widgets: `SlideContentWidget`, `VideoStreamingWidget`, and `AudioStreamingWidget`.

The programming model permits the specification of Annotations that allows for adding information about particular code instructions (see the keyword Annotation). They are specified at the generic code level by means of calls to the "do nothing" methods of the dedicated Annotation class. In this way, after preprocessing, annotations are encoded in the standard Java code through well recognizable method calls to allow for easy processing. For instance, in Fig. 4, the method call Annotation.slsAnnotation ("Cost(high), Features(full)"), first line of the connect method in the WiFi alternative, specifies that the WiFi connection, and hence the WiFi alternative, bears a high cost, but provides a high quality e-learning lesson. On the other hand, the method call Annotation.resourceAnnotation ("Battery(high)"), first line of the getLesson method, demands for a high battery state-of-charge, since the streaming of the video lesson along with its multimedia content calls for a considerable amount of energy to be consumed.

The scenario presented above clearly shows that for MAUS the architectural configuration cannot be assumed a priori (to assess dependability) but it is dynamically induced. As it is shown above, this can be done by exploiting information about the single components and their context of use, and the desired dependability.

```
adaptable public class e–learningMidlet extends MIDlet
                              implements CommandListener {
    /* life–cycle management methods */
    ...

    /* CHAMELEON specific management methods */
    ...

    /* e–learning specific methods */
    adaptable void connect();
    adaptable void getLesson();
    ...
}

alternative class GPRS adapts e–learningMidlet {
    Widget slideContentWidget = WidgetFactory.getWidgetStub(...);
    ...
    void connect() {
        Annotation.slsAnnotation("Cost(low),Features(limited)");
        connectViaGPRS();
    }

    /* streaming of the lesson slides */
    void getLesson() {
        ...
        // Calling SlideContentWidget interfaces
        result = ((SlideContentWidget)slideContentWidget).
                                   getTextLevel7(userName,textFile);
        ...
        contentField.setString(result);
        clientForm.append(contentField);
        ...
    }
}

alternative class WiFi adapts e–learningMidlet {
    Widget slideContentWidget = WidgetFactory.getWidgetStub(...);
    Widget videoStreamingWidget = WidgetFactory.getWidgetStub(...);
    Widget audioStreamingWidget = WidgetFactory.getWidgetStub(...);
    ...
    void connect() {
      Annotation.slsAnnotation("Cost(high),Features(full)");
      connectViaWiFi();
    }

    /* streaming of the video lesson with its multimedia content */
    void getLesson() {
        Annotation.resourceAnnotation("Battery(high)");
        ...
        // Calling SlideContentWidget, VideoStreamingWidget,
                             // and AudioStreamingWidget interfaces
        result = ((SlideContentWidget)slideContentWidget).
                                   getImageLevel2(userName,imageFile);

        int len = result.length();
        byte[] data = new byte[len];
        img = null;
        data = Base64.decode(result);

        // Create an image from the raw data
        img = Image.createImage(data, 0, data.length);
        show(img);
        ...

        VideoPlayer.Initialize(clientForm,
                       ((VideoStreamingWidget)videoStreamingWidget).
                                   getVideoSource(userName,mpegFile));

        AudioPlayer.Initialize(clientForm,
                       ((AudioStreamingWidget)audioStreamingWidget).
                                   getAudioSource(userName,mp3File));

        ...
    }
}
```

Fig. 4 An adaptable Midlet

Even though the CHAMELEON framework has been developed in and for Java [4, 5], other languages are eligible. To this end, we now discuss the portability of the framework on some of the well known platforms in the market: (i) Devices powered with Symbian Operating System (OS) can be programmed using different languages, among which Java Micro Edition. Applications are developed and deployed by using standard techniques and tools, such as the Sun Java Wireless Toolkit. CHAMELEON can be used as it is; (ii) The Google's Android OS uses the Dalvik virtual machine to run applications that are commonly written in a dialect of Java and compiled to the Dalvik bytecode. Even though different, the Dalvik bytecode and the J2ME bytecode present many similarities that make the portability of CHAMELEON straightforward; (iii) Concerning proprietary operating systems, such as the iPhone OS and the BlackBerry OS, applications are developed by following a close philosophy that does not require the flexibility of the CHAMELEON development process. In fact, for such OSs the exploitation of CHAMELEON might make no sense to address heterogeneity and resource limitation of the different execution environments. These issues can be a priori addressed since applications run on a priori known execution environments for which resource constraints can be tackled by using explicit hard-coded conditionals.

5 Concluding Remarks: Is There a Role for Software Architectures?

In light of the above, future research directions should address the challenges related to mobility and ubiquity by devising a dynamic composition process (*from user required dependability to system composition*) for the endless openness of MAUS. The process, possibly supported by a middleware for ubiquitous computing [6], has to sustain the dynamic connection of system components "best suited" according to the user-specified dependability. Indeed, the open and dynamic nature of MAUS makes requirements continuously evolve, especially regarding the context of use and the desired dependability. This calls for an approach that enables seamless and continuous software composition and adaptation. The dependability of the composed system can be then assessed in terms of its components' assumptions on the system context.

In this paper, by describing an e-learning scenario, we have shown that the role of the SA is to provide the *dynamic* composition rules that dictate how to compose (resp., reconfigure) the system in order to achieve (resp., keep) the wished dependability, despite the context changes.

Last but not least, the assembling process of MAUS can be no longer assumed to be handled by IT experts only. Rather, end users should be able to play an active role in the overall composition process, so that changes in requirements, as much as in context of use, can be adequately handled. In this direction, the goal of the CHOReOS project[1] (*Large Scale Choreographies for the Future Internet*), we are involved in, is to address these challenges—in the domain of Service Oriented Architectures—by devising a dynamic reuse-based development process, and associated methods, tools and middleware, to sustain the composition of services in the Future Internet and to move it closer to the end users. This again stresses the required move from static assembling to dynamic composition, effectively calling for adequate support for the dynamic reuse of components/services according to the user-specified dependability.

References

1. Autili, M., Di Benedetto, P., Inverardi, P., Tamburri, D.A.: Towards self-evolving context-aware services. In: Proc. of Context-Aware Adaptation Mechanisms for Pervasive and Ubiquitous Services (CAMPUS), DisCoTec'08, vol. 11 (2008). http://eceasst.cs.tu-berlin.de/index.php/eceasst/issue/view/18
2. Autili, M., Benedetto, P.D., Inverardi, P.: Context-aware adaptive services: The plastic approach. In: Chechik, M., Wirsing, M. (eds.) Proceedings of the International Conference on Fundamental Approaches to Software Engineering (FASE'09). LNCS, vol. 5503, pp. 124–139. Springer, Berlin (2009)
3. Autili, M., Benedetto, P.D., Inverardi, P.: A programming model for adaptable java applications. In: Proceedings of the 8th International Conference on the Principles and Practice of Programming in Java (PPPJ 2010) (2010, to appear)
4. Autili, M., Benedetto, P.D., Inverardi, P.: CHAMELEON project—SEA group. http://sourceforge.net/projects/uda-chameleon/
5. Autili, M., Benedetto, P.D., Inverardi, P.: CHAMELEON project—SEA group. http://di.univaq.it/chameleon/
6. Caporuscio, M., Raverdy, P.-G., Moungla, H., Issarny, V.: ubiSOAP: A service oriented middleware for seamless networking. In: Proc. of 6th ICSOC (2008)
7. IFIP WG 10.4 on Dependable Computing and Fault Tolerance: http://www.dependability.org/wg10.4/
8. Issarny, V., Zarras, A.: Software architecture and dependability. In: Bernardo, M., Inverardi, P. (eds.) Formal Methods for Software Architecture. LNCS, vol. 2804 (2003)
9. Schilit, B., Adams, N., Want, R.: Context-aware computing applications. In: IEEE Workshop on Mobile Computing Systems and Applications, Santa Cruz, CA, US (1994)
10. Weiser, M.: Open house. http://www.ubiq.com/hypertext/weiser/wholehouse.doc (1996)
11. Weiser, M., Brown, J.S.: Designing calm technology. http://www.ubiq.com/hypertext/weiser/calmtech/calmtech.htm (1996)

[1]EU project CHOReOS No: 231167 of the Integrated Project (IP) programme within the ICT theme of the Seventh Framework Programme for Research of the European Commission. Call (part) identifier: FP7-ICT-2009-5. Start date: October 1st, 2010.

A Bestiary of Overlooked Design Patterns

John Aycock

Abstract Designing effective software is good. Nowadays, patterns are touting tremendous efficacy. Regardless, naturally people always regret overlooked design yardsticks.

To this end, we collect some overlooked design patterns together for consideration.

1 Introduction

Ever since Gamma et al. radiated onto the software scene with design patterns [1], there has been a veritable gold rush of efforts to catalog all possible design patterns.[1] This can be seen to enhance the discipline of software engineering and act as an aid to both aspiring software designers as well as those trying to divert attention from the more egregious aspects of a steaming pile of software, e.g., "But look! It uses a Chain of Responsibility right there!" Design patterns have also allowed software developers to make statements aloud that were formerly restricted to runways in Milan: "Is that pattern a genuine *Gamma*?"

However, some design patterns that draw on observed human behavior for their inspiration have yet to be documented in the literature, a tragic oversight that we correct in the remainder of this paper.

2 List of Patterns

2.1 Unwanted Visitor Pattern

Any visitor which originally claims to be visiting "just a little while" but ends up grossly overstaying their welcome. Unwanted visitors often spend excessive time

[1] Ignoring the fate of many catalogs during the days of the Gold Rush.

J. Aycock (✉)
Department of Computer Science, University of Calgary, 2500 University Drive N.W., Calgary, Alberta, Canada T2N 1N4
e-mail: aycock@ucalgary.ca

K.K. Breitman, R.N. Horspool (eds.), *Patterns, Programming and Everything*,
DOI 10.1007/978-1-4471-2350-7_2, © Springer-Verlag London 2012

in critical sections—like the living-room couch in front of the television—and are seemingly oblivious to all attempts to remove them short of *force majeure*. They consume massive resources, especially beer, and while the resources are eventually released, they are not released in a form that anyone cares to reuse.

2.2 *False Facade Pattern*

False Facade patterns are the slimy salesmen of software development. A triumph of form over functionality, False Facades are often found in software cobbled together for demos. These patterns give all appearances of rich, robust software, but behind this exterior lies mostly hardcoded values, crossed fingers, and duct tape. Successful execution of software containing a False Facade demands the script of a Hollywood production and more precision than an aerobatic stunt team.

2.3 *Desperate Singleton Pattern*

A Desperate Singleton pattern is not polymorphic so much as polyester, and is generally found at the well-known Foo Bar. Unfortunately, interest in the Desperate Singleton's now-legacy code has waned substantially; it is painfully aware of its countdown timer and the limited remaining opportunities to spawn children.

2.4 *Biased Observer Pattern*

A Biased Observer is seemingly open-minded and keen to observe all state change events, but it becomes increasingly clear from continued interaction with a Biased Observer that it selectively accepts events that agree with its worldview and ignores those that don't. Granted, some state changes are less exciting than others—crossing between Nebraska and South Dakota, for example. A conglomeration of Biased Observers in a system often drives it into a red state.

2.5 *Interior Decorator Pattern*

Interior Decorators tend to consume many resources in their quest to inject non-functional yet aesthetically pleasing elements into a design. The result of an Interior Decorator instantiation is a tasteful mélange of an execution environment that is notably unsuited to the code running within it. Exceptions are bound to be raised, as `throw` pillows crop up seemingly from nowhere.

2.6 *Useless Adapter Pattern*

Useless Adapters are not so much allocated as accumulated, often in the detritus of kitchen junk drawers. They initially appear to be useful to adapt one interface into another, but practical usage is invariably denied due to some inexplicable corkscrew-shaped protuberance. Rare triumphs in applying a Useless Adapter to one interface are short-lived, by the discovery that the opposing end of the adapter suffers from gender identity disorder.

2.7 *Lazy-Spouse Initialization Pattern*

This pattern is typically characterized by a stubborn refusal to do anything with garbage, or to fix pointers that have been dangling for "some time now." Instances take one another for granted, and seldom exchange messages, preferring instead to use default arguments. Lazy Spouses usually use base 10; hex is infrequent.

2.8 *Disreputable Builder Pattern*

Disreputable Builder patterns are usually found in Design by Contractor methodologies. When Disreputable Builders finally begin computation, the resulting work is questionable at best—assuming the work is ever completed at all—and the caller will soon discover that the original time bounds they had been given were more of a fiction than *Moby Dick*. To their credit, Disreputable Builders do seem to have cracked the Halting Problem, as they have no problem stopping work at the slightest provocation.

2.9 *"Wanna-buy-a?" Bridge Pattern*

There is a sucker object instantiated every minute, as the Wanna-buy-a Bridge Pattern well knows. This pattern is notorious for giving away pointers to objects it doesn't own; comic hijinks ensue when the unsuspecting recipient of such a pointer tries to access it.

2.10 *Former Flyweight Pattern*

A Former Flyweight pattern was bullied by other, larger patterns while it was still young, pre-alpha software. This is reflected in its licensing, as the Former Flyweight was pantsed in front of the entire class one time, making it suddenly and reluctantly open source. A mature Former Flyweight pattern compensates for past injustices by allocating excessively large amounts of resources and doing lots of computation.

2.11 Industrial Mediator Pattern

An Industrial Mediator pattern is handy for resolving disputes between factory patterns, especially when it comes to deciding which variable refers to which value, i.e., binding arbitration. The destructor of a class implementing an Industrial Mediator is guaranteed to be called eventually, once the work of factory patterns is all offshored.

2.12 Failed State Pattern

Making use of a Failed State pattern in a project is somewhat of a coup. A typical application sees one corrupt, bloated design replaced by a leaner, more idealistic design that will itself become equally corrupt and bloated as its predecessor in the fullness of time. Some variants give at least lip service to processes being peers rather than hierarchically organized, and are usually accompanied by ranting, hours-long output streams.

2.13 Childproof Container Pattern

A Childproof Container is a container holding data that is impervious to all reasonable attempts to access it. The data may be extracted by multithreaded applications, where one thread pushes on the container and another twists the container simultaneously. The threads will at first seize up, in a manner reminiscent of severe constipation, before the container finally relinquishes its bounty. A far easier approach to accessing data in the container is to pass it off to a child process, which can get the container open instantly.

2.14 Unionized Factory Pattern

Unionized Factories are the jealous mistress in the producer/consumer relationship, not terribly interested in consumer choice or efficient production. They exhibit tremendous concern over imported objects, and they can output an endless stream of grievance objects if a worker thread in a Unionized Factory is terminated. Livelock is the preferred state of a Unionized Factory, because it assures an infinite amount of work. Ironically, a `union` construct is *never* used in a Unionized Factory because it implies that something can perform more than one role, which is strictly against union rules.

3 Conclusion

That the author should not be permitted within several hundred meters of software development activity went without saying beforehand, and really counts more as a passing observation than a *bona fide* conclusion. We can, however, conclude that the delicious potpourri that is the human experience is a wealth of untapped design pattern potential.

Acknowledgements Mike Zastre suggested the original design pattern names.

References

1. Gamma, E., Helm, R., Johnson, R., Vlissides, J.: Design Patterns. Addison-Wesley, Reading (1995)

End User Programming in Smart Home

Vilmos Bilicki, Zoltán Rak, Miklós Kasza, Ádám Végh, Róbert Béládi, and Tibor Gyimóthy

Abstract In the field of ubiquitous computing, one of the most important challenges is the proper involvement of end users in the control of the system. They should be aware of what is happening and why in the smart environment. A well known approach for end user involvement in the controlling of IT systems is end user programming. There are numerous approaches for enabling the end users to define the business logic starting with decision trees and ending with domain specific languages.

In order to enable the end user to program in the smart home we have ported the Drools toolkit and runtime, a well-known open source environment, to the Android platform, and we have integrated it with the PECES middleware. With the help of a smart home simulator, we benchmarked the response time of the solution. We have found that even in the case of an intensive data source such as a 3D movement sensor, the ADL (Activity of Daily Life) detecting DSL based algorithms are performing very well.

V. Bilicki (✉) · Z. Rak
FrontEndART Software Ltd, Zászló u. 3, 6722 Szeged, Hungary
e-mail: bilickiv@frontendart.hu

Z. Rak
e-mail: rakz@frontendart.hu

M. Kasza · Á. Végh · R. Béládi · T. Gyimóthy
Department of Software Engineering, University of Szeged, Dugonics tér 13, 6703 Szeged, Hungary

M. Kasza
e-mail: kaszi@inf.u-szeged.hu

Á. Végh
e-mail: azvegh@inf.u-szeged.hu

R. Béládi
e-mail: brobi@inf.u-szeged.hu

T. Gyimóthy
e-mail: gyimi@inf.u-szeged.hu

K.K. Breitman, R.N. Horspool (eds.), *Patterns, Programming and Everything*,
DOI 10.1007/978-1-4471-2350-7_3, © Springer-Verlag London 2012

1 Introduction

M2M (Machine-to-Machine) systems have recently gained new momentum thanks to the increasing availability of low-cost components, and to the growing demand for more automated and advanced user interaction with the surrounding environments. As the currently available solutions for intelligent places (e.g. home, workplace, etc.) are designed as the evolutions of traditional electric plants, they suffer from two main drawbacks: lack of interoperability and lack of intelligence beyond simple automation. There are a few commercial systems that are built from different sets of proprietary elements [13] but these systems are also closed and their intelligence is very limited. It is not easy to argue for a given customer installing a given sensor type twice because of the lack of interoperability of the domain specific service providers. This situation is evolving. The trend we are envisioning is similar to the trend we have seen in telecommunication. The so called last mile is now a service which is shared between the different service providers. In the same way, the M2M provider may provide an intelligent last mile offering controlled access to the shared M2M infrastructure. This way, the total cost of ownership could be reduced as the infrastructure could be shared between the different domain specific service providers. As an example, one can imagine a solution where the information coming from the wall mounted movement sensors is shared between the security and the telemedicine providers. From the business point of view, the intelligent last mile could be done via appliance or via utility model [6]. The service model is easier to implement, as in this case intelligence could be centralized and implemented in a dedicated place. The appliance model is trickier, as in this case the small atomic appliances should interact with each other and the intelligence of the system is distributed among them. We apply a hybrid model which provides the technological capability to cover both approaches. Due to the distributed nature of the M2M system (in the case of the appliance model), different middleware solutions are utilized by the M2M community in order to provide the necessary abstraction level for software developers. There is a wide variety of issues that a middleware should take care of. In the PECES FP7 project, we took part in the development of a role and rule based location neutral middleware. In this article, we will describe our reference software architecture based on the PECES middleware designed for M2M service providers. the middleware provides the following capabilities:

- Context based group forming and group based data oriented communication. The groups are tied to physical location of the sensors, the solution enables group communication among devices placed in different locations.
- End user capability of reviewing and defining the logic of the different ways of group forming.
- Seamless and secure integration of the dumb sensor and the sharing of sensors among multiple service providers.

The article has the following structure: in the second section, we describe the high level requirements that a M2M framework should fulfill, then based on the requirements several state of the art middleware solutions are analyzed. The third section describes the innovation content of the solution we have developed. In the next section, the high level software architecture and the utilized technologies are described. In the fifth section, we describe the implemented use-case which is then benchmarked and analyzed. The last section summarizes the key aspects of the reference software architecture.

2 High-Level Requirements and State of the Art

A significant percentage of the M2M solutions implements the so called smart environment or smart home service. There are several articles [6, 11, 13] discussing the challenges that a smart environment could face. In the followings, we will summarize the requirements described by the authors of articles [6, 11, 13, 14]:

- The end users are not expert IT programmers, but they should be able to understand and control the smart home (there is no system administrator, etc.). The system should be designed for domestic use. A significant number of the end users prefer a conditional logic like formalism (if/then) for describing the behavior of the system [11].
- The devices need to be rendered interoperable. (For example, middleware is required for dumb devices; proprietary protocols are used to provide for interoperability, etc.).
- Software developers require a notation that offers a high level of abstraction. One such abstraction is intelligent group forming which, based on the context, provides data oriented interaction among the group members.

There are few M2M middleware approaches focusing on the ability of the end user to review and control the behavior of the system. In most cases the end user is able only to tune the parameters but the business logic is hidden from him/her [1]. An ontology and SPARQL are commonly used to model and define business logic. The popular Hydra middleware [7] for example is based on self-managing components which are based on SPARQL rules. The middleware itself mostly focuses on the interaction between the sensors and the data and there is no real context based grouping capability. The authors of the article [18] are going one step forward; they envision a genetic algorithm based security optimization layer on the top of the Hydra platform. It is clear that these solutions could not provide the necessary transparency for the end user to review the system and control its behavior. The authors of the article [4] describe a similar ontology and a SPARQL based solution. Here, the ADL (activity of the daily life) algorithms are encoded into SPARQL queries. As a summary we can conclude that the ontology based modeling and SPARQL based rule definition is popular among the middleware developers but this approach cannot provide the necessary capability to the end user to overview and control the system.

3 Proposed Solution

We have seen in the previous section that the ontology based modeling and the SPARQL based filtering are popular approaches among the different middleware providers. Our solution also utilizes these technologies but in a novel way. Our software reference architecture is built on the PECES middleware which provides an easy to use low complexity context based grouping facility. The grouping service is based on roles and rules. The rules could be defined in SPARQL or in a domain specific language. With the domain specific languages one can support end user programming. This way, all the four dimensions of the ubiquitous system (device, security, application, and application logic configuration) could be overseen and managed by the end user. The support of the dumb sensor that cannot run the middleware (e.g. wall mounted movement sensors) is solved with the help of a local coordinator which uses the virtual sensor concept. As the context based groups are not limited by the local connectivity, multiple sites could be involved in the same context, and this way, multiple sites could take part in a data oriented group communication process. The security framework uses the same role and rule engine, and it enables the same abstractions. With the help of location neutral context aware and secure group forming the dumb sensor could be shared among different domain specific service providers in a secure way. As a summary, the novelty of this solution is:

- Domain Specific Language based rule definition of the context
- Support for context based data oriented communication between entities that need not necessarily be geographically close
- Boxing the dumb sensor into a virtual sensor, and this way, sharing it among different service providers

4 Architecture and Technologies

The abstract physical overview of the target M2M system is shown in Fig. 1. The ecosystem consists of different smart spaces implementing the intelligent last mile for the M2M service provider, and several domain specific service providers. Our goal is to enable the secure sharing of the raw and the processed information coming from different dumb sensors based on the context. In the figure, the devices inside the orange boxes with dotted lines show a given context where the participants of the context can use data oriented communication.

The telemedicine provider can receive the data coming from different movement sensors. An important abstraction shown in the figure is the coordinator of the smart spaces. This device acts as a gateway and enables the interaction among the different smart spaces and the central repository. In order to implement the ecosystem shown in Fig. 1 and the requirements described in Sect. 3, we elaborated the reference software architecture shown in Fig. 2. There are many different approaches for implementing end user programming [8, 12, 15–17]. We selected the Domain

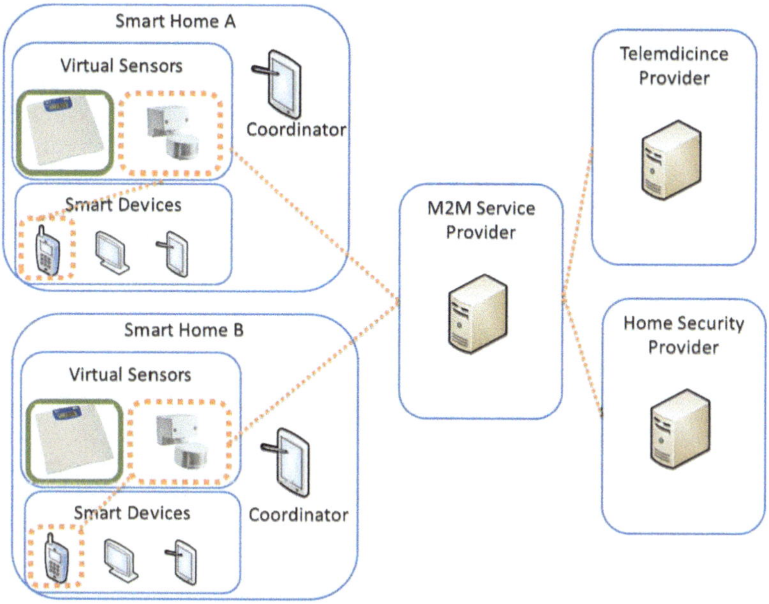

Fig. 1 M2M ecosystem

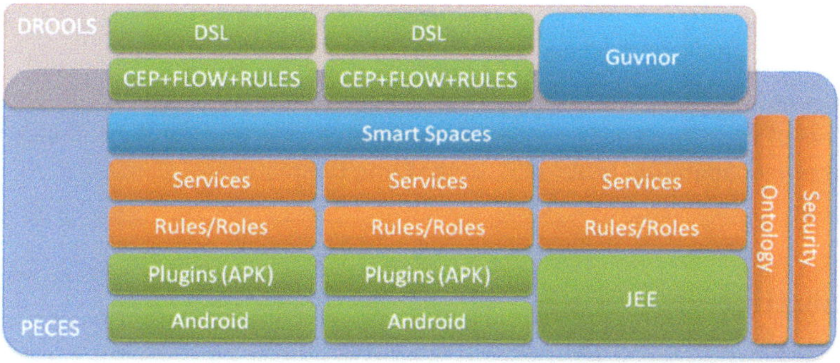

Fig. 2 Software stack

Specific Language approach, which has the capability to define the business logic with high-level tailored graphics or text based constructs. We applied the Drools toolkit which provides a rule engine with complex event processing capability and flow based logic description. As a basic runtime we selected the Android on the user side, while the central platform is based on the JEE container. Using the Android as a runtime in a smart home is a plausible idea as there are cheap and powerful embedded devices running this operating system. Selecting Domain Specific Language as a tool for implementing end user programming was motivated by the included complex event processing and the integrated flow and rule based logic engine. The template based DSL integrates these tools tightly enabling the customization of the syntax of the applied rules. Currently, the Drools environment is utilized mainly on the server side. We were able to port the framework to the Android platform enabling DSL based programming on tablets and even on high-level embedded devices. The runtime enables the remote deployment and monitoring of the DSL entities. With this solution in hand, one can manage the deployed business logic from a central location. The ported DSL framework itself is not enough for implementing smart home functionality. A framework which enables the seamless integration of the sensors and actuators placed in different locations with the tight security and high-level interaction capabilities is needed. Here, we applied the middleware developed in the PECES project. It provides ontology based modeling with SPARQL based logic description for defining the different configuration dimensions of a ubiquitous system. The details of the configuration handling capability are described in articles [2, 9, 10], here we would like to provide only a high level overview. The configuration capabilities of different ubiquitous systems are divided into three areas. Environment configuration defines the scope and the management mechanism of the middleware. Application configuration describes the configuration of the application using the middleware itself. Here, we can think about selecting the components of a component-oriented application based on the set of sensors. The goal of access configuration is to restrict the communication provided by environment configuration in order to fulfill security policies. PECES deals with these issues uniformly with the Generic Role Mechanism. Roles are assigned tags based on the evaluation of the rules defined in the SPARQL language on the background ontology model. With the help of the SPARQL logic definition, different rules could be described, and based on the rules roles for a given context could be assigned. Among the devices having the same role assigned, data oriented communication could be initiated. Due to the high costs of the SPARQL language, it is not suitable to provide the end user with a programming capability. Here, DSL comes into the picture.

5 Evaluation

The data intensity of the data sources found in a M2M system varies from a single measurement per month to several dozen measurements per second. Here, we introduce a real life scenario that we implemented in order to validate the feasibility of the reference software architecture described in the previous section. The use case scenario is based on the real life monitoring of the daily habits of an elder patient. The habits and daily activities are detected with the help of movement sensors mounted on the walls and 3 dimensional acceleration sensors built into the smart phone. We implemented two applications on the top of the infrastructure. The first one is in the field of telemedicine where the goal of the application is to monitor the activity of daily life (ADL). The second application is in the field of personal security. If the monitored person leaves the flat and motion is sensed, the application sends an alarm to the closest relative or friend. Both applications utilize a hierarchy of rules implemented in a DSL designed for this field. The hierarchy is built from

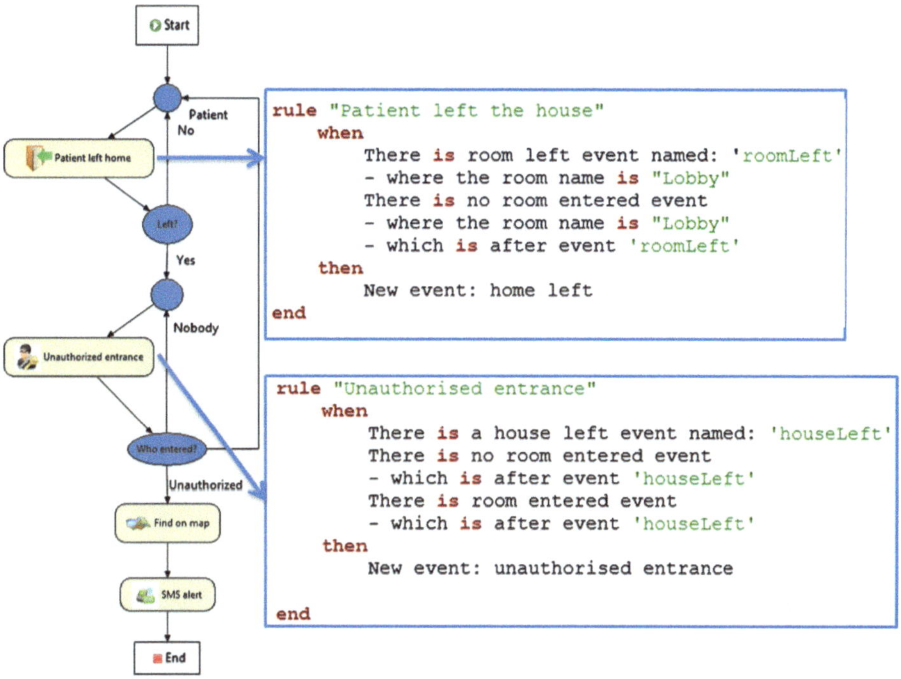

Fig. 3 DSL flow and DSL rule

rules detecting atomic events such as movement from one room to another, and from complex rules such as measuring the length of being in one room or measuring the number of visits in a room. The temporal reasoning engine of the Drools framework uses memory intensive data structures in order to minimize the processor utilization. In a server environment this could be a good strategy but on an embedded device can easily run out of the memory. In order to avoid this we applied a dynamic object based state transfer between the first and the second tier. In this solution the result of the first tier is boxed into dynamic objects and the rules of the second tier are based on these objects. On the top of this two tier rule structure there are the flows which describe the actions and workflows based on the events are rules shown on Fig. 3. We can notice the custom syntax for both the flow and rule. A simple end user can better understand these construct than a SPARQL query.

During our measurements, we used a simple java based simulator to simulate a test environment. It was a realistic flat with preinstalled motion sensors, door sensors, and an accelerometer which was bundled in the private mobile device of the monitored person. The accelerometer and the sensors were implemented to act like in real-life, i.e. detect the magnitude and direction of a proper acceleration (g-force) as a vector quantity. When at rest, they measured a downward force of 1 g upwards ($-9{,}81\ m/s^2$ or $[0, 0, -9{,}81]$ as represented within the Simulator). The movement of the Actor was attached to alter this vector by obeying the following relation: "acceleration = gravity + linear acceleration". Motion sensors had the following

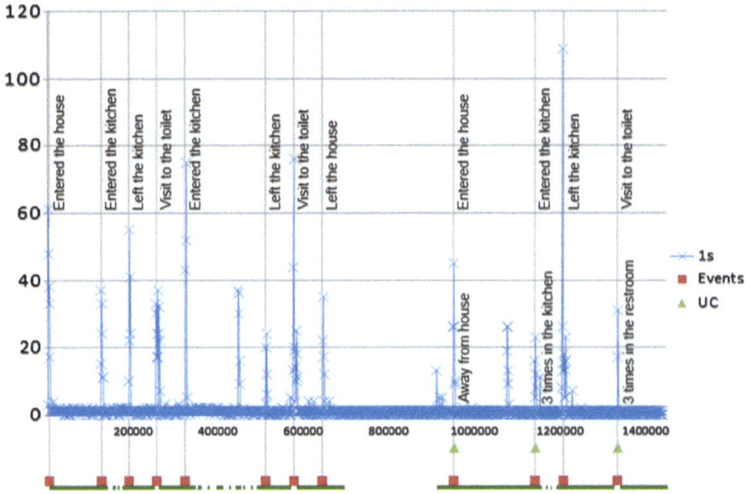

Fig. 4 Runtime values and details for 1 s measurement

properties: coordinate within the Scene, the angle of the sensor (i.e. which direction they are looking at, in degrees, with 0° facing East), the range of the sensor (in meters) and the field of view (in degrees). They also held a Boolean property—cleared before each frame—on whether a motion was detected by them (0 for no movement, 1 for any movement). Door sensors also had their coordinates and a state: whether they are open or closed. Upon running the simulator an output file was generated for 24 minutes (1/60th of a day). The use cases were shrunk down to this magnitude, i.e. a condition for a daily use case was set to 30 seconds instead of 30 minutes. The actor in the simulation followed a pre-set routine: 3 visits to the kitchen, 3 visits to the toilet afterwards and leaving the house once for 5 minutes. Each line of the generated data file held the events generated by the sensors in 200 ms resolution. Each event had the timestamp it occurred, the type of the event and data related to that type (e.g. in case of a motion sensor the three-dimensional vector values). This data file was parsed on an Android device (Samsung Galaxy Tab, Android 2.2, 592 MByte RAM, C110, 1 GHz, Cortex A8 Hummingbird Application processor) that was used to conduct the measurements. The events were fed to the Drools knowledge session with several approaches: real-time (i.e. every 200 ms) and batched (every 1 s, 30 s, 1 m, 5 m, 10 m and all at once (24 m)). The elapsed time was measured for both inserting the data to the session and firing all rules. Figure 4 shows a detailed chart for the 1-second interval measurement. The x axis shows the logical time in the simulator. The green dots are the movements in a given point of time. The red squares are the atomic events (mainly movement from one room to another). Atomic events, second-level events and high-level events (use case completions) are shown with description. Spikes in run time are clearly visible near higher-level events. The description of the event is shown on the vertical lines. The blue × symbols show the insert delay of the environment the y axis show this value in milliseconds. We can notice that it Standalone high values are the result of

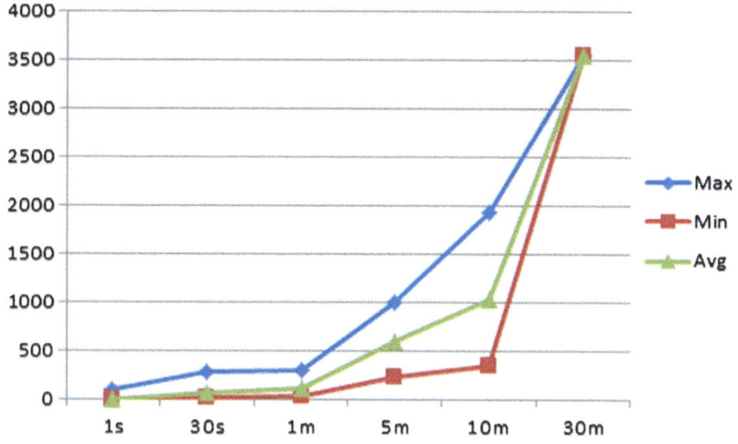

Fig. 5 Runtime values

Garbage Collecting. In all circumstances the maximum run times were way below the batch interval times meaning all intervals are feasible for executing the rules. The energy consumption of the wireless devices is influenced significantly by the usage of the wireless interface. In most cases the best strategy is to make periodic transfers with short data bursts and long sleeping periods (or periods with wireless interface turned off). In our second experiment we studied the effect of the burst on the performance of the Drools runtime. Figure 5 shows the results of the measurements. We use the same data set we have previously described but instead of inserting the events one-by-one we simulated the burst with a time window. This time window contained the events from 1 second to half hour. The red plot on the chart shows the maximal insertion time for a given window, the red and the yellow plots show the average and the minimum delay respectively. We can notice a threshold around ten minutes where the delay increases significantly. In this case the memory consumption reaches a given limit and the garbage collector runs very frequently.

6 Conclusions

In this article we have described a reference software architecture for an M2M service provider infrastructure which enables the end users to overview and to control the system. Beside this capability we have shown a solution how to integrate the already existing dumb sensors and how to share the data among different service providers in an easy and secure way. In order to properly benchmark the proposed architecture we defined real life use cases and ADL detecting rules. The results show that the solution is feasible, the delay was lower than 100 ms. We believe that there is huge potential in the DSL based M2M solutions. One potential field is the telemedicine where one can describe the recommendations applied by the general practitioners by domain specific rules [3]. We would like to focus on the authoring capability of the end users in our next R&D project. Currently Guvnor [5] (an opensource web based framework for rule storage and management) is used for this purpose but it is not suitable for non-programmer end users.

Acknowledgement The work presented was partly funded by the National Innovation Office, Hungary (project No. OMFD-00735/2005 BELAMIH), and PECES (Pervasive Computing in Embedded Systems), funded by the European Commission under FP7 with contract number FP7-224342-ICT-2007-2.

References

1. Allerding, F., Schmeck, H.: Organic smart home: architecture for energy management in intelligent buildings. In: Proceedings of the 2011 Workshop on Organic Computing, pp. 67–76. ACM, New York (2011)
2. Apolinarski, W., Handte, M., Marrón, P.J.: A secure context distribution framework for peer-based pervasive systems. In: Pervasive Computing and Communications Workshops (PERCOM Workshops), 2010 8th IEEE International Conference on, pp. 505–510. IEEE, New York (2010)
3. Bilicki, V., Végh, A.Z., Szűcs, V.: Klinikai döntéstámogató rendszerek és a telemedicina. IME: Inform. Menedzsment Egészségügyben **X**(7), 50–54 (2011)
4. Bonino, D., Corno, F.: Rule-based intelligence for domotic environments. Autom. Constr. **19**(2), 183–196 (2010)
5. Drools Guvnor—JBoss Community. http://www.jboss.org/drools/drools-guvnor.html
6. Edwards, W., Grinter, R.: At home with ubiquitous computing: Seven challenges. In: Ubicomp 2001: Ubiquitous Computing, pp. 256–272. Springer, Berlin (2001)
7. Eisenhauer, M., Rosengren, P., Antolin, P.: A development platform for integrating wireless devices and sensors into ambient intelligence systems. In: Sensor, Mesh and Ad Hoc Communications and Networks Workshops, 2009. SECON Workshops' 09. 6th Annual IEEE Communications Society Conference on, pp. 1–3. IEEE, New York (2009)
8. Günther, S.: Agile dsl-engineering and patterns in ruby. Otto-von-Guericke-Universität Magdeburg, Technical report (Internet) FIN-018-2009 (2009)
9. Handte, M., Wagner, S., Schiele, G., Becker, C., Marrón, P.J.: The base plug-in architecture-composable communication support for pervasive systems. In: 7th ACM International Conference on Pervasive Services (July 2010) (2010)
10. Haroon, M., Handte, M., Marrón, P.J.: Generic role assignment: A uniform middleware abstraction for configuration of pervasive systems. In: Pervasive Computing and Communications, 2009. PerCom 2009. IEEE International Conference on, pp. 1–6. IEEE, New York (2009)
11. Holloway, S., Julien, C.: The case for end-user programming of ubiquitous computing environments. In: Proceedings of the FSE/SDP Workshop on Future of Software Engineering Research, pp. 167–172. ACM, New York (2010)
12. Ko, A.J., Abraham, R., Beckwith, L., Blackwell, A., Burnett, M., Erwig, M., Scaffidi, C., Lawrance, J., Lieberman, H., Myers, B., et al.: The state of the art in end-user software engineering. ACM Comput. Surv. **43**(3), 21 (2011)
13. Nikayin, F., Skournetou, D., De Reuver, M.: Establishing a common service platform for smart living: Challenges and a research agenda. In: Toward Useful Services for Elderly and People with Disabilities, pp. 251–255 (2011)
14. Solaimani, S., Bouwman, H., Baken, N.: The smart home landscape: A qualitative meta-analysis. In: Toward Useful Services for Elderly and People with Disabilities, pp. 192–199 (2011)

15. Tuchinda, R., Szekely, P., Knoblock, C.A.: Building mashups by example. In: Proceedings of the 13th International Conference on Intelligent User Interfaces, pp. 139–148. ACM, New York (2008)
16. Van Deursen, A., Klint, P., Visser, J.: Domain-specific languages: An annotated bibliography. ACM SIGPLAN Not. **35**(6), 26–36 (2000)
17. Vasudevan, N., Tratt, L.: Comparative study of dsl tools. Electron. Notes Theor. Comput. Sci. **264**(5), 103–121 (2011)
18. Zhang, W., Schütte, J., Ingstrup, M., Hansen, K.: A genetic algorithms-based approach for optimized self-protection in a pervasive service middleware. In: Service-Oriented Computing, pp. 404–419 (2009)

Reconceptualizing Bottom-Up Tree Rewriting

K. John Gough

Abstract Bottom-up tree rewriting is a widely used method for code selection in programming language compilers. The use of dynamic programming allows such rewriters to emit code sequences that are optimal with respect to some prescribed cost metric, at least for tree-structured computations. The semantics of rewriting are specified by the production rules of a tree grammar. In this paper, it is shown that a suitable reinterpretation of the meaning of the non-terminal symbols of such grammars provides a significant increase in the expressivity of the rewriting system. In particular, the generation of instructions for flow of control may be subsumed into the rewriter. Likewise, transformation rules normally associated with peephole optimization are also conveniently expressible.

1 Background

Bottom-up tree rewriting is a general mechanism for tree-to-tree transformation. In this paper we restrict consideration to the use of rewriting for instruction selection in a programming language compiler.

The context in which instruction selection by bottom-up tree rewriting is framed is as follows: we are given a set of production rules of a tree grammar, each of which has some known application cost. Each application has a "semantic action" which leads to the emission of zero or more machine instructions. Given some expression tree, the goal of rewriting is to find a sequence of rule applications that emits instructions to evaluate the expression with minimal cost relative to the given cost metric. The "rewriting" aspect of the transformation is clear if the resulting instruction sequence is represented as a tree, with the dependencies between instructions explicit rather than being implied by the use-definition relation between instructions in the linear sequence.

By analogy with context-free string grammars we define the patterns of the rules using *terminal symbols* and *non-terminal symbols*. Terminal symbols correspond

K.J. Gough (✉)
School of Computer Science, Queensland University of Technology, Brisbane, Australia
e-mail: j.gough@qut.edu.au

K.K. Breitman, R.N. Horspool (eds.), *Patterns, Programming and Everything*,
DOI 10.1007/978-1-4471-2350-7_4, © Springer-Verlag London 2012

Reg = *add*(Reg, Reg) *// Adding two Reg values creates a Reg value*
Reg = *add*(Reg, Imm13) *// Adding a Reg and 13-bit immediate creates a Reg*
Reg = Imm32 *// A 32-bit immediate may be loaded into a Reg*
Imm32 = Imm13 *// A 13-bit immediate may be used as 32-bits*

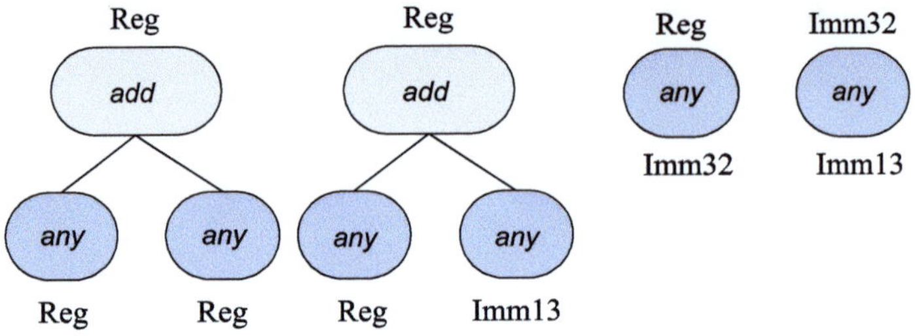

Fig. 1 Example rule patterns, and corresponding "tree tiles"

to the *kind* of the nodes. For an expression tree grammar this would be a finite alphabet of operator tags such as "literal", "add" and "assign". Non-terminal symbols correspond to *syntactic categories* of the tree. Each non-terminal expresses an assertion on a node. For an expression tree grammar two non-terminal symbols might be "Reg" and "Imm13" encapsulating the assertions "the tree rooted at this node has been evaluated into an integer register" and "the tree rooted at this node is an integer literal that fits in 13 bits" respectively. In the context of expression trees we may refer to the non-terminal symbols as *forms* since they are often named to indicate the form or storage class of the location into which the tree is deposited.

Figure 1 shows some examples of production rules (without semantic actions) for some instructions for the *SPARC* architecture.

In this figure the comments given with each pattern give the textual meaning of the rule. In the graphic, each pattern is shown as a tree fragment of one or more nodes. The leaf nodes marked "*any*" may have any operator tag at all, provided that the value of the tree rooted at that node may be put in the form stated *under* the node[1]. The result form of the pattern is written *above* the root of the pattern.

The last two rules have a non-terminal symbol on both sides of the rule. We call such rules *chain-rules*, since they are rules that allow a tree in some particular form to be transformed into a different form.

The actions associated with these rules have not been shown. However, it should be clear that the action for the first and second rules would be to emit a single "`add`" instruction (after performing some housekeeping actions to define a destination register). The action for the third rule would be to emit either one or two instructions to load the immediate value, the required number depending on the size of the immedi-

[1]Of course, in some cases this constraint may lead to a very small choice. For example, probably nothing but a "*literal*" node can be put into one of the immediate forms.

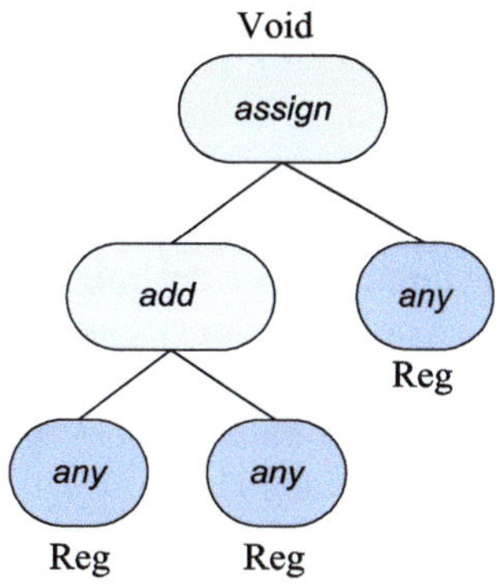

Fig. 2 Tree-tile for the *SPARC* "`stw`" instruction with a two-register *lvalue*

ate value. Finally, the last rule requires no action: it simply states that an immediate value that fits into 13-bits also fits in 32-bits.

Given the representation of production rules as "tree-tiles" we may think of the instruction selection problem as finding an optimal tiling which covers the given tree subject to the following constraint: the form of each tile leaf must match the form of the sub-tree rooted at that node.

The applicability of a particular pattern at a particular tree node depends on successfully matching the terminal symbol of the node, and being able to put the subtrees rooted at the leaves into the specified form. Thus the applicability of a pattern depends recursively on the applicability of other patterns further down the tree. This is the reason that trees are matched "bottom up".

From this perspective selection of a derivation may be thought of as an attempt to cover the given tree with "tiles" corresponding to each rule. The tree must be completely covered, and the points of contact between the tiles must have matching non-terminal labels.

Tiles may be more complicated than the examples in Fig. 1. For example, the tile corresponding to one variant of the *SPARC* "`stw`" (store word) instruction is shown in Fig. 2.

In this pattern the *lvalue* which denotes the destination of the assignment is formed from the sum of two register values. The "Void" form asserts "the tree has been evaluated and all side-effects executed". The declaration of this production would state the pattern thus—

Void = *assign*(*add*(**Reg** a1, **Reg** a2), **Reg** src)

This example introduces another feature of the specification metalanguage adopted here: each leaf of a pattern has a declared *form*, but may also be given an optional name. If leaves are given meaningful names the pattern is more readily understood, and semantic actions may refer to leaves by name rather than by the positional references used by many other rewriter-generators.

1.1 Dynamic Programming

Almost all tree grammars have multiple derivations for even the most simple expression trees. The choice of derivation is thus driven by the cost metric. According to circumstance this might be (some estimate of) least execution time, smallest code size or least power consumption.

As it turns out, the selection of the productions from a given tree grammar to discover a minimal cost covering of any given tree may be performed by *dynamic programming* [1, 3].

It is worth noting that the availability of an efficient algorithm that solves the minimal cover problem applies only to trees. The corresponding problem for an arbitrary directed acyclic graph (*DAG*) is known to be *NP*-hard [2, 13]. Thus, for code selection, the choice and placement of shared subexpressions must rely on heuristic considerations. See Koes and Goldstein [12] for a more recent approach to this problem.

The underlying principle that allows dynamic programming to work for tree rewriting is the *principle of optimality*. A statement of the principle is as follows—

> Suppose we have a tree T rooted at some node R, and we have a covering of the tree that rewrites T into the non-terminal form F with minimal cost. Now, if P is the production rule that is applied at the root R, then at each leaf of the P pattern the sub-tree rooted at that leaf must have been rewritten into the required form at minimal cost.

As a rough approximation of the principle we may say "every part of a least-cost covering must itself be least-cost".

The principle gives us the possibility to perform a bottom-up computation on the tree which is relatively economical. Starting from the leaves of the tree we find the minimal cost of rewriting the node into any of the forms that are feasible. Recursing up the tree we compute the minimal cost of rewriting other nodes in terms of the known, minimal costs for the lower sub-trees, together with the cost of application of the matching rule.

Rewriter generators are software tools that take a tree-grammar specification and emit a compiler module that performs instruction selection. The dynamic programming may take place at rewriter-generation time [8], or at compiler runtime. The former method is faster, but less flexible. In this paper we consider only the second possibility.

1.2 Labelling and Reducing

Rewriter generators which perform dynamic programming at compiler runtime include *iburg* [7], *lburg* [6] and *mburg* [9, 11].

In such rewriters the rewriting of each tree takes place in two steps. First, all the nodes of the tree are *labelled*, then the tree is *reduced* to the required non-terminal form.

The labelling phase visits every node in the tree in a bottom-up order. Labelling computes, for every non-terminal form of the grammar, the least cost of rewriting into that form. This step requires matching the tree structure immediately below the current node against all the rule patterns to see which rules match the structure. If a structure matches, and if the sub-trees of the pattern are able to be rewritten into the required form then the pattern is *applicable*. If the pattern is applicable, and if the cost of the rewriting is less than any previous cost of rewriting the tree to the same form then the new minimal cost is recorded. The index of the production that achieves the new minimum is recorded also.

Reduction is performed on a labelled tree by invocations of a *Reduce* method. Typically this method takes two arguments. The first is a reference to the root-node of the tree, the second is the form that is required. The computation proceeds by examining the labels of each node starting at the root. Each label has a list of the minimal cost of rewriting for every feasible form, and the rule that must be used to achieve that best rewriting. Thus the rewriter fetches the rule that is used to achieve the demanded form, and executes the *reduction action* of the rule.

The reduction action of each rule has two parts: the reduction must recurse to the sub-trees so that they get rewritten also, and the user-specified semantic action of the rule must be executed. Thus *Reduce* is called on every node that corresponds to a leaf of the selected pattern, with the form demanded in the recursive call specified by the leaf form of that rule. For a tree node that is being rewritten using the first rule of Fig. 1 each sub-tree of the current node will be passed to a recursive call of *Reduce* together with the demanded form “Reg”. For the chosen production the user-specified semantic action would be to allocate a destination register and emit an instruction that adds the two source registers together. The identity of the two source registers is determined by the semantic actions of the sub-tree rewritings.

Most bottom up tree rewriter-generators restrict the structure of the semantic actions that may be declared in the grammar. Traditionally the semantic action is executed *after* an implicit recursion to the sub-trees. As shown below, in order to gain the greater expressivity proposed here it is necessary to allow arbitrary interleavings of sub-tree recursion and user-specified semantic actions.

2 Predicated Patterns

An innovation in *mburg* was a facility for attaching predicates to patterns. A *predicated pattern* is one that has a an auxiliary condition attached to its applicability. A typical use of predicated patterns is to specify special-case translations, applicable only if certain algebraic conditions are met.

Some other rewriter generators achieve the same effect by *disallowing* the use of particular productions in undesired cases. This is achieved by declaring a cost function that returns “infinite” cost for the undesired cases. It is not that the pattern is held to be non-applicable, it is just that the infinite cost means that the undesired production can never be part of a minimal cost cover of a tree. The use of explicit predicates seems rather more natural.

Here is a simple example, specifying a strength reducing rewriting. Remembering that (non-trapping) multiplication by powers of two may be implemented by shifting, we declare—

Reg = *mult*(**Reg** lhs, **Imm** lit) &(*IsPowerOfTwo*(lit.value))

where the semantic action (not shown in the figure) would be to emit a left-shift, rather than a multiplication instruction.

An ampersand in a rule introduces a parenthesised predicate. The predicate, in this example, declares that this rule is applicable not just when the sub-trees are available in the required form but when, in addition, the value of the immediate expression denoted *lit* is a power of two.

In other cases predicates simply give an alternative to introducing an additional non-terminal form. For example, in the grammar fragment given in Fig. 1, instead of having separate forms for immediate values of different sizes (*Imm13* and *Imm32*) we *might* have chosen to declare a single form *Imm* and constrain the patterns with a predicate when required. Thus the second rule in Fig. 1 would be expressed as—

Reg = *add*(**Reg** lhs, **Imm** lit) &(-4096 <= lit.value && lit.value <= 4095)

However, in the case of the *SPARC* instruction set the use of the "fits in 13-bits" constraint is so widespread that it is almost certainly better to directly model these values as a separate form.

Predicates are evaluated during the labelling pass, as part of the applicability computation for a predicated rule. Thus the predicate may only depend on data that is available during the labelling traversal.

2.1 Using Predicated Patterns

Predicated patterns may be used to produce a variety of special case translations that are only applicable when particular properties hold. Here is a simple example, to demonstrate the general idea.

A programming idiom of *Pascal* family languages involves integer expressions of the form

$$(x + n)\,\mathrm{div}\,m \times m, \qquad \text{where } m = n + 1,$$

where div is integer division, x is an integer variable, and n and m are integer literals. This expression rounds up x to the next higher multiple of m.

In the common case that m is a power of two, say 8, many *C*-programmers would write `(x + 7) & (-8)` without a second thought. It is less obvious in the case that m is an arbitrary number, 13 say, that the following *C* code returns the required result—

```
int tmp = x + 12; result = tmp - tmp % 13;!
```

In both cases, the *C* computation is better than the *Pascal* idiom, even if the division and multiplication are strength-reduced.

In any case, a predicated production may recognize the rounding idiom, with the semantic action emitting whichever optimized instruction sequence is applicable—

> **Reg** = *mul*(*div*(**Reg** t, **Imm** m1), **Imm** m2)
> &(m1.value == m2.value)
> {*Emit "mask by –m" or "subtract remainder" code*}.

This production replaces the *Pascal* idiom and a number of other related rounding operations with an equivalent but faster computation.

3 What Are Forms?

In the traditional use of bottom-up tree rewriting for code selection the *forms* that are represented by the non-terminal symbols of the tree grammar denote the "location-kind" of the value computed at a node. In some cases there is some *property* of the value that is also indicated by the naming of the form. Thus we have forms such as: "*IReg*" denoting that the expression has been evaluated into an integer register; "*DReg*" denoting that the expression has been evaluated into a floating point double register; "*Void*" denoting that the expression has been evaluated for its side effects.

3.1 Forms and Post-Conditions

There is nothing about the use of dynamic programming or the principle of optimality that requires such a narrow view of the role of the non-terminal symbols. Indeed, the role of the non-terminals is simply to introduce an additional finite-cardinality dimension into the state space within which the optimization proceeds. A much more useful way to attach meaning to the form enumeration is to identify each form with a quite general *post-condition* that is asserted by the corresponding node of the rewritten form of the tree. All of the forms used as examples above clearly fit easily into such a conceptualization of the role of the forms.

The reconceptualization of forms as post-conditions allows a wider range of expressions to be rewritten by the technique, and fits easily with the way that programmers think about hand-written code.

The first step in generalizing the kind of post-condition that a form may assert might be to include some property of the value computed, or some invariant of the computation. We have already used a form, *Imm13*, to assert a value range limit. Consider however the possibility of introducing a form that guarantees that all instances of the expression will be evaluated into a register without observable side-effect and, in particular, *without raising an exception*. Let us call this form *SafeReg*.

A sketch of the productions that might conservatively generate such a form is as follows. Loading scalar local variable values, value parameters, static scalars and immediate values are all trap-free. Non overflow-tested add, subtract, multiply and all the bit-wise logical operations on trap-free operands are also trap-free. And so on.

Having defined evaluations that assert such a post-condition, we next consider an example use for such a form.

3.2 Full Evaluation of Boolean Expressions

It has been known since the 1960s that short-circuit evaluation of Boolean expressions is not always optimal [14]. In the last fifty years, as branch penalties have grown relative to machine cycle times this venerable observation is even more relevant.

The full evaluation of a short-circuit Boolean expression will be computationally equivalent to the short-circuit evaluation provided that each speculative operation is trap-free and has no observable side-effect. In the manner of the *SafeReg* form introduced above we define two new forms. *RegBool* asserts the post-condition "the expression has been evaluated into a machine register, and is known to be a Boolean value". *SafeBool* is a refinement of *RegBool* and asserts, in addition, that the evaluation is trap-free and has no observable side-effects.

Given such post-conditions, we may immediately add rules—

RegBool = *orElse*(**RegBool**, **SafeBool**)
{*"Evaluate both terms, then do bitwise OR"* }.
SafeBool = *orElse*(**SafeBool**, **SafeBool**)
{*"Evaluate both terms, then do bitwise OR"* } .

Here, the "semantic actions" just contain a description of the operational semantics. Notice that in the first production the evaluation of the first disjunct does not need to be safe. This is correct, since the first expression is always evaluated in the canonical, branching evaluation. The second disjunct is speculatively evaluated and hence must be safe. The second production states that if both disjuncts are safe the entire expression is safe.

There are corresponding productions for evaluating the "short circuit" *AND* in a jump-free manner.

These productions compute when it is *safe* to emit jump-free code. However, when is it *profitable* to do so? The answer is simple: if the cost metric is accurate, dynamic programming will choose precisely those cases where the jump-free case is superior.

Having introduced the notion of trap-free evaluation, there are a whole raft of special, peephole-style patterns that may be defined. Here is just the simplest such rule, for a special case of the (ternary) conditional expression $p\ ?\ e\ :\ 0$ where e is trap-free, and the value of the expression when p is false is zero (or null)—

Reg = *cndExp*(**RegBool** p, **SafeReg** t, **Imm** f) &(f.value == 0) .

The semantic action for this rule is amusing. The Boolean value p is arithmetically negated, transforming it into a mask word of either all ones or all zeros. This mask is bitwise and-ed with the register value computed by the speculative evaluation of the "true" sub-tree t.

3.3 Conditional Execution

In the same vein, the elimination of branch penalties, we may consider instruction selection for those machine architectures that provide for conditional execution, such as *ARM* [4]. Dynamic programming seems to promise a quantitative basis to choose between branching and conditional execution in such cases.

In the previous example we speculatively executed an evaluation, only to sometimes nullify the result with a masking operation in the semantic action. With conditional execution the machine fetches and decodes instructions, but does not perform any evaluation if the specified condition is not met. Such conditional code is more widely applicable than our result-nullifying trick, since the evaluations need not meet the rather stringent requirement of freedom from side-effects or traps.

Nevertheless, for *ARM* there is still a constraint on the computations that can be made conditional. *ARM* has only one set of condition code registers, so that (generally speaking) conditional code sequences may not be nested, and should not modify the condition codes.[2]

The extent to which such a formulation will explode the number of non-terminals for an *ARM* instruction selector is still under evaluation. Here however is a simple case following from the previous example of evaluation of conditional expressions—

Reg = *cndExp*(**Flag** cc, **Nullable** t, **Nullable** f) .

Instead of the constraint that the expressions must be "safe", that is, trap-free, we have the milder constraint that each instruction of the evaluation must be eligible for conditional execution. The semantic action makes the first evaluation conditional on the true value of the flag, with the inverse condition on the second evaluation.

In the example, the *Flag* form asserts that the predicate has been evaluated into the condition code flags. The *Nullable* form asserts that every instruction in the evaluation of the expression is eligible for conditional execution.

3.4 Emitting Jumping Code

Consider the problem of honoring the semantic demand "Evaluate Boolean expression E and branch to some given label if the value is true, otherwise control must fall through to the following instruction". We see that the semantic demand calls for the establishment of the evaluation post-condition "If true, control has passed to the

[2]There are actually some special case exemptions, but we do not treat these here.

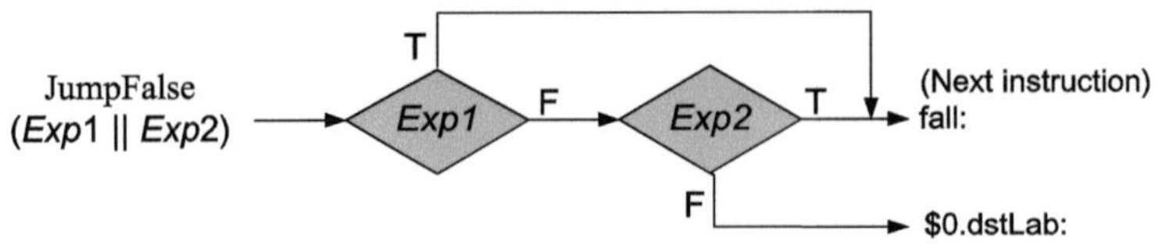

Fig. 3 Control flow for *JumpFalse* of a Boolean *OR*

given label, otherwise control has fallen through". Let us denote this post-condition "*JumpTrue*" where the target label is an *inherited*[3] attribute of the evaluation. We assume the existence of a corresponding "*JumpFalse*" denotation.

Now let us further suppose that in some particular case the Boolean expression is $(E_1 \,|\,|\, E_2)$ where "| |" denotes short-circuit evaluation of Boolean *OR*. Every experienced programmer would immediately decompose this problem as the prescription—

- Emit code to evaluate E_1 and conditionally branch to the given label if the value is true, otherwise fall through to the next instruction.
- Emit code to evaluate E_2 and conditionally branch to the given label if the value is true, otherwise fall through to the next instruction.

Notice how the natural description of the decomposition is phrased in terms of exactly the kind of post-conditions that we associate with non-terminal symbols. The prescription appears to be simply a repetition of the "jump if true" pattern for each sub-expression in turn.

The natural decomposition of this problem corresponds to the rewriting pattern—

JumpTrue = *orElse*(**JumpTrue** lOp, **JumpTrue** rOp)

where *orElse* is the node-tag for the "| |" operator.

Of course, this description has glossed over the manipulation of the "given" label values. The given label is an inherited attribute of the *orElse* node that is the root of expression E. This same label must be passed on to *both* of its child nodes *prior* to the recursive reduction of the two sub-trees. These label manipulations are part of the semantic actions of the rules. Such manipulations require no action during the *labelling* traversal and have no influence on the determination of minimality.

The logically reversed branch for the same operator decomposes into a similar rewriting pattern—

JumpFalse = *orElse*(**JumpTrue** Exp1, **JumpFalse** Exp2)

in this case the label manipulations are slightly more complicated. Figure 3 has a representation of the control flow. We wish for control to end up at the "given" label only if both expressions evaluate to false. In the event that the first expression evaluates to true we should immediately jump to the next instruction following the

[3] In the language of attribute grammars, an inherited attribute is one that is passed down the tree from an ancestor node.

entire evaluation. Since this "next instruction" location is the target of a jump from the evaluation of the first disjunct, it is necessary to allocate and name a new label for this location. In the figure this label has been named "fall".

The first disjunct is evaluated to establish the "JumpTrue" post-condition with the "fall" label as the target. If control falls through to the evaluation of the second disjunct the "JumpFalse" post-condition is established with our original inherited label as target.

The dual problem, where the expression E is $(E_1 \; \&\& \; E_2)$ and where "&&" denotes short-circuit evaluation of Boolean *AND* decomposes in similar ways—

JumpTrue = *andThen*(**JumpFalse** lOp, **JumpTrue** rOp)
JumpFalse = *andThen*(**JumpFalse** lOp, **JumpFalse** rOp)

where *andThen* is the node-tag for the "&&" operator.

Just to complete the Boolean rewriting overview, consider the following patterns for the Boolean negation "*not*" operator—

JumpFalse = *not*(**JumpTrue** child)
JumpTrue = *not*(**JumpFalse** child) .

Of course! We evaluate the same child expression, but reverse the sense of the branch. These two rules will have zero application cost, since they require no runtime action. In both cases the only semantic action of the rule will be to copy the destination label from the root node to the child node at compiler runtime.

It should be noted that the derivation of branching control flow for arbitrary (short circuit) Boolean expressions is unambiguous. Indeed, the instructions generated by these productions exactly duplicate those generated by the (deterministic) recursive *FallTrue/FallFalse* encoding pattern. See Gough [10, Chap. 9] for an example.

There is no need for dynamic programming to generate the code in this particular case. Nevertheless, the generation of control flow by a tool-generated rewriter has some advantages. In particular, it provides a uniform mechanism for instruction selection, including the fall-back code generation that is necessary when some otherwise profitable optimization of a Boolean evaluation is stubbornly unsafe.

4 Consequential Changes

The small example of the previous section hints at a radical expansion of the tasks that tree rewriting might be used to perform. However, any such expansion requires a few other generalizations of the framework.

4.1 Computing the Cost

In order to compute the cost of evaluation of a particular expression tree rooted at some node N we start with two pieces of information: the minimal costs of evaluation of each sub-tree into the form required by the specified rule, plus the cost of application of the rule that we are considering using at node N. The way in which these values are aggregated together is trivial in the case of a fully evaluated expression: we simply add the cost of application to the sum of the known costs of the sub-expressions.

However, if the expression is *not* fully evaluated in every execution of the emitted code, then we shall need a different way of aggregating the known cost values, at least for metrics that seek to model runtime execution cost.

In the case of a short-circuit expression evaluation the first sub-expression is always evaluated, and hence always exacts its full cost. However, the second sub-expression is only sometimes evaluated. Thus the aggregated cost will be the full cost of the first sub-expression, together with some discounted cost for the second sub-expression. Of course, each of the sub-expressions may themselves be subject to partial discounting.

In summary, the notion of the cost of a rewritten tree must be understood in a *statistical* sense, rather than the absolute sense that applies for fully evaluated expressions. In such cases the simple additive aggregation of sub-tree costs must be replaced by either a heuristic discounting factor or perhaps a profile-directed weighting.

4.2 Handling Inherited Attributes

For fully evaluated expressions the use of *synthesized*[4] attributes of the rewriting is sufficient. For example, if a rule calls for the emission of a register to register add the source registers of the instruction will have been allocated during the rewriting of the sub-trees, and thus will be available when the "`add`" instruction needs to be emitted.

By contrast the examples in the previous section show that when flow of control instructions are generated, label values need to be copied and/or allocated *prior* to the recursive call of *Reduce* which triggers the emission of the sub-expression evaluation code. For these examples label values are inherited attributes, source registers are synthesized attributes.

Thus, in order to support the wider range of possible rewritings the way in which semantic actions are specified for rules must be generalized. In particular the propagation of both inherited and synthesized attributes must be supported. Allowing arbitrary interleaving of user-specified computations and reduction recursions provides an easy path to handle both cases.

Previous rewriter-generators have supported rewriting patterns where *Reduce*() is implicitly called on the sub-trees rooted at the pattern leaves *prior* to the emission of the code explicit in the semantic action of the active production rule. In the new

[4]In the language of attribute grammars, a synthesized attribute is one that is passed up the tree from a descendant node.

framework actions may need to be performed before, after and even between reductions of the sub-trees. If follows that the positions of the recursions must be *explicit* in the semantic actions.

The work described in this paper began as a project to reimplement the 1997 program *mburg* [11] so as to generate *C#*. However, as the ideas described here have evolved, so the new tool has passed through several iterations. The current version, "*GPBurg*", is written in *C#*, and produces rewriters targetting the *.NET* framework.

Compared to other rewriters, *GPBurg* adds the following new features to its input metalanguage—

- Support for predicated productions.
- Explicit markers locating sub-tree recursion within semantic actions.
- Support for overriding the default cost aggregation rule.
- Support for productions with variable arity.

The rewriter has been used in a code emitter for an experimental *C#* version 3 compiler with an extensible type system [5]. The emitter output is standard *.NET ILASM*. Most of the concepts introduced here, such as substitution of alternate encoding patterns and safe full-evaluation of Boolean expressions, have been tested. For the experimental emitter *all* flow of control is generated by the rewriter, validating the claims of Sect. 3.4.

4.3 Future Work

The demonstration of these ideas in a framework that emits virtual machine code has an obvious limitation: since the *JIT* has still to work its magic, the cost metric is necessarily imprecise. A new implementation, still under construction, will emit *ANSI-C* and will be tested with a rewriting grammar targetting *ARM*. This will provide a flexible framework for rapid experimentation with grammar variants and standard embedded benchmarks. We will quantify the gains that are possible using conditional execution, and the compile-time costs of the additional complexity of the grammar.

5 Conclusions

The key concept in the reconceptualization of bottom-up tree rewriting is the recognition of *forms* as being a finite set of rather general postconditions on the emitted code. This concept has been validated by preliminary experiments. The quantitative utility of this insight is a matter that is still being explored.

The consequences of such a reconceptualization can also be seen, at least in outline. If rewriting is used to generate (or replace) flow of control, then the meaning of the cost metric must also be radically reconsidered. Costs must be now understood in a statistical sense, and take into account the execution probabilities of each instruction path. Furthermore, the simple rule for aggregation of costs by addition of sub-tree costs must also become more nuanced.

It should be noted however that if tree-rewriting is used to generate flow of control, but not to choose between branching and non-branching implementations the situation is much simpler. As remarked earlier, the branching flow of control generated for short-circuit Boolean evaluation is deterministic. Therefore the allocation of costs and the cost aggregation strategy cannot influence the outcome, and may be chosen arbitrarily.

Finally it should be reiterated that the implementation of these ideas requires a generalization of the mechanisms for specifying semantic actions in the grammar. The specification must be able to compute inherited as well as synthesized attributes, and must thus be able to specify the position of the sub-tree recursions in each semantic action.

References

1. Aho, A.V., Johnson, S.C.: Optimal code generation for expression trees. J. ACM **23**(3) (1976)
2. Aho, A.V., Johnson, S.C., Ullman, J.D.: Code generation for expressions with common subexpressions. J. ACM **24**(1) (1977)
3. Aho, A.V., Ganapathi, M., Tjiang, S.W.K.: Code generation using tree matching and dynamic programming. ACM Trans. Program. Lang. Syst. **11**(4) (1989)
4. ARM: ARM Architecture Reference Manual. ARM Limited. http://infocenter.arm.com/help/index.jsp?topic=/com.arm.doc.ddi0406b/index.html
5. Craik, A.J., Kelly, W.A.: Using ownership to reason about inherent parallelism in object-oriented programs. In: Gupta, R. (ed.) CC 2010, 19th International Conference on Compiler Construction, Paphos, Cyprus. LNCS, vol. 6011 (2010)
6. Fraser, C.W., Hanson, D.R.: A Retargetable C Compiler: Design and Implementation. Benjamin/Cummings, Redwood City (1995)
7. Fraser, C.W., Hanson, D.R., Proebsting, T.A.: Engineering a simple, efficient code generator generator. Lett. Program. Lang. Syst. **3**, 213–226 (1992)
8. Fraser, C.W., Henry, R.R., Proebsting, T.A.: BURG—Fast optimal instruction selection and tree parsing. SIGPLAN Not. **27**(4) (1992)
9. Gough, K.J.: Bottom-up tree rewriting tool MBURG. SIGPLAN Not. **31**(1) (1996)
10. Gough, J.: Compiling for the NET Common Language Runtime. Prentice-Hall PTR, Upper Saddle River (2002)
11. Gough, K.J., Ledermann, J.: Optimal code-selection using MBURG. In: ACSC 20, Australasian Computer Science Conference, Sydney (1997)
12. Koes, D.R., Goldstein, S.C.: Near-optimal instruction selection on DAGs. In: CGO'08, Boston, Massachusetts, April 2008
13. Proebsting, T.: Least-cost instructions selection in dags is NP-complete. http://research.microsoft.com/~toddpro/papers/proof.htm
14. Wulf, W.A., et al.: The Design of an Optimizing Compiler. American Elsevier, New York (1975)

Automated Adaptation of Component Interfaces with Type Based Adaptation

Thomas Gschwind

Abstract The construction of software can be improved by building software from reusable parts, which are typically referred to as software components. Software components can be developed independently from each other, thus decreasing the overall development time of a project. A disadvantage of software components, however, is that due to their independent development, component interfaces do not necessarily match and thus need to be adapted. In this paper, we present type based adaptation an adaptation technique that, unlike other techniques, supports the automated adaptation of component interfaces by relying on the component's type information and without requiring knowledge about the component's implementation. In this paper, we describe how we have achieved this kind of functionality and we will show how we have applied type based adaptation in practice.

1 Introduction

The essential idea of software engineering is to systematically construct software out of parts that we call components [14]. A key benefit of software components is that they can be developed independently from each other. Components may be developed by different groups who may be working on different parts of the same application or even by groups that may not even know about each other's efforts. Only this independent development enables the construction of large software systems.

Most component models available today, such as the CORBA Component Model (CCM) [19–21], the JavaBeans component model [7], the Enterprise JavaBeans (EJB) component model [3, 18], or COM [4] rely on black box components with well-defined and publicly available interfaces, a contract that the component promises to fulfill. Components only interact through the use of these component interfaces and do not require any knowledge of the implementation of the component itself. Software components are perfectly suited for object-oriented software

T. Gschwind (✉)
Zurich Research Laboratory, IBM, Säumerstrasse 4, 8803 Rüschlikon, Switzerland
e-mail: thg@zurich.ibm.com

K.K. Breitman, R.N. Horspool (eds.), *Patterns, Programming and Everything*,
DOI 10.1007/978-1-4471-2350-7_5,

development since their interfaces integrate nicely with the type system provided by object-oriented programming languages. As a result, software components have gained especial importance for the development of object-oriented software applications.

Although software components provide several benefits new problems arise with the use of software components. One such issue is the adaptation of software components that conceptually may interact with each other but which cannot due to syntactical incompatibilities between their component interfaces. In the context of distributed object technologies where the components that need to interact with each other cannot be known a-priori, the adaptation of components is of major importance. To solve these adaptation problems, we have developed type based adaptation.

The design goal of type based adaptation is to provide a means for the automated adaptation of software components and to be usable in combination with the component models available today. Except for the type information of the component interfaces today's component models do not provide any additional semantic or formal description. As we will show in this paper, it is sufficient to use the type information of the component-interfaces *expected* and those *provided* by a component, information provided by any modern component model. Information about the provided interfaces can be obtained from the component model's environment. The extraction of the information about the expected interfaces, will be shown later in this paper.

The remainder of this paper is structured as follows. Section 2 presents a set of application domains that can benefit from using type based adaptation. In Sect. 3, we describe component adapters the basis of our adaptation approach. These adapters are able to convert between different component interfaces or just individual parts thereof. In Sect. 4 we explain how these adapters can be composed to form more powerful adapters. By storing component adapters in a repository that enables them to be retrieved and combined, the process of adaptation can be automated. The requirements for such a repository are given in Sect. 5. In Sect. 6 we present our implementation of type based adaptation and how we have applied it to an Internet Bookstore application. We have also used this implementation to empirically verify our adaptation technique. In Sect. 7, we discuss the limitations of our approach and how we plan to eliminate them in future versions. We discuss related work in Sect. 8 and draw our conclusions in Sect. 9.

2 Application Domains

Distributed systems are one application domain for type based adaptation. In a distributed system, clients look up the components they need to interact with at a naming or trading service [5]. Only if the component required is available and provides the interface expected by the client intercommunication is possible. Using type based adaptation, however, it is also possible to communicate with a component that uses a syntactically different interface.

One application where such functionality might be useful is an Internet store that allows users to browse through the products available and to select and buy those of interest. At the checkout phase the user is asked to select a shipping address from an address book component which typically is a part of the Internet store. Using type based adaptation it is possible to let the user specify an address book component of his choice and to adapt the component interface of this component to the one required by the Internet store. Now, the user may select the shipping address from those addresses managed by his address book component.

Type based adaptation is also ideal for maintaining compatibility to older versions of a system whenever the interface of a component changes. In the Java Programming Language, this problem has been solved by allowing developers to declare a method as deprecated [2]. When the developer uses a deprecated method, the Java compiler emits a warning message. Although this approach allows the deprecated methods to access the component's internal state, the legacy code necessary to maintain compatibility to older systems is still part of the component.

The advantage of type based adaptation is that it allows the decoupling of the component's legacy code from its implementation by providing a separate adapter that implements the legacy code. Now, the old and new versions of the interface can be used simultaneously without the user noticing it. After all the users have upgraded to the new interface, the adapter providing the old component interface can be discarded easily without having to change the component again. Hence, the developer can focus on the new version of a component without having to deal with legacy code that only provides compatibility to older versions of the system.

Another application domain is pervasive computing where the components are installed on the individual pervasive computing devices which need to interact with each other. Since new devices are constantly entering and leaving the environment, it is necessary to be able to interact with a large number of software components, even if they use syntactically differing interfaces.

The user of a PDA, for instance, that frequently has to make appointments with other people might want the calendar component of his PDA to contact that of another PDA to come up with a possible date for an appointment. Since it is likely that not every PDA user will be using the same calendar component and that the calendar components will use different component interfaces to query for available dates, the component of the other PDA needs to be adapted to meet the requirements of the expected component interface.

The intercommunication of software components of large software systems that are composed by components contributed by different vendors is also a perfect choice for type based adaptation.

Consider a hospital system where the patient management system is bought from one vendor, the blood analysis system from another one, and the accounting software is bought from a third one. When certain blood tests are requested using the patient management system, they need to be forwarded to the blood analysis system and the test results need to be returned to the patient management system. Additionally, a record for the accounting software has to be generated. Unfortunately, there are a lot of different component interfaces used by such software. This is due to the large number of systems available and due to different regulations in different countries. So far, these systems are being adapted on an individual basis; a solution that is cumbersome for clients and vendors.

3 Adapters

Today's component models allow a program to query for the interfaces implemented by a given software component and for the component features defined by the component interfaces. Depending on the component model, this information can be provided using an interface repository [21], a type library [4], or reflection [13].

With the term *feature*, we refer to the externally visible interaction points of a component [19] such as the methods that may be invoked, the properties a component provides, and the events it may trigger. Since most component models map component interfaces onto a corresponding interface in an object-oriented programming language, properties and events are frequently realized using methods adhering to a certain naming convention. For instance, a property `x` is specified using a `getX()` and `setX()` method. This due to the fact that many type systems limit the definition of an interface to a set of methods.

In the following discussion, we will first focus on the interfaces provided by a software component and subsequently extend our approach to be applied to the individual features of a component. Like an interface in an object-oriented programming language, an interface of a software component represents a contract that the component promises to abide to [16]. Thus, the knowledge of the component interface provides already information to reason about the component's semantics. The missing information, however, is how to adapt one component interfaces to another conceptually compatible but syntactically different component interface.

Today's component models do not provide any semantic description of the components. Additionally, it is unclear whether it is possible to derive the algorithm to adapt a component on the basis of such a description alone. Hence, we have chosen a different approach to component adaptation. Instead of dealing with the description of the component's semantics, we focus on the specification of how one component interface can be adapted to another semantically compatible component interface. As we will show our approach can use this information to build more complex component adaptations and to infer on the basis of this information whether a component can be replaced with another component.

To provide this adaptation information, type based adaptation uses *component adapters*. These adapters algorithmically describe how to translate different component interfaces, and thus types, into each other. An adapter that sits between two components provides on the one side the interface expected by a component A and on the other side makes use of the interface provided by another component B that A wishes to interact with. An adapter translating between component interfaces, we write as shown in equation 1 where T_{to} represents the component interface expected by a component A and T_{from} that provided by a component B.

$$\Gamma \vdash a : T_{\text{from}} \succ T_{\text{to}} \tag{1}$$

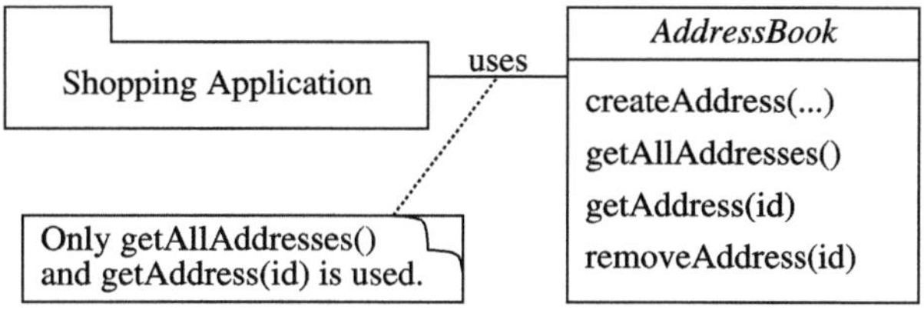

Fig. 1 Sample application requiring an address book component

Using this approach, we can compose two adapters a and b if the type translated to by adapter a matches that expected by adapter b. More details on the composition of adapters will be shown in Sect. 4.

So far, we have focused on entire component interfaces. In some cases, however, it will not be possible to implement an adapter that provides the functionality of the entire component interface T_{to} on the basis of T_{from}. In addition, many applications that require a component with the component interface T_{to} will not make use of all of the functionality provided by the component interface. This is due to the fact that components try to be highly versatile and thus will typically provide much more functionality than required by a single application.

Consider the shopping application of Fig. 1 for example. This application has been programmed with a specific address book component in mind but only uses two of the component's methods. Hence, an adapter that is only able to provide the functionality of the `getAllAddresses()` and `getAddress(id)` methods of the *AddressBook* component would be sufficient.

To support such cases we can break a component interface up into its individual component features (e.g., methods, properties, and events). Subsequently, type based adaptation supports adapters that do not translate the whole component interface but that only provide specific features of a component interface on the basis of specific features of another component interface. An adapter that translates one set of features into another set of features, we write as shown in Eq. (2). Again, the features required by an adapter are written on the left hand side and those provided on the right hand side. The name of a feature is represented by f_i and its type by T_i. $\mathcal{I}$ and $\mathcal{J}$ represent index sets.

$$\Gamma \vdash a : \{f_i : T_i\}^{i \in \mathcal{I}} \succ \{f_i : T_i\}^{i \in \mathcal{J}} \tag{2}$$

It is important to note that the semantics of a feature is only well defined if the name of the feature includes the name of the given component. For example, just specifying that an adapter provides the `saveAs`() feature is not sufficient since different components will have such a feature but with different semantics attached to it. Only if we say the adapter provides the `saveAs`() feature as provided by the Microsoft Word component, the semantics of the adapter is well defined.

One problem that needs to be solved with this approach is that from the compiler's point of view, the type safety of an application is judged on the basis of the component interface alone and not on the basis of the features used. Thus, from a compiler's point of view any substitute has to provide the complete interface even if the application uses only a subset of its functionality. We will show in Sect. 6

how our implementation deals with this problem, its possible solutions, and their advantages and disadvantages.

Currently, we require a developer to implement component adapters. Unlike a computer, a developer easily understands two component interfaces T_{to} and T_{from} and is able to define the necessary adaptations. Since our approach is able to automatically combine component adapters, developers only need to implement a small number of such adapters.

Code similar to the one that needs to be written for such adapters exists already in many of today's software systems in the form of wrappers or in the form of subclasses. One drawback is that such wrappers are usually part of a bigger component and thus cannot exist on their own, especially when subclassing is being used. Sometimes, these wrapper classes provide more functionality than is necessary for the sole purpose of adaptation. In this case, the adaptation functionality could be factored out into a separate adapter class to be usable as a component adapter.

For the implementation of a component adapter we could have defined a mapping language similar to the one used by the Polylith system [22, 23], the Object-Oriented Interoperability approach [10]. Unfortunately, many of these languages are hard to read or lack expressiveness. To alleviate this problem some of these languages allow functions to be defined using traditional programming languages such as C and to use these functions as part of the mapping language.

For our approach we consider the choice of such a language to be of lesser importance since we focus on the combination of adapters and not on their construction. Hence, we allow developers to define such adapters in whatever language is convenient for them provided that we can determine the component interfaces T_{from} and T_{to} that an adapter translates. In the prototype we have developed, we have successfully used the Java programming language for the definition of component adapters.

4 Adapter Composition

An important aspect of type based adaptation is the ability to combine component adapters to build more powerful adapters. To do that, we define the composition ($\circ$) and the combination ($\cup$) of two adapters a and b. Before we can do this, however, it is necessary to define the subtype relation ($<:$) between types (component interfaces). This relation indicates that any variable of type A can be viewed as type B if A is a subtype of B ($A <: B$). According to [1], the subtype relation is reflexive, antisymmetric, and transitive. The basic rules of subtyping are for an environment Γ that consists of typing assumptions for variables (v), each of the form $v : T$, are as follows:

Reflexiveness:

$$\frac{\Gamma \vdash A}{\vdash A <: A}$$

```
class Adaptera implements TTo {
  Ty componentToBeAdapted;
  // ... provide Ty on the basis of
  // componentToBeAdapted ...
}

class Adapterb implements Tx {
  Tfrom componentToBeAdapted;
  // ... provide Tx on the basis of
  // componentToBeAdapted ...
}
```

Fig. 2 Pseudo code of two adapters

Transitivity:

$$\frac{\Gamma \vdash A <: B \quad \Gamma \vdash B <: C}{\Gamma \vdash A <: C}$$

Subsumption:

$$\frac{\Gamma \vdash v : A \quad \Gamma \vdash A <: B}{\Gamma \vdash v : B}$$

In typical object-oriented programming languages as used by today's component models, a type is identified by a name. This name identifies the contract, and thus the semantics, the component is bound to [16]. For two types to be equal not only their structure but also their names have to be equal. Additionally, the subtype relation is defined explicitly. Thus, A is only a subtype of B if it has explicitly been defined that way.

Using the rule of subsumption we can identify that a subtype of a component has to fulfill the same requirements as its supertype. This rule leads to the Liskov substitution principle [11, 12] that states that a program accepting a type B has to exhibit the same behavior when operating on a type A if it is a subtype of B ($A <: B$).

Using the same rule, we can define the composition of component adapters. Given an adapter b that is able to translate a type T_{from} to T_{x} and an adapter a that is able to translate a type T_{y} to T_{to}, it is possible to first apply adapter b and than adapter a given that T_{x} can be substituted by T_{y}. The result of this combination is an adapter that translates T_{from} into T_{to}, as shown in Eq. (3).

$$\frac{\Gamma \vdash a : T_{\mathrm{y}} \succ T_{\mathrm{to}} \quad \Gamma \vdash b : T_{\mathrm{from}} \succ T_{\mathrm{x}} \quad \Gamma \vdash T_{\mathrm{x}} <: T_{\mathrm{y}}}{\Gamma \vdash a \circ b : T_{\mathrm{from}} \succ T_{\mathrm{to}}} \tag{3}$$

To illustrate this adapter composition, Fig. 2 shows some pseudo code of two adapters a and b. Adapter a can use any component (or component adapter) of type T_{y} or a subtype thereof. Otherwise, it would not be possible to assign the reference of that component interface to the adapter's `componentToBeAdapted` attribute. Thus, for adapter a to use a component that has been adapted by adapter b, the component interface T_{x} has to be a subtype of T_{y}.

$$\frac{\Gamma \vdash a : \{f_i : T_i\}^{i \in I} \succ \{f_i : T_i\}^{i \in J} \qquad \Gamma \vdash b : \{f_i : T_i\}^{i \in K} \succ \{f_i : T_i\}^{i \in L}}{\Gamma \vdash a \cup b : \{f_i : T_i\}^{i \in I \cup K} \succ \{f_i : T_i\}^{i \in J \cup L}} \tag{4}$$

Since we also want to be able to form composite adapters operating on individual component features, we can define the composition of such adapters analog to those operating on component interfaces. Since we have only defined the subtype relation for component interfaces so far, we extend this definition to sets of component features.

A set of features $F := \{f_i : T_i\}^{i \in \mathcal{I}}$ can be substituted with another set of features $F' := \{f_i : T_i\}^{i \in \mathcal{J}}$ if F' provides at least the functionality provided by F. This is the case if $\mathcal{I}$ is a subset of $\mathcal{J}$ ($\mathcal{I} \subset \mathcal{J}$). This looser definition is probably more restrictive than necessary since it might be sufficient if for every component feature f_i in F a component feature in F' can be located that is a supertype of f_i. This definition would require to define a subtype relation between individual component features. Before we can adopt this looser definition, however, it is necessary to gain more experience with our current adaptation approach.

The combination operator specifies that we can apply two adapters a and b that translate between two sets of component features at the same time. As shown in Eq. (4), the combined adapters then translate from the union of the feature sets required by the adapters to the union of the feature sets provided by them. If a feature is provided by both adapters we can use the one provided by either implementation. One approach to determine which implementation to favor over the other is to use some kind of performance estimates. This decision, however, is an implementation detail. Our current implementation uses for reasons of simplicity the implementation of the feature of the first component adapter.

5 Adapter Repository

An important aspect of type based adaptation is that the adapters are stored in a repository with meta information about the individual adapters. This meta information comprises the types (features) that the adapters translate and may also contain performance characteristics and other properties of an adapter.

On the basis of the component interfaces and features required by an application, those provided by the available components, and the adapter repository we can automatically determine whether it is possible to adapt a component to the requirements of the application. The algorithm to determine how the existing adapters need to be composed and combined can be described as follows.

1. We start out with the component interface or features required by the application and place this set of requirements together with an empty adapter into a queue.
2. If any component or set of component fullfills the set of requirements of the element at the head of the queue, the algorithm returns the corresponding adapter and terminates.
3. We take the first set of requirement off the queue and try to apply each adapter (either by composition or combination) that is stored in the adapter repository. If no adapter can be applied, no adaptation is possible and the algorithm terminates.

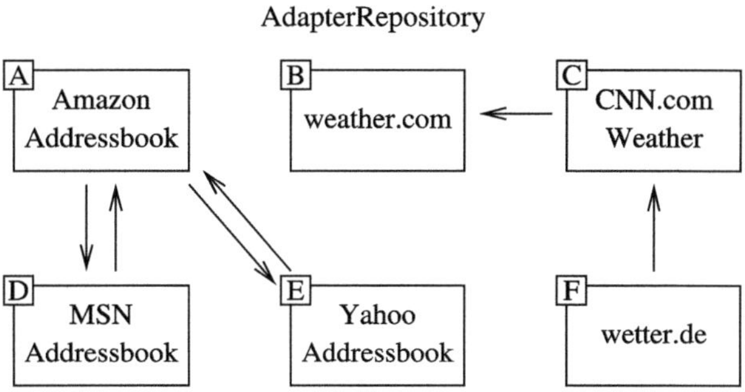

Fig. 3 A sample adapter repository

4. For each adapter a that can be applied, we do the following: The component interfaces and features provided by a and listed in the set of required ones are replaced with those provided by a. The new set of requirements together with the new composite adapter is added to the end of the queue.
5. Continue with step 2.

To illustrate a simplified version of the above algorithm, Fig. 3 shows a simplified version of an adapter repository which is restricted to manage adapters operating on component interfaces only. This repository consists of the adapters AD, DA, AE, and EA which are able to convert between the component interfaces A, D, and E and the adapters CB and FC, that translate between the component interfaces B, C, and F.

This adapter repository can be seen as a directed graph where the component interfaces are represented by the vertices and the adapters by the edges. The composition of adapters can be compared to the concatenation of neighbouring edges. Thus, given this adapter repository, we can use a shortest path algorithm to determine whether one component interface can be adapted to another one. The path between the two component interfaces indicates the adapters that need to be composed. For instance to adapt the component interface D into E, we the algorithm would compose the adapters AE and DA (AE ∘ DA). Since our implementation also supports adapters that operate on individual component features, our algorithm is more complicated.

Our algorithm can be tuned to only consider adapters that have specific properties. In some cases for instance, it might be sufficient, if an adapter provides an approximation of the required component interface. For example, consider an address book component that stores the name of a person in a single string. If that component needs to be converted into one that uses separate strings for the first name and last name, an adapter might assume that the first component stores names in the form *firstname lastname* or in the form *last name, first name*. Depending on the application domain, such heuristics may be sufficient or not. In other cases it might be adequate for an adapter to query the user for additional information if necessary but not provided by any of the available components.

```xml
<adapters>
  <adapter>
    <requires interface="java:at.ac.tuwien.infosys.vcard.IVCard" />
    <provides interface="java:at.ac.tuwien.infosys.bookstore.AddressBook" />
    <implementation class="at.ac.tuwien.infosys.adapters.IVCard2BookstoreAddressBook" />
    <description>Translates a IVCard interface into a bookstore AddressBook component</description>
  </adapter>
  <adapter>
    <requires interface="iostream:org.gnome.GnomeCard" />
    <provides interface="java:at.ac.tuwien.infosys.vcard.IVCard" />
    <implementation class="at.ac.tuwien.infosys.adapters.GnomeCard2IVCard" />
    <description>Translates a GnomeCard interface into a IVCard interface</description>
  </adapter>
  <adapter>
    <requires interface="java:at.ac.tuwien.infosys.ejb.AddressBook" feature="getAllAddresses" />
    <requires interface="java:at.ac.tuwien.infosys.ejb.AddressBook" feature="getAddress" />
    <provides interface="java:at.ac.tuwien.infosys.bookstore.AddressBook" feature="getListOfAddresses" />
    <provides interface="java:at.ac.tuwien.infosys.bookstore.AddressBook" feature="getAddress" />
    <implementation class="at.ac.tuwien.infosys.adapters.EJBAddressBook2BookstoreAddressBook" />
    <description>Provides a list of addresses and addresses on the basis of an EJB address book component
    interface</description>
  </adapter>
  <!-- Other adapters we have implemented translate between
    -- * an Enterprise JavaBeans address book and the I/O stream based GnomeCard interface (this adapter
    --   only translates the EJB component's getAllAddresses and getAddress features),
    -- * an Microsoft's Outlook address book and GnomeCard's component interface, and
    -- * a component using the alias database of the mutt email client to our bookstore's address book
    --   component.
    -->
</adapters>
```

Fig. 4 Meta description of an adapter

6 Evaluation

We have implemented the approach presented in this paper and verified it empirically by applying it to an Internet Bookstore. Using our approach, we were able to extend the application in a way that allows it to interact with different address book components. The advantage of using type based adaptation is that the application does not have to be changed to interact with other address book components since the components are automatically adapted to match the requirements of the application.

For our implementation we have used the Java programming language. Before we started with the implementation, however, we defined how the adapters used by our system need to be described. For the description of the adapters we have chosen to use an XML based syntax because of the tools available to parse such files. As we have explained in the previous sections, it is necessary to describe the component interfaces or features required by an adapter, those provided, its properties, and its implementation.

Two sample adapter descriptions are shown in Fig. 4. The first description shows an adapter that translates the `IVCard` interface implementing the VCard standard to an `AddressBook` interface used internally by our bookstore application. The "`java:`" in front of the name of the interface indicates the name of the type system. This allows developers to implement adapters that are at the same time able to bridge between different component models.

Since the type system is part of the name of a component adapter, adapters may also bridge between different component models. To verify this functionality, we have implemented adapters that allow the adaptation between Java types and components using a stream based communication mechanism. Although such services do not provide interfaces in a pure object-oriented sense they are used by many components available today. Such components wait for commands on one stream and return the results on another stream. The format of the requests and answer is defined in a protocol which can be regarded as the component's interface. Sample such well known protocols are IMAP, or SMTP. In our adapter description, such components are prefixed by "`iostream:`".

The third adapter specifies an adapter that translates some of the features of an EJB address book component to some of the features of the component interface used by our bookstore application. Using such adapters, we can loosen the substitutability requirements. For the adaptation process, it is sufficient if we provide only those features from a component used by the application itself. Hence, it is not necessary to provide all the features, even if they are not being used by the application.

To be able to use this looser definition of substitutability, however, we need to solve the following two challenges. The first is to identify the actual features used by the application since the component lookup operations only allow us to derive the name of the component interface required. To solve this problem, we have extended our component infrastructure to allow the application to explicitly state the features it requires from a given component interface. Since this approach introdues additional redundancy that might lead to software errors, we plan to analyze the byte code of an application to derive the set of features used. Another approach would be the use Architectural Description Languages (ADLs) [15]. ADLs explicitly lists the connectors and thus the features used by an application.

The second, bigger challenge is Java's type system. Java's type system requires a substitute component to implement all the features provided by the component interface, even if they are not being used by the application. Although the introduction of a separate interface for each individual component feature might solve this problem from a theoretical point no programmer would adopt this solution. Unfortunately, we have not yet found a clean solution to this problem that does not introduce too much overhead. Hence, we are currently supplying dummy implementations for the component features not being used by the application.

After we have implemented the infrastructure for type-based adaptation, we have implemented the six adapters shown in Fig. 4. If combined using our adaptation technique, these adapters enable the adaptation of the following component interfaces.

Bookstore's Address Book: This is the component interface internally expected by the bookstore application we have implemented.

EJB Address Book: This is the component interface of an Enterprise JavaBean address book component that we have downloaded from the Internet.

VCard Interface: This interface allows to retrieve business cards stored using the VCard standard.

GnomeCard I/O Stream Interface: GnomeCard provides an I/O stream based protocol that allows a VCard database to be queried for its business cards via a network socket. The protocol used is somewhat similar to HTTP.

Outlook I/O Stream Interface: This is an I/O stream based server that allows for the access of contact information stored within Microsoft's Outlook application. Originally, Outlook is a COM component but since we cannot access COM components from UNIX we have added a simple socket based interface to it.

Mutt's Alias Database: This is simple Java component that allows us to access the alias database maintained by the mutt email client. We have added this component interface to allow us to experiment with a component that only provides a subset of the required information.

It is interesting to note that Microsoft Outlook and the GnomeCard application have a similar component interface. It seems that Microsoft Outlook is, like GnomeCard, roughly based on the VCard standard for the representation of business cards. As a side-effect, the implementation of the Outlook to GnomeCard and the GnomeCard to IVCard adapters were straight-forward.

The implementation of the IVCard to our application's internal address book component interface was a little bit more complicated because the VCard standard supports to store several types of addresses for a given person whereas our application only supports to store a single address per entry. This problem was solved by storing the person multiple times and including the type of address as part of the entry's identifier.

As the next step, we have implemented the bookstore application. We implemented the application as a web store that allows users to browse through the available books and to put books of interest into a shopping basket. When the user decides to buy the books, he is asked to supply the shipping address and payment information. By default, our application uses its internal address book component but also allows users to specify their own address book component to use. After the user has specified the reference of the address book component to be used, the web application contacts the user's addressbook service and presents a list of the mailing and shipping addresses to the user. Additionally, the component's reference is stored in the user's profile and the corresponding component will be used during subsequent visits to the store.

A component reference looks similar to a web URL. It consists of three parts separated by a colon. The first part specifies the name of the component model. The second represents the name of the component interface (or the protocol used by the component). The third one indicates which instance of the component to use and is specific to the component. This last part is used by the component adapter that is able to adapt the corresponding type of component. The component reference of the EJB address book component, for instance, looks as follows:

```
java:
at.ac.tuwien.infosys.ejb.AddressBook:
sequ.infosys.tuwien.ac.at:1099/AddressBookEJB
```

Using the adapters we have implemented, our system was able to transparently adapt between the different address book components we have presented. This was the case no matter whether the adapters were translating the whole component interface or just some features thereof.

Since the adapter translating from mutt's email database was only able to provide the person's name and email address, the adapter had to query interactively for the missing address information. The problem we encountered here was that the adapter was trying to query the user sitting on the server machine for the address information. Hence, a better approach would be to execute the code responsible for the adaptation on the client machine using an applet for instance.

7 Future Work

One limitation of our current approach is that an application that uses type based adaptation may have to list the component features it relies on. Otherwise type based adaptation has to assume that the application uses all of the features provided by the component which typically is not the case. Explicitly listing all the component features, however, introduces a source of programming errors. If a developer forgets to list one of the component features used, this might lead to a runtime error since type based adaptation is free to select an adapter that does not provide this feature.

In future versions, we will try to analyse the program to infer the required component features. Another approach would be the use of an Architectural Description Language (ADL). ADLs have the advantage of explicitly listing the component connectors [15] and thus the features required.

Another focus today is to verify whether a component adheres to its specification. This can be done by stating the pre- and postcondition of the methods defined in the component interface with a formal description language. On the basis of these conditions and the component's implementation [28], it is possible to infer whether the specification is met. Since these conditions also have to be met by an adapter that is able to provide the same component interface on the basis of another component, it must be possible to use this information to prove the correctness of an adapter and subsequently a composition of adapters.

8 Related Work

The problem of software adaptation is not new and hence several other techniques have been developed that try to tackle this issue. A comparison of such techniques that require the manual adaptation by software developers can be found in [8]. The most prominent of these techniques is wrapping where a wrapper encapsulates the original component and thus may alter the component interface. In [6], wrapping is also referred to as Adapter or Decorator design patterns.

Our approach can be seen as an extension of the adapter pattern [6, 17]. The difference, however, is that in our approach the adapters are first-class objects described on their own and that there is an adapter repository which has full knowledge about the adapters available and the transformations they describe. On the basis of this information the adaptation process can be automated.

Bridging [26] is another manual adaptation technique. Bridging does not address the adaptation of the interface itself but maps the protocol used by one component technology to that of another component technology. Such a bridge, for instance, might allow to interact with CORBA components like they were COM components. One disadvantage of bridging, however, is that a different bridge is required for every different pair of component models.

The interworking problem between different components has already been identified with the NIMBLE [23] language which is part of the Polylith [22] system as well as by the Conciliation approach presented in [24]. Unlike Conciliation, NIMBLE does not take the object-oriented view into account and solely operates on a procedural level. Compared to type-based adaptation, however, both of these approaches are static and their adaptations cannot be combined to form more complex adapters. In dynamic distributed systems, however, it is important that the adaptation is performed at run-time since the components that need to interoperate with each other cannot be known a-priori.

A semi-automated approach for the adaptation of component interfaces is presented in [27]. This approach does not make use of the name of the component interface but instead augments component interfaces with an additional description of the protocol underlying the interface. It describes the legal orderings of the messages that may be sent and received by the component by means of a finite state grammar. Additionally, this approach uses an interface mapping language that allows developers to describe mappings from one interface to another. Based on the description of the component interface's protocol and the interface mapping it can be verified that the adaptation is safe and hence that the communication protocols used by the components are compatible.

The advantage of type based adaptation, however, is that the interface mappings define how the protocol of component interface A communicating with component interface B has to be adapted and hence such a description has been provided for every two components that possibly need to interact with each other. The adapters used by type based adaptation, however, define how a component interface B' can be simulated on the basis of a component interface B. Since our adapters do not depend on the knowledge of how B' is used by component A our adapters may be combined to form more complex adapters. With regards to safety, we rely on the component adapters to be implemented such that they abide to the contract defined by the component interface in a way similar that [27] relies on the correctness of the component's protocol description.

An approach that supports the automated synthesis of interface adapters has been presented in [25]. This approach, however, is purely syntactic and is only concerned with the structure of interface signatures and ignores semantic issues. Given a component type B that has to be used to emulate a component type B', this approach analyses the structure of B and B' and finds a mapping of B's structure to that of B'. If ambiguities due to the existance of multiple such mappings arise or due to additional attributes, they require user intervention.

The disadvantage of this approach is that it requires the availability of the original and the substitute component in order to derive the component adapter. Additionally, it cannot derive an adapter for structurally different but semantically compatible components. For instance, a component that uses a tree structure for data storage cannot be adapted to one that uses a linear list even though they provide the same functionality.

The adaptation of software components is not restricted to the adaptation of component interfaces. Aspect-oriented programming [9], for instance, allows the adaptation of components to add new functionality to a component itself. This kind of adaptation is useful in the presence of cross cutting concerns such as security or logging. Aspect-oriented programming allows to encapsulate these concerns into a separate module and to weave these concerns into the necessary software components during compile time.

9 Conclusions

The contribution of this paper is type based adaptation, a simple but flexible and powerful adaptation technique. Type based adaptation enables the automated adaptation of a software component that provide a syntactically different but semantically compatible component interface. Such adaptations are necessary for components that have been developed independently and only match on a semantical level.

The basis of type based adaptation are component adapters. These adapters define how two component interfaces or individual parts thereof can be adapted. The problem of typical other such approaches is that they require $O(n^2)$ different adapters. Our approach, however, requires a much smaller number of adapters since it supports the composition of component adapters to enable more powerful adaptations than those provided by each individual adapter.

As we have shown in this paper, the adaptation can be automated by placing such simple component adapters into a repository together with a description of the adaptation they perform. On the basis of this repository, the component interface required by an application and those provided by the components an algorithm can determine which adapters that need to be composed. This kind of type information is already maintained by today's component models. Thus, our adaptation technique can be used in combination with today's software systems as we have shown in Sect. 6.

Since the adaptation can be performed automatically during run-time, it is an ideal adaptation approach for systems were the components that need to interact cannot be known a-priori. Additionally, our adaptation technique enables the definition of adapters that adapt between components that have been developed for different component models which increases the number of components that may be used in combination with such systems.

Finally, we have demonstrated the feasibility of type based adaptation for the use in web applications. Our results, however, indicate that it can be used in a variety of other application domains as well. As we have shown with our example automatic adaptation is important since it adds more flexibility to component based software applications and does not require all of the components to be known at development time.

Acknowledgements This work was performed while the author was Technische Universität Wien as part of his PhD thesis. The author gratefully acknowledges the financial support provided by the European Union as part of the EASYCOMP project (IST-1999-14151).

References

1. Abadi, M., Cardelli, L.: A Theory of Objects. Springer, Berlin (1996)
2. Arnold, K., Gosling, J.: The Java Programming Language (Java Series), 2nd edn. Addison-Wesley, Reading (1997)
3. DeMichiel, L.G., Yalçinalp, L.Ü., Krishnan, S.: Enterprise JavaBeans Specification, Version 2.0. Sun Microsystems, April 2001. Proposed Final Draft 2
4. Eddon, G., Eddon, H.: Inside Distributed COM. Microsoft Press, Redmond (1998)
5. Emmerich, W.: Engineering Distributed Objects. Wiley, New York (2000)
6. Gamma, E., Helm, R., Johnson, R., Vlissides, J.: Design Patterns: Elements of Reusable Object-Oriented Software, 1st edn. Addison-Wesley, Reading (1995)
7. Hamilton, G.: JavaBeans. Sun Microsystems, August 1997. Version 1.01-A
8. Heineman, G.T.: Adaptation of software components. Technical Report WPI-CS-TR-99-04, Worcester Polytechnic Institute, Computer Science Department, February (1999)
9. Kiczales, G., Lamping, J., Mendhekar, A., Maeda, C., Lopes, C.V., Loingtier, J.-M., Irwin, J.: Aspect-oriented programming. In: Akşit, M., Matsuoka, S. (eds.) Proceedings of the 11th European Conference on Object Oriented Programming (ECOOP'97), pp. 220–242. Springer, Berlin (1997)
10. Konstantas, D.: Object oriented interoperability. In: Nierstrasz, O. (ed.) Proceedings of the 7th European Conference on Object Oriented Programming (ECOOP'93), pp. 80–102. Springer, Berlin (1993)
11. Liskov, B.H., Wing, J.M.: Specifications and their use in defining subtypes. In: Paepcke, A. (ed.) Proceedings of the Conference on Object-Oriented Programming Systems, Languages, and Applications (OOPLSA'93), pp. 16–28. ACM Press, New York (1993)
12. Liskov, B.H., Wing, J.M.: A behavioral notion of subtyping. ACM Trans. Program. Lang. Syst. **16**(6), 1811–1841 (1994)
13. Maes, P.: Concepts and experiments in computational reflection. In: Meyrowitz, N.K. (ed.) Proceedings of the Conference on Object-Oriented Programming Systems, Languages, and Applications (OOPSLA'87), pp. 147–155. ACM Press, New York (1987)
14. McIlroy, M.D.: Mass produced software components. In: Proceedings of the Nato Software Engineering Conference, pp. 138–155 (1968)
15. Medvidovic, N., Taylor, R.N.: A classification and comparison framework for software architecture description languages. IEEE Trans. Softw. Eng. **26**(1), 70–93 (2000)
16. Meyer, B.: Applying "Design by Contract". IEEE Comput. **25**(10), 40–51 (1992)
17. Mezini, M., Seiter, L., Lieberherr, K.: Component integration with pluggable composite adapters. In: Aksit, M. (ed.) 2000 Symposium on Software Architectures and Component Technology: The State of the Art in Research and Practice. Kluwer Academic, Dordrecht (2000)
18. Monson-Haefel, R.: Enterprise JavaBeans, 2nd edn. O'Reilly & Associates, Sebastopol (2000)
19. OMG: CORBA Components—Volume I, August 1999. OMG TC Document `orbos/99-07-01`
20. OMG: CORBA Components—Volume II: MOF-Based Metamodels, August 1999. OMG TC Document `orbos/99-07-02`
21. OMG: CORBA Components—Volume III: Interface Repository, August 1999. OMG TC Document `orbos/99-07-03`
22. Purtilo, J.M.: The Polylith software bus. ACM Trans. Program. Lang. Syst. **16**(1), 151–174 (1994)

23. Purtilo, J.M., Atlee, J.M.: Improving module reuse by interface adaptation. In: Proceedings of the International Conference on Computer Languages, pp. 208–217 (1990)
24. Smith, G., Gough, J., Szyperski, C.: Conciliation: The adaptation of independently developed components. In: Gupta, G., Shen, H. (eds.) Proceedings of the 2nd International Conference on Parallel and Distributed Computing and Networks. IASTED, Calgary (1998)
25. Thatté, S.R.: Automated synthesis of interface adapters for reusable classes. In: Proceedings of the Symposium on Principles of Programming Languages (POPL'94), pp. 174–187. ACM Press, New York (1994)
26. Wegner, P.: Interoperability. ACM Comput. Surv. **28**(1) (1996)
27. Yellin, D.M., Strom, R.E.: Interfaces, protocols, and the semi-automatic construction of software adaptors. In: Proceedings of the Ninth Annual Conference on Object-Oriented Programming Systems, Languages, and Applications (OOPSLA'94), pp. 176–190. ACM Press, New York (1994)
28. Zaremski, A.M., Wing, J.M.: Specification matching of software components. ACM Trans. Softw. Eng. Methodol. **6**(4), 333–369 (1997)

The Benefits of Bad Teaching

Derrick G. Kourie

Abstract It is proposed that IT academics are inclined to put too much time and effort into teaching well. The result need not necessarily redound to the benefit of either the teacher or the student. It may rob the teacher of time that could be more valuably spent on other academic activities. It tends to deprive the student of the benefits of self-discovery, intellectual ownership and responsibility.

1 Prologue

This somewhat notorious *bad teaching* talk was presented as a keynote address at the 2001 Southern African Computer Lecturers Association (SACLA) conference. SACLA conferences have been held annually in South Africa since 1971. Although recent conferences incorporate formal refereed tracks and produce formal proceedings, this was not the case in 2001. On the contrary, SACLA has a tradition of being an informal forum for exchanging educational ideas about Computer Science and Information Systems. Because of this informality, this *bad teaching* talk never found an ISSN or ISBN publication home.

Nevertheless, electronic copies of the talk spread, and as a result it has been read and discussed more widely than most of my technical publications. A hard-copy version mailed to me by an educationalist colleague was amply annotated with comments of agreement and disagreement. A deputy vice-chancellor dismissed it as merely the opinion of a disaffected staff member. Numerous colleagues have applauded it, even to the extent of advocating it as obligatory induction material for new faculty members. It was mentioned in at least two subsequent SACLA talks; it has been cited by IT educationalists in New Zealand [4, 5]; and a PhD thesis in Education offers it as an example of how " ...academics are suffering under the burden of additional loads, and often resent the 'quality burden' thrust on them" [2].

Judith Bishop, too, has referenced the *bad teaching* talk. This she did in her delightful contribution to a festschrift in my honour. In a playful yet thought-provoking

D.G. Kourie (✉)
Fastar Research Groups, Department of Computer Science, University of Pretoria, Pretoria, South Africa, 0001
e-mail: dkourie@cs.up.ac.za

K.K. Breitman, R.N. Horspool (eds.), *Patterns, Programming and Everything*, DOI 10.1007/978-1-4471-2350-7_6, © Springer-Verlag London 2012 article entitled "The Lazy Programmer" [1], she points to my laziness "in the Dijkstrasian sense: if a program can be written correctly the first time, surely we can save a lot of trouble in debugging, and all go home early?" She then cites the *bad teaching* talk as further evidence of my proclivity towards measured laziness. I plead guilty as charged! Indeed, republishing the talk in this festschrift dedicated to Judith reinforces the charge. In mitigation, I appeal to the widely commended software engineering practice of reuse.

In a more profound sense, however, it is singularly appropriate that one of my best-known efforts at writing should find a home in a festschrift for Judith—a deeply cherished longstanding friend and colleague. For Judith has played a singularly important role in my academic life (and, indeed, in much of my personal life). She has pushed and shoved and jostled my natural proclivity towards laziness, never allowing me to rest on my laurels, and continually urging me on. She has roped me into various committees; she has introduced me to a steady stream of international academics; she has shifted and shaped my efforts at managing an academic department; she has influenced the character and content of courses I have taught; and she leveraged me into a twenty year spell as editor of the South African Computer Journal.

My first encounter with Judith was at a student conference in the early 1970s. The mind-image of her that has remained vividly with me ever since is of a bouncy lass whose rapid, resolute, fixed step betrayed her personality: an ordered, strong character, constantly and firmly *en route* to some well-considered objective. That resolute, ordered, ever-advancing nature continues to characterise her. It is said of the controversial Victorian author, Hillaire Belloc, that he had no opinions, only convictions! That, in part, is how I experience Judith. (I recall making this point to Niklaus Wirth on one of his several Judith-arranged visits to South Africa. Though he laughed heartily at the aphorism, he concurred with the description, repeating several times to himself: "She has no opinions, only convictions!")

However, that is only part of Judith. There is another very soft side to this powerful lady, a side that embodies so many archetypally feminine attributes: attention to the detail, person-centred, feeling-aware, service-oriented, sometimes even disarmingly vulnerable. Her friends and colleagues, her students, her sons and family know these attributes well, for Judith's richly contrasting personality is also largely an extroverted one.

We have seen her working furiously to meet a deadline for the next new book; and we have seen her preparing jelly in moulds of hollowed out orange skins for a child's birthday party. We have listened to her strategising about the optimal sequence of moves to get the dean to agree to her latest academic proposal; and we have seen her as a Miss Marple-like figure in a hat and blue Cub Mistress uniform with little ten-year old boys scampering about her feet as they dib-dib-dib and promise to do their best. We have watched as she confidently orchestrates the logistics of major international conferences; and we have overheard her speaking quiet words of encouragement to a floundering and disheartened student as we pass by her office door. Most of all, so many of us have been the beneficiaries of Judith's abundantly exuberant generosity in respect to her time, energy, contacts and resources.

It is therefore a joy, an honour and an irony that my *bad teaching* talk should finally find a more formal home in the festschrift of one who is so incorrigibly energetic, thorough and productive. But for the occasional contextualising footnote, the talk is lazily reproduced in its original form.

If a thing is worth doing, it's worth doing badly.

G. K. Chesterton

2 Introduction

The theme of this presentation derives from the widely held perception that the various IT-related academic disciplines at universities (Computer Science, Information Systems, Information Science, Computer Engineering, etc.) are under severe stress. On the one hand, the courses are more popular and are growing at a faster rate than other fields. On the other hand, university bureaucracies and policies are not merely ill-equipped to respond to fast growth, but actually benefit financially by delaying a response to the growth for as long as possible. Furthermore, the popularity of IT courses stems precisely from the fact that IT qualifications are in high demand in industry, which leads in turn to a shortage of IT academic staff to teach the courses, even when posts are available.

The net result is that fewer people teach more courses, so that IT departments rake in ever-increasing amounts of state subsidy for their universities. These profits, euphemistically labeled "contribution to overhead costs", are deployed in various ways: cross-subsidization of non-profitable departments; maintenance of general facilities; salaries for administrative personnel, etc. Sweeteners of generous physical resources for the IT departments may be provided. But I know of no university in South Africa where significant concessions have been made in terms of industry-related remuneration. At best, small subventions are provided. As a result, shortages of quality staff remain acute in most IT departments.[1]

Simultaneously, universities are in strong competition to raise their so-called research profiles. The public measure of a South African university's research prowess has become the number of publications on the list (of journals used by the Department of National Education for subsidy purposes). Academics who produce publications on the list are looked upon favourably for promotion, while those who do not, tend to be treated in a concessionary, if not condescending fashion. They have to motivate vigorously the value of their conference contributions and other IT outputs to selection committees, often dominated by skeptical academic power brokers

[1] Readers will recall the wildly frenetic nineties. Student numbers were exploding as the computer gaming industry took off, as the web became ever-more popular, and as Y2K doomsday scenarios focussed attention on IT as a lucrative area of specialisation. Even though now, a decade after the 2001 *bad teaching* talk, the hump of the so-called hype-curve has long been crossed, IT in academia remains under pressure, albeit somewhat less severe than before.

from the more traditional departments whose continued survival is underwritten by IT's contribution to overhead costs.

For there should be no doubt about the following—that the value of research in South African universities is primarily at the level of prestige and image-building, not of direct income generation. This claim does not deny the link between image and income, nor that patented research may sometimes pay handsome dividends. But, from a subsidy point of view, research only brings in something like 2 % of total subsidy income. It is an abiding irony, but an academic reality, that promotion is based not on one's contribution to income generation but on the contribution to image advancement.[2] It cuts no ice to argue the case for promotion based on a good teaching track record. This is usually dismissed with a dogmatic assertion that one cannot be a good teacher without being a good researcher (a highly dubious notion, in my opinion).

Thus, the IT academic wishing for promotion is on an Homeric journey. She has to navigate between the Scylla and Charybdis—between the six-headed monster of academic purism continually snapping: "Where are your journal publications?" and the lure of being sucked deeper into the vortex of ever increasing teaching commitments. (The use of the feminine pronoun is here not only politically correct. It is probably also more appropriate. It would seem that women tend to be the ones who most often rescue departments where new teaching needs arise. They do so either voluntarily—having an affinity for the human-centered activity that is implied—or succumb more readily than their male counterparts to pressure from authority.)

There are many strategies that could facilitate the journey. For example, IT departments could limit both student intake and range of courses presented. Here, a complimentary strategy is offered: teach less well. I contend that "bad" teaching not only improves one's research and therefore one's promotional opportunities, but that it might, paradoxically, result in better educated students.

3 A Personal Historical Perspective

Permit a brief and personal historical perspective on the notion that universities should teach well. (It is personal, in the sense of being the truth as I see it, without purporting to be the full and complete truth. In our post-modern world, I am under the impression that giving such a perspective is a perfectly respectable academic thing to do.) The emphasis on good teaching is a relatively recent one. It is a product of mass education that came about in the second half of the twentieth century. Prior to that, the emphasis was on the knowledge of the professor, not on how well he got

[2]Note that the figure of 2 % refers to research income due to state subsidy of publications in approved journals. Because the subsidy amount per publication has been increased quite considerably in recent times, this figure now stands at approximately 10 % of subsidy income. Research income from the state therefore continues to lag behind tuition income, notwithstanding the more generous state subsidy of research publications.

across the knowledge. That would often take place on a one to one basis, as in the Oxbridge model still existing today. The ancient universities of Europe were places where small elite groups of truth-seekers gathered at the feet of luminaries to imbibe their wisdom and follow their prescription about what to read and study. Pedagogy and didactics were secondary matters.

Even in the sixties and seventies, when some of us were students, there did not seem to be too much of a premium on good teaching. Large numbers of students were admitted into popular degrees such as civil engineering, medicine and physics. Gray-haired professors taught large first year chemistry, mathematics and physics classes with relatively little concern for the ability of students to cope. They seemed blithely unconcerned about high failure rates. Some naturally taught well, and others less so. For students, it was a case of sink or swim. External examiners (an outmoded British notion carried over from a yet earlier era) were appointed to prevent flagrant injustices but whether they ever seriously intervened, we will never know. It was a time when universities were subsidized on the basis of intake, rather than throughput. It was a time when the bald and brawny 25-year old rugby player who sat (sometimes!) in my Chemistry 1 class could cheerfully countenance his fifth failure of the subject while continuing his respected rugby career in the university's first team.

Then, at the start of the eighties, the subsidy formula changed. It now rewarded throughput rather than intake. The attitude of university authorities changed accordingly. Students who failed too often were either excluded or had to pay higher fees. In an effort to improve teaching, staff members were sent on courses, run by educationalists. We were shown how to design courses, partition them into study units and specify learning objectives for each study unit. Study notes were required to illuminate study units. Continual assessment was emphasized and re-examination procedures strengthened to improve the chances of marginal students. While good researchers were always valued, academics who acquired qualifications in education were also rewarded. Indeed, some people seemed to move quite high up into the academic hierarchy on the basis of their teaching ability alone (although—in the case I have in mind—it might have been that Broederbond[3] affiliations also played a role).

As we marched into the New South Africa, there was renewed interest from the state in improved tertiary teaching. The beneficiaries were to be the growing number of historically disadvantaged students who were entering universities. It was felt that courses should be standardized, structured and refashioned to produce specific outcomes. We were told to submit to organs of the state (SAQA) a list of our degree programs, their courses, their contents and their expected outcomes in terms of skills and values. Somehow this would all redound to the benefit of the historically disadvantaged. We are not sure what happened to all these carefully drawn up submissions. Mercifully, individual universities have retained their freedom to teach

[3]The Broederbond was the secret Afrikaner organisation that served as a brains trust and the strategic underpinning for the Nationalist Government during South Africa's Apartheid years.

what they please, and we even seem free to change what we teach without revising our erstwhile SAQA submissions.

Latterly the minister of education has set the cat amongst the pigeons. He has announced measures to differentiate universities into five categories, based primarily on their research output. Once again research prowess—never really lost as a value in most universities—has shifted to center stage.[4] SAQA and all its outcomes-based requirements seem to have faded slightly into the background. This, then, seems to be a good moment to reassess the meaning and value of good teaching!

4 Good Teaching

Broadly, a well-taught course may be characterized by the selection of appropriate course material, good organization, good delivery, good reinforcement procedures and good assessment procedures. A brief elaboration of these characteristics follows.

4.1 Appropriate Course Material

It is important to select course material that is consistent with international trends. It should build on prior knowledge of students and avoid repetition. While some might argue on the extent to which course material should directly address industry needs, we would agree that the knowledge acquired should empower the student. Of course, the prescribed book should be selected with utmost care: it should be well written; should cover the relevant topics; should be pedagogically sound; etc.

4.2 Good Organization

The times and venues for lectures, tests and examinations should be pre-announced, and a lecturing schedule should be provided. The weighting of marks for tests, assignments, practical classes, examinations, etc should also be known in advanced. To assist students in their time-management, the number of assignments and projects and their respective due dates should be prespecified. The prescribed book should have been chosen well in advance of the course and should be available at bookstores before the start of the course. Supporting notes (either in hardcopy format or on an intranet) should be made available, if not in advance, then at least in synchrony with material delivered in lectures.

[4]It is worth noting the original model proposed by the late minister of education, Kadar Asmal, for differentiating universities in relation to their research output never really took off. Neither has pressure to publish abated. If anything, it has increased as high-ranking research universities vie for position, and lower ranking universities aspire for recognition.

4.3 Good Delivery

The lecturer ought to make full use of existing technologies—especially visual technologies—available for teaching. A minimum requirement seems to be to rely on printed (as opposed to hand-written) transparencies—coloured, if possible. An even better option is to rely on a slide show presentation (Power Point or equivalent), tastefully designed to use sound, colour, and animation. While the lecturer's personal style of speaking is not readily changed (actually, more can be done here than most people imagine!), the lecturer should be thoroughly familiar with the material and should not be caught out by unexpected questions. Each lecture should be carefully structured; it should start with a statement of what was covered in the previous lecture and give an indication the material to be covered in this lecture; it should end with a brief recapitulation of the lecture's main points and a pointer to what will bc coming in the next lecture.

4.4 Good Reinforcement Procedures

The material covered in the lectures should be reinforced by carefully selected homework and practical assignments. The statement of work to be done should be clear and unambiguous. Completed work should be promptly handed in at the due date, speedily and conscientiously marked and should be accompanied by thoughtful and encouraging comments indicating where and why the student has gone wrong. Students should be given access to memoranda of the marking schemes and/or to model answers of all assignments.

4.5 Good Assessment Procedures

The student should have access to self-test procedures. All tests (class, semester, practical and final examinations) should be fair and unambiguous. Questions should, as far as possible, examine all aspects of the syllabus in a balanced and uniform fashion. Time allotted for the testing should be reasonable. Marks allotted to questions should be balanced and fair. An external examiner should moderate the final examinations.

The above does not purport to fully characterize good teaching. No doubt one could add many other features: a friendly and approachable lecturer disposition, regular solicitation of student opinion, mechanisms to enhance class participation, etc.

5 Bad Teaching

For the present purpose, which is to sing the praises of bad teaching, there is no need to itemize in detail the notion of bad teaching. Logically, one could merely say that the further one moved from the prescriptions above, the worse one would be teaching. Now, I am not so naïve as to propose that one should deliberately aim to teach as badly as possible. But I do claim that many of the kinds of prescriptions listed above are unnecessary. They are time-cost inefficient. They may be underplayed, neglected or ignored without causing great harm to your students. In fact, you might actually be advancing your students' academic maturity by not paying too much attention to good teaching. Allow me to pick up on some of the prescriptions given above.

5.1 Appropriate Course Material

Of course it is advisable to select material that is appropriate. However, the long term impact of any given course on the efficacy of our graduates in the IT marketplace is open to wide debate. There is a case to be made for the claim that the critical factor is the process of learning rather than the content of what is learnt. Graduates should be people who can learn and adapt. I contend that the primary quality that is certified by any degree, IT-based or otherwise, is the ability of the graduate to draw on her own internal resources to learn and find ways to solve problems. It is therefore not an unmitigated disaster if one occasionally includes inappropriate material into a course.

Neither is it such a bad thing to occasionally get it wrong by prescribing a bad book for a course. If this happens, students should be helped to see where the book falls short. It should be used as an occasion to hone the student's skills in adjudicating between good and bad. Students should be encouraged to critique written material, both good and bad. This is especially necessary for students from disciplinarian (Afrikaner) or disadvantaged (Black) backgrounds. Such students are inclined to believe that if it is written down, if it is published, then it must be good. If they don't understand something, they are inclined to believe in their own inadequacy or stupidity, rather than in the possibility that some illustrious author might have explained poorly or even made an error. To show them that authors sometimes fall short is good for their morale and develops their critical skills.

5.2 Good Organization

Once again, one could hardly criticize someone who makes all the arrangements relating to a course before its delivery, as indicated in the paragraph above. However, one should be wary of turning such pre-organization into absolute prescriptions. It might be perfectly reasonable to have JIT cut-backs or augmentations of the syllabus, rather than to stick rigidly to a pre-arranged schedule. Sometimes it might be reasonable to be forgiving about slippages on hand-in times or to cancel assignments. At other times it might make sense to add in additional assignments, even though the poor students will be put under greater stress. I personally particularly dislike the notion that one should rigidly stick to pre-assigned weightings for various categories of deliverables. Who has not experienced the disastrous semester test where one has misjudged the students' knowledge and—for whatever reason—they fail in large numbers? I prefer to have the flexibility to re-assign weightings should they appear *ex post facto* to be inappropriate.

5.3 Good Delivery

Most of us academics are not gifted performers. We tend to be a little shy and introverted. Despite our best efforts and intentions, we do not sparkle in the lecture room but drone on and bore the students to tears. It is an illusion to think that the use of transparencies or slide show presentations changes this. I believe that these media, now regarded as baseline requirements for any lecture, can be, and in fact often are, counter-productive. They tend to serve primarily as notes for the speaker. They let us off the hook. I do not wish to be dogmatic about this point. I merely ask: are we not wasting an awful lot of time in preparing slide and projection-based presentations in the belief that they enhance our teaching when they do not? Are the time-cost/benefits really worth it? I remark, additionally, that some people (I am one such) find transparency lighting rather sharp and unpleasant. And we should note that the dimmed lights in a boring slide show can be deliciously soporific.[5]

5.4 Good Reinforcement Procedures

Part of my skepticism about emphasizing delivery too strongly is that the lecture is merely the introductory part of the learning process (albeit a more important part than many students seem to believe). Most learning takes place thereafter. We learn by doing, studying and reflecting more than by merely listening. To this extent, doing various kinds of assignments can importantly aid a student in assimilating the material. However, one should beware of misplacing responsibilities in the learning process: the lecturer's primary responsibility is to specify what is to be learnt and to certify that this has happened; the student's primary responsibility is to do the learning. Explaining the material lies closer to the lecturer's core responsibility.

[5]It is interesting that the injudicious use of slide shows has come under increasing fire in recent times. See, for example, [3] for one of many scholarly works on the topic. A Google search of the string "powerpointless" in the past year yielded 11700 hits.

Doing other things (such as homework exercises) to facilitate the learning process seems closer to the student's core responsibility. In this sense, it is something of a concession that lecturers should spend time selecting and marking assignments so that students may better understand the material. Ultimately, the student should take responsibility for getting to know the material, even if no assignments were to have been specified.

5.5 Good Assessment Procedures

No-one would dispute that assessment should be fair, balanced and thorough. The real question is: have we not gone overboard? We know fairly early on that Jones is a distinction candidate and that Smith will be lucky to pass. Yet we have a plenitude of assessment procedures, which constantly reassert and reaffirm Jones to be good and Smith to be poor. At great cost to ourselves, we set and grade class and semester test after class and semester test, homework and practical assignment after homework and practical assignment, project after project. The correlation between a student's marks from one grading to the next remains very high indeed. And then we set and mark a final examination, asking an external examiner to check our efforts lest we have made a mistake. At the end of it all, we congregate in committees to agonize over whether Smith's final mark of 48 % should be condoned to 50 %—after all he did have a semester mark of 52 %! Perhaps he should be re-examined. It is perfectly reasonable to ask whether the quality and fairness of our assessment would decrease if we did it less frequently? I sincerely doubt that it would. I believe that the final outcome—who passes, who gains distinctions, who fails—would remain very close to what we have today.[6]

6 Conclusion

In summary, it seems to me that we have bought into a plethora of prescriptions, imposed on us by higher authorities or by our own sense of diligence and commitment, about what should be done in order to teach a course well. These prescriptions have

[6]Educationalists have critiqued this paragraph because it fails to recognise that assessment instruments in general, and tests / examinations in particular, serve an important educational role other than mere assessment. It has been impressed upon me that the very act of taking the test engages the student in a learning activity which serves to consolidate and reinforce concepts. While I grant the point, it does not undermine the broader argument: that we are in danger of over-examining students, and of being too literal about the meaning of a mark. In some sense, the consequences of narrowly interpreting marks have become more dire. This is because there has been a drift to slice and dice larger courses into ever-smaller course units. Each of these fine-grained courses is now individually examined and needs to be individually passed. If I am ever asked to give a keynote address at SACLA again, I am likely to zoom in on the evils of the fashion for such micro-courses.

become a stumbling block for the lecturer who has to do research to be promoted. They also tend to spoon-feed students; they provide an unrealistic but neat shrink-wrapped context for problem solving; and they underemphasize the importance of taking responsibility for ones own learning.

This leads me to the iconoclastic conclusion that some of us should sometimes take the liberty of teaching less well. That will ensure that graduates are exposed to and survive a multiplicity of learning situations. They will be men and women of proven initiative and responsibility. We should avoid being gray ISO9000 teaching units producing monotone ISO9000 graduates. We may safely leave that task to the burgeoning e-learning institutions. Let us differentiate ourselves as universities by being the places of freedom, responsibility, challenge, variety and colour that we should be.

References

1. Bishop, J.: The lazy programmer. In: Gruner, S., Watson, B.W. (eds.) Colloquium and Festschrift at the Occasion of the 60th Birthday of Derrick Kourie (Computer Science), March 2009, University of Pretoria (2009). http://137.215.9.22/handle/2263/9222
2. Fresen, J.W.: Quality assurance practice in online (web-supported) learning in higher education: An exploratory study. PhD thesis, Faculty of Education, University of Pretoria, Pretoria, South Africa (2005)
3. Klemm, W.R.: Computer slide shows: A trap for bad teaching. Coll. Teach. **55**(3), 121–124 (2007)
4. Potgieter, C., Burrell, C.: Perfect storm of literature studies by international students. In: Mann, S., Verhaart, M. (eds.) Proceedings of the 1st Annual Conference of Computing and Information Technology Education and Research in New Zealand (CITRENZ): Incorporating the 23rd Annual Conference of the National Advisory Committee on Computing Qualifications, pp. 356–357. National Advisory Committee on Computing Qualifications (NACCQ), Hamilton (2010). URL http://researcharchive.wintec.ac.nz/927/. Conference held 6–9 July, 2010, in Dunedin, New Zealand
5. Potgieter, C., Ferguson, B.: Managing international students attendance with consideration of completion and satisfaction. In: Mann, S., Verhaart, M. (eds.) NACCQ 2009: Proceedings of the 22nd Annual National Advisory Committee on Computing Qualifications. National Advisory Committee on Computing Qualifications, Hamilton, pp. 87–90. (2009). URL http://researcharchive.wintec.ac.nz/242/. Conference held 10–13 July, 2009, in Napier, New Zealand

SSA-Based Simulated Execution

Jonas Lundberg, Mathias Hedenborg, and Welf Löwe

Abstract Most scalable approaches to inter-procedural dataflow analysis do not take into account the order in which fields are accessed, and methods are executed, at run-time. That is, they have no inter-procedural flow-sensitivity. In this chapter we present an approach to dataflow analysis named *Simulated Execution*. It is flow-sensitive in the sense that a memory accessing operation (call or field access) will never be affected by another memory access that is executed thereafter in all runs of a program. This makes Simulated Execution strictly more precise than the most frequently used flow-insensitive approaches. We also outline a proof of correctness using abstract interpretation. Finally, although we present Simulated Execution as a dataflow algorithm applied to context-insensitive Points-to Analysis, it can be applied on any inter-procedural dataflow problem and in a context-sensitive manner.

1 Introduction

The theoretical basis for static program analysis is the theory of monotone dataflow frameworks [15, 20]. A program is represented by a program graph, its nodes correspond to operations in the program and its edges to control and data dependencies between them. For each node, the analysis computes an analysis value, in our case a set of references to abstract objects. Starting with an appropriate initialization, the analysis iteratively updates the analysis values in each node by (i) merging analysis values from predecessor nodes and (ii) applying transfer functions representing the abstract program behavior at these nodes wrt. the analysis problem. Provided the transfer functions are monotone, this approach is guaranteed to terminate in a fix

J. Lundberg (✉) · M. Hedenborg · W. Löwe
School of Computer Science, Mathematics, and Physics, Linnaeus University, 351 95 Växjö, Sweden
e-mail: jonas.lundberg@lnu.se

M. Hedenborg
e-mail: mathias.hedenborg@lnu.se

W. Löwe
e-mail: welf.lowe@lnu.se

K.K. Breitman, R.N. Horspool (eds.), *Patterns, Programming and Everything*,
DOI 10.1007/978-1-4471-2350-7_7,

point. Furthermore, a dataflow analysis is considered to be *flow-sensitive* if it takes control-flow information into account [8].

Points-to analysis is a static program analysis that extracts reference information from a given input program, e.g., possible targets of a call and possible objects referenced by a field. Throughout the chapter, we use Points-to analysis as an example to explain simulated execution and to discuss differences to classic dataflow analysis.

In Sect. 2 we present the foundations of Points-to analysis. Section 3 presents our simulated execution approach. In Sect. 4, we discuss the flow-sensitivity of our approach, and, in Sect. 5, we outline how abstract interpretation can be used to proof the correctness of Simulated Execution. Section 6 presents related works and Sect. 7 concludes the chapter and discusses issues for future work.

2 Foundations of SSA-Based Points-to Analysis

In this section, we introduce the representation of analysis values, which are sets of abstract objects and a heap-memory abstraction, and our program representation called Points-to SSA. They are then used in the actual analysis algorithm, which is described in Sect. 3.

2.1 Analysis Values

In points-to analysis, we need to represent references to abstract objects and an abstraction of the heap-memory.

An *abstract object* o is an analysis abstraction that represents one or more runtime objects. In this chapter, we use the following abstraction: each *syntactic creation point* s corresponds to a unique abstract object o_s. Thus, the set of all allocation sites in a program defines a finite set of abstract objects denoted O, and every abstract object $o_s \in O$ can be seen as an analysis abstraction representing *all* runtime objects created at the corresponding allocation site s in *any* execution of the analyzed program.

In the analysis, reference variables will in general hold references to more than one abstract object. Hence, we assume that each *points-to value* v in the analysis of a program is an element in the *points-to value lattice* $L_V = \{V, \sqcup, \sqcap, \top, \bot\}$ where $V = 2^O$ is the power set of O, $\top = O$, $\bot = \emptyset$, and $\sqcup, \sqcap$ are the set operations $\cup$ (union) and $\cap$ (intersection). The height of the points-to value lattice is $h_o = |O|$. We use the notation $Pt(a)$ to refer to the points-to value that is referenced by the expression a.

Each abstract object $o \in O$ has a unique set of *object fields* $[o, f] \in OF$ where $f \in F$ is a unique identifier of a field (capturing references). Each object field $[o, f]$ is in turn associated with a *memory slot* $([o, f], v)$ where v represents the abstract object references stored in object field $[o, f]$.

The abstraction of the heap-memory associated with an analyzed program, referred to as *abstract memory*, *Mem*, is defined as the set of all memory slots $([o, f], v)$. We think of the abstract memory as a mapping from object fields to points-to values. The memory is therefore equipped with two operations $Mem.get(OF) \rightarrow V$ and $Mem.addTo(OF, V)$ with the interpretation of reading the points-to value stored in an object field $[o, f] \in OF$, and merging the points-to value $v \in V$ with the points-to value already stored in an object field $[o, f] \in OF$, respectively. Note that we never override previously stored object field values in memory store operations, i.e., we never execute strong updates. Instead, we merge the new value with the old one using the points-to value lattice's join operation, i.e., we perform weak updates.

The abstract memory is updated as a side effect of the analysis. In order to quickly determine the fixed point, we use memory sizes indicating whether or not the memory has changed. In what follows, we refer to the size of the abstract memory as a *memory size* $x \in X = [0, h_m]$ where h_m is the maximum memory size. It corresponds to the case where all object fields contain all abstract objects, hence, $h_m = |OF| \cdot |O|$.

In order to apply the theory of monotone dataflow frameworks to memory size values as well, we introduce a lattice L_X referred to as the *memory size lattice*. The memory size lattice L_X is a single ascending chain of integers, i.e., $L_X = \{X, \sqcup, \sqcap, \top, \bot\}$ where $X = \{0, 1, 2, \ldots, h_m\}$, $\top = h_m$, $\bot = 0$, $x_1 \sqcup x_2 = \max(x_1, x_2)$, and $x_1 \sqcap x_2 = \min(x_1, x_2)$. The height of L_X is h_m.

2.2 Points-to SSA

Points-to SSA is our graph-based program representation. In Points-to SSA, local variables are resolved to dataflow edges connecting operations (nodes) that define variables to operations (nodes) that use these variables. As a result, every def-use relation via local variables is explicitly represented as an edge between the defining and using operations. Join-points in the control flow where several definitions may apply are modeled with special φ-nodes using possible definitions valid in the different branches and introducing new definitions.

Figure 1 shows a simple "Linked List" implementation (class `L`) and the corresponding Points-to SSA graphs. Each method is represented by a graph and each node in the graph represents an operation in the method. We have for example `Entry` and `Exit` nodes representing method entry/exit points, and `Store` and `Load` nodes representing field write/read operations. The ports at the top of a node represent operation input values (e.g., memory size `x`, target address values `a`, and the values `v` to store in the `Store` nodes) and the ports at the bottom represent operation results (e.g., a new memory size `x` in the `Store` nodes). Edges connecting node ports represent the flow of values from defining nodes (operation results) to using nodes (operation input values). An out-port $out_i(n)$ may be connected to one or more outgoing edges. An in-port is always connected to a single incoming edge.

```
public class L {
  V value = null;
  L next = null;

  public L (V v) {
    value = v;
  }

  public void append(V v) {
    if (next == null)
      next = new List(v);
    else
      next.append(v);
  }

  public void putAt(int n, V v) {
    int count = 0;
    L l = this;
    while (count < n) {
      l = l.next;
      count++;
    }
    l.value = v;
  }
}
```

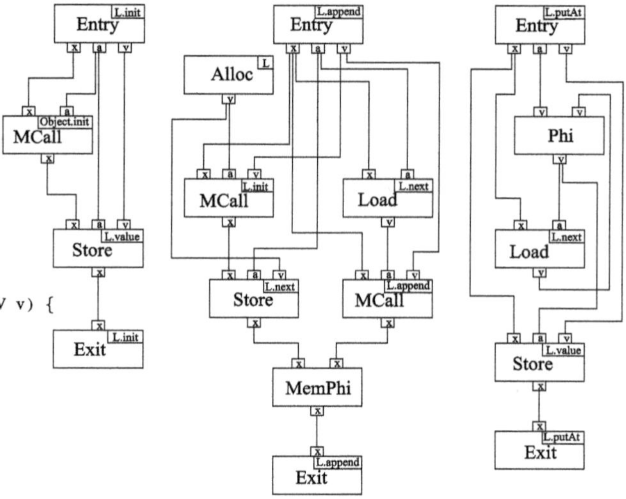

Fig. 1 Source code fragment and corresponding Points-to SSA graphs

The last property reflects our underlying SSA approach—each value has one, and only one, definition.

The constructor `L.init` starts by calling its super constructor `Object.init` and notice that object creation, in method `L.append`, is done in two steps: we first allocate an object of class `L` and then call the constructor `L.init`. φ-nodes are used in `L.append` to merge the memory size values from the two selective branches, and in `L.putAt` as the loop head of the iteration.

A Points-to SSA method graph can be seen as an abstraction of a method's semantics, an SSA graph representation specially designed for points-to analysis. It is an abstraction since we have removed all operations not directly related to reference computations, e.g., operations related to primitive types. Moreover, we abstracted from the semantics of the remaining operations by giving them an abstract analysis semantics.

Another feature of Points-to SSA is the use of memory edges to explicitly model (direct, indirect, and anti-) dependencies between different memory operations. An operation that may change the memory *defines* a new memory size value, and operations that may access this updated memory *use* the new memory size value. Thus, memory sizes are considered as data, and memory size edges have the same semantics—including the use of φ-nodes at join points—as def-use edges for other types of data. The introduction of memory size edges in Points-to SSA is important since they also imply a correct order in which the memory accessing operations are analyzed, which ensures that the analysis is a flow-sensitive abstraction of the semantics of the program. Flow-sensitivity will be discussed in Sect. 4.

Certain node types have attributes that refer to node specific, static information. For example, each $Alloc^C$ node is decorated with a class identifier C that identifies the class of the object to be created.

Finally, each type of node is associated with a unique *analysis semantics* (or *transfer function*) which can be seen as a mapping from in-ports to out-ports that may have a side-effect on the memory. As an example, Algorithm A1 shows the analysis semantics for the $Store^f$ node, which abstracts the actual semantics of a field write statement $a.f = v$.

A1 $Store^f : [x_{in}, a, v] \mapsto x_{out}$

$x_{out} = x_{in}$
for each $o \in Pt(a)$ **do**
  $prev = Mem.get([o, f])$
  if $v \not\sqsubseteq prev$ **then**
    $Mem.addTo([o, f], v)$
    $x_{out} = Mem.getSize()$
  end if
end for
return x_{out}

For each abstract object o in the address reference a, we look up the points-to value previously stored in object field $[o, f]$. If the new value to be stored changes the memory (i.e., if $v \not\sqsubseteq prev$), we merge v with the previous value and save the result. Notice also that we compute a new memory out-port value (a new memory size) if the memory has been changed during this operation.

3 Simulated Execution

Our dataflow analysis technique, called *simulated execution*, is an abstract interpretation of the program based on the abstract analysis and program representation discussed in the previous section. It simulates the actual execution of a program where the analysis of a method is interrupted when a call occurs, and later resumed when the analysis of the called method was completed. This analysis approach would be very costly if we could not find a way to interrupt a large number of all call sequences. In fact, it would never terminate in case of recursive calls.

The simulated execution approach can be seen as a recursive interaction between the analysis of an individual Points-to SSA method graph and the transfer function associated with monomorphic calls, which handle the transition from one method to another. Polymorphic calls are handled as selections over possible target methods m_i, which are then processed as a sequence of monomorphic calls targeting m_i.

3.1 Method Graph Processing

For each method graph, we have a pre-computed node order that is determined by the data and memory dependencies between the nodes. We compute a topological sorting for forward edges. To order the nodes in loops, we use a so-called *interval analysis* [1, 19] where we identify inner and outer loops and their loop heads (always φ-nodes).

The method processing starts in the method entry node, follows the node ordering, and iterates over loops until a fixed point is reached. Inner loops are stabilized before their outer loops. Consequences of this approach are: (1) All nodes in a method graph g_m are analyzed at least once every time method m is analyzed. (2) All nodes, except the loop head φ-nodes, have all their predecessor nodes updated before they are analyzed themselves. (3) The order in which the nodes are analyzed respects all control and data dependencies and is therefore an abstraction of the control-flow of an actual execution. The final point is a crucial step to assure flow-sensitivity in the SSA-based simulated execution technique.

The above properties of analyzing single method graphs is taken into consideration by *processMethod* as given in Algorithm A2. It should only be considered as a rough outline of the approach actually implemented. The idea is simple: We start by initializing the method entry node with the method input to be used in this particular method *activation*. We then analyze the method nodes repeatedly until we reach the method exit node. Therefore, we *compute* a node's transfer function given by the node type, *update* the successor in-ports, and determine the *next* node to analyze to get its values stable.

A2 $processMethod : (m, [x_{in}, a, v_1, \ldots, v_n]) \mapsto [x_{out}, r]$

$n = m.entryNode$
$in(n) = [x_{in}, a, v_1, \ldots, v_n]$
do
  $n.computeTransferFunction()$
  $n.updateSuccs()$
  $n = n.next()$
while $n \neq m.exitNode$
return $in(n)$

The statement *n.computeTransferFunction()* makes a transition from one method to another if the node n is of a monomorphic call type ($MCall^{m,cs_i}$). Note that the processing of a call in turn may lead to the analysis of the call target method m as defined in *processMethod*.

3.2 Call Processing

Our approach to analyzing individual calls (see Algorithm A3) describes the handling of a call to method m in a context ctx^m. For the understanding of our call processing, it is safe to assume that all calls to m are associated with only *one* context ctx^m, i.e., that we perform a context-insensitive analysis. This is generalized to more contexts in [14].

A3 $processCall(ctx^m, [x_{in}, a, v_1, \ldots, v_n]) \mapsto [x_{out}, r]$

```
- - if ctx^m was already analyzed with larger parameters before
if [x_in, a, v_1, ..., v_n] ⊑ ctx^m.prev_args then
    return ctx^m.prev_return
end if
ctx^m.prev_args = ctx^m.prev_args ⊔ [x_in, a, v_1, ..., v_n]
- - if ctx^m is on the analysis stack
if ctx^m.is_active then
    ctx^m.is_recursive = true
    return ctx^m.prev_return
end if
ctx^m.is_active = true
[x_out, r] = processMethod(m, ctx^m.prev_args)
- - if ctx^m was not recursively called within processMethod
if ¬ ctx^m.is_recursive then
    ctx^m.prev_return = [x_out, r]
    ctx^m.is_active = false
    return [x_out, r]
end if
- - while ctx^m's recursive call results haven't reached fixed point
while ctx^m.prev_return ⊏ [x_out, r] do
    ctx^m.prev_return = [x_out, r]
    [x_out, r] = processMethod(m, ctx^m.prev_args)
end while
ctx^m.is_recursive = false
ctx^m.is_active = false
return [x_out, r]
```

The processing of (recursive) method calls must guarantee that the analysis terminates and that the analysis values reach a global fixed point.

The crucial step to ensure termination is that each context ctx^m is associated with two attributes *prev_args* and *prev_return* where we store previous input and return values of the calls to m in that context ctx^m. The former of these attributes is used to decide whether we have seen a more general call targeting m in the same context ctx^m before, i.e., if $[x_{in}, a, v_1, \ldots, v_n] \sqsubseteq prev\_args$, in which case we interrupt the call processing and reuse the previous result from *prev_return*.

The alternative, a call targeting m in ctx^m with new arguments, leads to a new method activation where we process the target method m by invoking *processMethod* using the merged input $prev\_args \sqcup [x_{in}, a, v_1, \ldots, v_n]$. We also update the two attributes *prev_args* and *prev_return* in preparation for the next call targeting m in ctx^m.

Termination of our analysis is ensured since we incrementally merge our arguments $prev\_args \sqcup [x_{in}, a, v_1, \ldots, v_n]$ before we start processing a method m. Thus, the sequence of arguments $args_i$ used for a given context ctx^m forms an ascending chain satisfying $args_0 \sqsubset args_1 \sqsubset \cdots \sqsubset args_n$.

Each such chain must have finite length since our value lattices have finite heights (both L_X and L_V are finite). Thus, each method can only be processed a finite number of times, and analysis termination is guaranteed. This argument also holds for calls involving recursion; terminations is guaranteed for these programs as well.

In order to guarantee that the fixed point is reached, especially in loops induced by recursive method calls, we need a few more attributes associated with each context: *is_active* is used to check if we are processing a call in a context that is currently being analyzed, i.e., if m is called recursively in ctx^m. In this case, we directly return *prev_return* for the recursive call (or undefined $[0, \bot]$ if we have no previous results). Also we set $is\_recursive = true$ which indicates, upon return from *processMethod*, that we have seen a recursive call during *processMethod*. In this case, we need to stabilize the results by iteratively reinvoking *processMethod* until the fixed point is reached.

4 Flow-Sensitivity

An analysis is *flow-sensitive* if it takes into account the order in which statements in a program are executed [23]. However, there does not seem to exist a consensus about the precise definition of flow-sensitivity [16]. Many people require so-called *strong* updates as a criteria for flow-sensitivity [23]. Strong updates occur when an assignment supersedes (or kills the results of) an earlier assignment. The problem with strong updates is that they are only permitted if the ordering of the reads and writes of a given variable is sure and if the variable identifies a unique memory location. For local variables, these cases can be detected using a *def-use* analysis, i.e., an analysis that computes for every *definition* of a variable all *uses* of that variable along a definition free control-flow path.

The flow-insensitivity leads to an *intra-procedural* (local) precision loss whenever we have *multiple definitions* of a reference variable v. Each definition adds new values to the point-to set $Pt(v)$ and every use of v will transport all values stored in $Pt(v)$. This problem is solved in our SSA-based analysis by the introduction of reference edges connecting the operations (nodes) where values are defined to operations where they are used. Thus, every use of a variable has exactly one definition and the mixing of points-to values due multiple definitions is avoided. It is not a new idea that using an SSA-based program representation implies an intra-procedural flow-sensitivity, it has been demonstrated in [7] in a points-to analysis for C.

We might also have a precision loss due to *inter-procedural* flow-insensitivity, i.e. taking into account certain inter-procedural control-flow paths that never can occur at run-time.

To demonstrate the effects, in Fig. 2, we show a scenario with a sequence of three calls $r_i = a_i.m(v_i)$ targeting the same method m

$$m(V\ v)\ \{\text{return } v;\} \mapsto V$$

(which just returns the argument). A classic data-flow approach which neglects the call order would, in addition to the three correct control-flow paths $start_i \rightarrow m \rightarrow$

Fig. 2 A flow-insensitive scenario

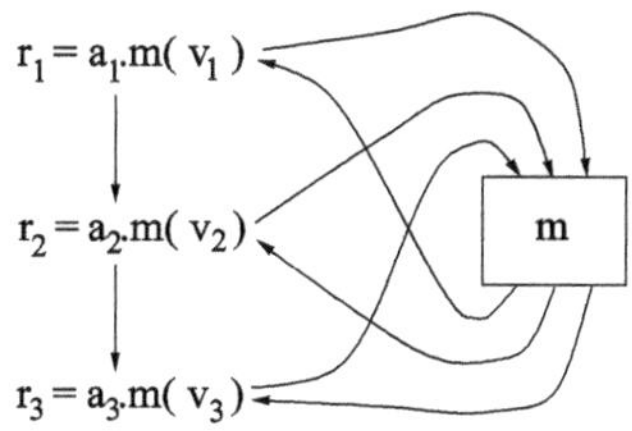

end_i, $i = 1, 2, 3$, utilize the following six non-correct paths $start_i \rightarrow m \rightarrow end_j$, $i \neq j$. These additional paths come with a precision loss since the return value received at *each* call site is the union of *all* return values induced by the different call-sites. For example, all call sites in Fig. 2 will receive the same value

$$Pt(r_1) = Pt(r_2) = Pt(r_3) = Pt(v_1) \cup Pt(v_2) \cup Pt(v_3)$$

It should be noted that the problem of mixed return values can be reduced (not removed) by adding a finite depth context-sensitivity.

A similar problem occurs whenever we have multiple field accesses targeting the same object field $[o, f]$. All read operations will receive the union of *all* values added by the different store operations targeting the same object field.

Our SSA-based simulated execution approach has two important ingredients that add flow-sensitivity to the analysis:

1. We have intra-procedural memory edges imposing an ordering among all memory accessing operations (calls and field accesses) within a method. This ordering is strictly obeyed by our method graph processing algorithm. The result is that a memory access $a_1.x$ will never be affected by another memory access $a_2.x$ that is processed strictly after $a_1.x$ in all program runs.
2. We have the simulated execution technique that follows the inter-procedural control-flow from one method to another. This will extend the above mentioned ordering of memory accessing operations to hold between any two operations in the program.

The major advantage of our approach is the reduced mixing of values returned by calls targeting the same method. Since each call is treated separately, each return only contains contributions from previously processed calls. That is, the first call to a method has no mixing of the return values and only the final call has the same degree of mixing as the classic data-flow approach. For example, the call sites in Fig. 2 will receive values that are unaffected by calls that take place later on:

$$Pt(r_1) = Pt(v_1),$$
$$Pt(r_2) = Pt(v_1) \cup Pt(v_2),$$
$$Pt(r_3) = Pt(v_1) \cup Pt(v_2) \cup Pt(v_3)$$

Another interesting (but rather strange) effect is the result of multiple calls targeting the same method that take place in different branches of a selective statement. The result will in these cases depend on the order in which we process the different branches. The branch first processed will have no mixing and the final branch will be completely mixed. This is still a conservative result since only one branch will be executed in reality, and the precision is still better than in the classic data-flow approach where all calls will be completely mixed.

The same idea of progressively increased mixing holds also for multiple field accesses targeting the same object field $[o, f]$. A read operation targeting $[o, f]$ will receive all values stored in $[o, f]$ up to this point, but will be unaffected by store operations that we still have not processed.

In summary, our SSA-based simulated execution approach is flow-sensitive in the meaning that a memory accessing operation (call or field access) $a_1.x$ will never be affected by another memory access $a_2.x$ that is executed after $a_1.x$ in all program runs. This makes our approach strictly more precise than the classic data-flow approach where the analysis follows more non-correct control-flow paths.

5 Correctness of Simulated Execution

In this section we will outline a proof of correctness based on abstract interpretation [3, 20]. Within this framework, it is sufficient to show that the analysis correctly abstracts the data (references and heap and stack memory), that the analysis transfer functions correctly abstracts the concrete semantics, and that fixed-point iteration over-approximates the concrete execution traces. The subsequent sections will discuss these proof obligations.

5.1 Data Abstraction

The analysis abstracts from all value data types like Integer and Boolean.

In Sect. 2, we stated that each syntactic object creation point s corresponds to a unique abstract object (reference) o_s. This defines a many-to-one abstraction (α) where each object o_s^i created at run-time at s is mapped to a unique analysis abstraction o_s. We have also implicitly defined a reverse concretization mapping (γ) that associates each abstract object o_s to *all* run-time objects created at site s in *any* execution of the analyzed program. The two mappings α and γ obviously form a Galois connection satisfying $\{o_s^i\} \subseteq \gamma(\alpha(o_s^i))$ for each run-time object o_s^i and $\alpha(\gamma(o_s)) = \{o_s\}$ for each abstract object o_s.

Similarly for the heap memory, each run-time memory slot $([o_s^i, f], o_p^j)$ is mapped (α) to an abstract memory slot $([o_s, f], v)$ where $o_s = \alpha(o_s^j)$ and $\alpha(o_p^k) \in v$. The reverse mapping $\gamma(([o_s, f], v))$ is defined by the set of all run-time memory slots $\{([o_s^i, f], o_p^j) \mid o_s^i \in \gamma(o_s) \wedge \exists o_p \in v : o_p^j \in \gamma(o_p)\}$. The two mappings α and γ again form a Galois connection satisfying $\{([o_s^i, f], o_p^j)\} \subseteq \gamma(\alpha(([o_s^i, f], o_p^j)))$ for each run-time memory slot $([o_s^i, f], o_p^j)$ and $\alpha(\gamma(([o_s, f], v))) = ([o_s, f], v)$ for each abstract memory slot $([o_s, f], v)$.

The final part of run-time memory that needs to be abstracted is the activation frames in the call stack. At run-time the frames represent the target object reference and the actual parameters associated with a method call. We deliberately omit the discussion of return address (represented by back-edges in the method call graph) and local variables (represented by the method's SSA graph edges). In our context-insensitive analysis, all activation frames (addresses) created for any method call $a.m(\ldots)$ targeting method m are mapped to a context ctx^m. And in reverse, a context ctx^m represents any call targeting m, in any execution of the program. Let $o_s^i.m(o_p^j, \ldots, o_q^k)$ be a concrete call (frame). It is abstracted (α) by $(m, \{o_s\}, \{o_p\}, \ldots, \{o_q\})$ where $o_s = \alpha(o_s^i)$ and $o_p = \alpha(o_p^j), \ldots, o_q = \alpha(o_q^k)$. An abstract frame $(m, s, p, \ldots, q)$ is mapped (γ) to a set of concrete frames

$$\big\{o_s^i.m\big(o_p^j, \ldots, o_q^k\big) \mid o_s \in s, o_s^i \in \gamma(o_s) \\ \wedge o_p \in p, o_p^j \in \gamma(o_p) \ldots o_q \in q, o_q^k \in \gamma(o_q)\big\}.$$

Again α and γ form a Galois connection: $\alpha(\gamma((m, s, p, \ldots, q))) = (m, s, p, \ldots, q)$ and $\{o_s^i.m(o_p^j, \ldots, o_q^k)\} \subseteq \gamma(\alpha(o_s^i.m(o_p^j, \ldots, o_q^k)))$.

5.2 Transfer Functions

The analysis abstracts from all operations that are related to value data types.

Object allocation operations are taken care of by the analysis abstraction leading to abstract objects, which we discussed already. Field store and method call are the only operations that have an effect on the memory. We show the correctness of the store (call) transfer functions wrt. the concrete semantics of store (call).

The Algorithm A1 defines the transfer function for $Store^f$ nodes as a *weak* update of abstract heap memory slots. Let $a = \{o_1, \ldots, o_k\}$ and v be two sets of abstract objects and let $([o_i, f], v_i), o_i \in a$ denote abstract heap slots before the execution of a update $Store^f(a, v)$. Then the abstract heap slots after this update are defined by $([o_i, f], v_i \cup v), o_i \in a$.

In a concrete run, $Store^f$ performs a *strong* update of heap memory slots. Let $([o_s^i, f], o_p^j)$ be a heap memory slot before the execution of an operation $Store^f(o_s^i, o_q^k)$. Then $([o_s^i, f], o_q^k)$ is the memory slot after its execution.

The transfer function of $Store^f$ is a correct abstraction of its concrete semantics: Let $([o_s^i, f], o_p^j)$ be a concrete heap memory slot and $([a, f], v)$ an abstract one with $\{([o_s^i, f], o_p^j)\} \subseteq \gamma(([a, f], v))$. Then $Store^f(o_s^i, o_q^k)$ and $Store^f(a, v')$ lead to slots $hs = ([o_s^i, f], o_q^k)$ and $hs_a = ([a, f], v' \cup v)$, resp., and $\{hs\} \subseteq \gamma(hs_a)$.

Algorithm A3 defines the transfer function for $Call^m$ nodes. We discuss the control flow associated with calls in Sect. 5.3. Here, we focus on their effect on concrete and abstract stack frames.

For each concrete call $o_s^i.m(o_p^j, \ldots, o_q^k)$, a corresponding stack frame is *created*. The abstract transfer function of $Call^m$ updates an abstract stack frame

$(m, s, p, \ldots, q)$. The transfer function of $Call^m$ is a correct abstraction of its concrete semantics: Let $(m, s, p, \ldots, q)$ be an abstract stack frame and trivially $\emptyset \subseteq \gamma((m, s, p, \ldots, q))$. Then $Call^m(o_s^i, o_p^j, \ldots, o_q^k)$ and $Call^m(m, s, p, \ldots, q)$ lead to stack frames $sf = o_s^i.m(o_p^j, \ldots, o_q^k)$ and $sf_a = (m, s \cup \alpha(o_s^i), p \cup \alpha(o_p^j), \ldots, q \cup \alpha(o_q^k))$, resp., and $\{sf\} \subseteq \gamma(sf_a)$.

5.3 *Execution Traces*

An execution trace is a sequence of program states, i.e., the initial memory (empty heap and stack) and its stepwise updates caused by the operations of a program. Each concrete trace $tr = (m_0, m_1, \ldots, m_i, \ldots)$, i.e., each sequence of memory states induced by the concrete semantics of operations in a concrete program run, is correctly abstracted by an abstract trace $tr_a = (M_0, M_1, \ldots, M_j, \ldots)$, i.e., by a sequence of abstract memory states induced by updates according to the transfer functions of operations in a simulated execution. This means that for each such pair of traces and corresponding memory state contained, we require that M_j is a correct abstraction for m_i.

For individual memory state transitions, this correctness has been discussed for each individual operation in Sect. 5.2. As the sequences of operations visited in simulated executions is still an over-approximation of operation sequences that possibly occur in any concrete execution as discussed in Sect. 4, the correctness argumentation is complete.

6 Related Work

In this section we present current research related to flow-sensitive dataflow analysis in general, and to points-to analysis of object-oriented programs in particular. For brevity we focus our efforts on works explicitly dealing with the analysis of object-oriented programs. However, it should be noted that most works targeting object-oriented programs have an "imperative counterpart" which often pre-dates the object-oriented work. People interested in more general reviews of the area should take a look at [6, 8, 21, 23].

First of all, Simulated Execution has been implemented, briefly presented, and used in [14]. Although focusing on presenting a new approach to context-sensitive points-to analysis, that paper demonstrates that Simulated Execution scales to programs containing hundreds of classes.

An analysis is *flow-sensitive* if it takes into account the order of execution of statements in a program. Only a few papers report on flow-sensitive approaches to points-to analysis for object-oriented programs [2, 5, 27]. The major theoretical obstacle in a flow-sensitive analysis is the question when it is safe to perform strong updates. A strong update occurs when an assignment supersedes (or kills) all previous assignments. The alternative, *weak update*, uses incremental updates of all values.

Both [5] and [27] use weak updates for every assignment involving fields and method parameters. The more recent of the two works [27] reports increased precision at a reasonable cost. A more ambitious approach is taken in [2]. They compute inter-procedural def-use information, which is later used to decide whether strong updates are safe or not. They report high precision but at an unacceptable cost. Our approach is flow-sensitive but restricted to weak updates.

Most approaches to points-to analysis of object-oriented programs are based on a sparse whole program points-to graph (WPP2G), [6, 9, 11, 12, 18, 24, 28]. WPP2Gs contain three different node types: abstract objects, reference variables, and object fields. Edges represent assignments of abstract objects, variables and fields to (other) variables and fields. To handle calls, edges are added that correspond to assignments of address, arguments (and return values) to the implicit variable *this*, formal parameters (and receiving variable). The result is one large graph representing the whole program.

A straight forward dataflow analysis applied on this type of whole program graph would result in a flow-insensitive analysis. And, as pointed out in Sect. 4, they have an intra-procedural precision loss in case of multiple variable definitions, and an inter-procedural precision loss since they take into account certain inter-procedural control flow paths that never can occur at run-time. Our SSA-based Simulated Execution approach has no such intra-procedural precision loss, and reduces the inter-procedural precision loss.

In a *context-insensitive* program analysis, call arguments of different calls to the same method are propagated and mixed there. The analysis result for a given method is then the merger of *all* calls targeting that method. A *context-sensitive* analysis addresses this source of imprecision by distinguishing between different calling contexts of a method. It analyzes a method separately for each calling context [23]. The above mentioned sources of flow-insensitivity can be reduced (but not removed) by adding a finite depth context-sensitivity.

The number of papers explicitly dealing with context-sensitive points-to analysis of object-oriented programs is continuously growing [2, 11, 14, 18, 22, 28, 29]. The papers experiment with different context definitions and techniques to reduce the memory cost associated with having multiple contexts for a given method. New context-sensitive analysis techniques designed for object-oriented programs are: *object-sensitivity* [17, 18], *this-sensitivity* [14], and a k-call-string based analysis with no fixed upper limit (k) that only takes acyclic call paths into account [28, 29]. These new approaches have been compared in a number works [10, 11, 14, 18]. They found that 1-this-sensitivity is similar in precision, but much faster, than 1-object-sensitivity [14], which was found to be "clearly better" both in terms of precision and scalability than the k-call-string approach [11]. Many papers use approximative method summaries to reduce the cost of having multiple contexts [2, 22]. Sometimes, ordered binary decision diagrams (OBDD) are used to efficiently exploit commonalities of similar contexts [11, 25, 28], which allows handling of a very large number of contexts at a reasonable memory cost.

Our program representation Points-to SSA is closely related to Memory SSA [25, 26]. Memory SSA is an extension to the traditional approach to SSA, as presented in [4, 19]. Memory SSA is a low intermediate representation capturing the complete program semantics whereas in Points-to SSA we deliberately abstract from the exact program semantics. We have removed all features that are related to primitive types and raised the abstraction level by merging patterns of primitive RISC operations into single complex operations. Another difference is that we use memory sizes instead of memory configurations as our memory values making our approach scale to a few hundreds of classes as opposed to a few hundreds of lines of code for points-to analyses based on Memory SSA [13].

7 Summary, Conclusion and Future Work

In this chapter we present a novel flow-sensitive approach to dataflow analysis named *Simulated Execution*. Although we present Simulated Execution as a dataflow algorithm applied to context-insensitive Points-to Analysis, it can be applied on any inter-procedural dataflow problem and in a context-sensitive manner. Simulated Execution is based on Points-to SSA, a sparse SSA-based program representation that explicitly models dependencies, direct or indirect, between different memory store and load operations. Points-to SSA has def-use information for local variables encoded from the start and adds therefore *local flow-sensitivity* to the analysis.

Our dataflow algorithm simulates an abstract execution of the program where the processing of a method is interrupted when a call occurs, and later resumed when the processing of the called method is completed. The fact that we follow the control-flow from one method to another adds a *global flow-sensitivity* to the analysis. This added flow-sensitivity makes Simulated Execution strictly more precise than the classic data-flow approach where the analysis follows more non-correct control-flow paths.

In the future we will continue the work with the outline of the proof of our theorem. This will then include a more detailed look into simpler models for simulated execution and also an exploration of the details about the SSA graph modelling and more general models. We also plan an experimental evaluation comparing Simulated Execution with flow-insensitive approaches to see if the added analysis precision due to flow-sensitivity is significant also in practise.

References

1. Aho, A., Sethi, R., Ullman, J.: Compilers: Principles, Techniques, and Tools. Addison-Wesley Reading (1986)
2. Chatterjee, R., Ryder, B., Landi, W.: Relevant context inference. In: Symposium on Principles of Programming Languages (POPL'99), pp. 133–146 (1999)

3. Cousot, P., Cousot, R.: Abstract interpretation: A unified lattice model for static analysis of programs by construction of approximations of fixed points. In: Conference Record of the Fourth Annual ACM SIGACT/SIGPLAN Symposium on Principles of Programming Languages, January, pp. 238–252 (1977)
4. Cytron, R., Ferrante, J., Rosen, B., Wegman, M., Zadeck, K.: Efficiently computing static single assignment form and the control dependence graph. ACM Trans. Program. Lang. Syst. **13**(4), 451–490 (1991)
5. Diwan, A., Moss, J.E.B., McKinley, K.S.: Simple and effective analysis of statically typed object-oriented programs. In: Proceedings of the Conference on Object-Oriented Programming Systems, Languages, and Applications (OOPSLA'96), October (1996)
6. Grove, D., DeFouw, G., Dean, J., Chambers, C.: Call graph construction in object-oriented languages. In: Proceedings of the Conference on Object-Oriented Programming Systems, Languages, and Applications (OOPSLA'97), pp. 108–124 (1997)
7. Hasti, R., Horwitz, S.: Using static single assignment form to improve flow-insensitive pointer analysis. In: Proceedings of the Conference on Programming Language Design and Implementation (PLDI'98), June, pp. 97–105 (1998)
8. Hind, M.: Pointer analysis: Haven't we solved this problem yet? In: Workshop on Program Analysis for Software Tools and Engineering (PASTE'01), pp. 54–61 (2001)
9. Lhoták, O., Hendren, L.: Scaling Java points-to analysis using spark. In: Proceedings of the International Conference on Compiler Construction (CC'03), April, pp. 153–169 (2003)
10. Lhoták, O., Hendren, L.: Context-sensitive points-to analysis: Is it worth it? In: Mycroft, A., Zeller, A. (eds.) International Conference on Compiler Construction (CC'06). LNCS, vol. 3923, pp. 47–64. Springer, Berlin (2006)
11. Lhoták, O., Hendren, L.: Evaluating the benefits of context-sensitive points-to analysis using a BDD-based implementation. ACM Trans. Softw. Eng. Methodol. **18**(1), 1–53 (2008)
12. Liang, D., Pennings, M., Harrold, M.: Extending and evaluating flow-insensitive and context-insensitive points-to analysis for Java. In: Proceedings of the Workshop on Program Analysis for Software Tools and Engineering (PASTE'01), June, pp. 73–79 (2001)
13. Liekweg, F.: Compiler-directed automatic memory management. In: 3rd Workshop on Semantics, Program Analysis, and Computing Environments for Memory Management (SPACE). ACM/SIGPLAN, New York (2006)
14. Lundberg, J., Gutzmann, T., Edvinsson, M., Löwe, W.: Fast and precise points-to analysis. J. Inf. Softw. Technol. **51**(10), 1428–1439 (2009)
15. Marlowe, T., Ryder, B.: Properties of data flow frameworks: A unified model. Acta Inform. **28**, 121–163 (1990)
16. Marlowe, T.J., Ryder, B.G., Burke, M.G.: Defining flow sensitivity for data flow problems. Laboratory of Computer Science Research Technical Report, Number LCSR-TR-249 (1995)
17. Milanova, A., Rountev, A., Ryder, B.G.: Parameterized object sensitivity for points-to and side-effect analyses for Java. In: Proceedings of the International Symposium on Software Testing and Analysis (ISSTA'02), July, pp. 1–11 (2002)
18. Milanova, A., Rountev, A., Ryder, B.G.: Parameterized object sensitivity for points-to analysis for Java. ACM Trans. Softw. Eng. Methodol. **14**(1), 1–41 (2005)
19. Muchnick, S.S.: Advanced Compiler Design Implementation. Morgan Kaufmann, San Francisco (1997)
20. Nielsen, F., Nielsen, H.R., Hankin, C.: Principles of Program Analysis, 2nd edn. Springer, Berlin (2005)
21. Palsberg, J.: Object-oriented type inference. In: Proceedings of the Workshop on Program Analysis for Software Tools and Engineering (PASTE'01), July, pp. 20–27 (2001)
22. Ruf, E.: Effective synchronization removal for Java. In: Proceedings of the Conference on Programming Language Design and Implementation (PLDI'00), pp. 208–218 (2000)
23. Ryder, B.G.: Dimensions of precision in reference analysis of object-oriented programming languages. In: International Conference on Compiler Construction (CC'03). LNCS, vol. 2622, pp. 126–137. Springer, Berlin (2003)

24. Streckenbach, M., Snelting, G.: Points-to for Java: A general framework and an empirical comparison. Technical report, Lehrstuhl für Softwaresysteme, Universität Passau, Germany, November (2000)
25. Trapp, M.: Optimierung objektorientierter programme. PhD thesis, Universität Karlsruhe, December (1999)
26. Trapp, M., Lindenmaier, G., Boesler, B.: Documentation of the intermediate representation Firm. Technical report 1999-14, Fakultät für Informatik, Universität Karlsruhe, Germany (1999)
27. Whaley, J., Lam, M.S.: An efficient inclusion-based points-to analysis for strictly-typed languages. In: Proceedings of the Static Analysis Symposium (SAS'02) (2002)
28. Whaley, J., Lam, M.S.: Cloning-based context-sensitive pointer alias analysis using binary decision diagrams. In: Proceedings of the Conference on Programming Language Design and Implementation (PLDI'04), June, pp. 131–144 (2004)
29. Zhu, J., Calman, S.: Symbolic pointer analysis revisited. In: Proceedings of the Conference on Programming Language Design and Implementation (PLDI'04), June, pp. 145–157 (2004)

Towards a Calculus of Object Programs

Bertrand Meyer

Abstract Verifying properties of object-oriented software requires a method for handling references in a simple and intuitive way, closely related to how O-O programmers reason about their programs. The method presented here, a Calculus of Object Programs, combines four components: *compositional logic*, a framework for describing program semantics and proving program properties; *negative variables* to address the specifics of O-O programming, in particular qualified calls; the *alias calculus*, which determines whether reference expressions can ever have the same value; and the *calculus of object structures*, a specification technique for the structures that arise during the execution of an object-oriented program.

The article illustrates the Calculus by proving the standard algorithm for reversing a linked list.

1 Addressing the Specifics of Object-Oriented Software

Object-oriented programming predominates today; the verification methods we apply should reflect its distinctive properties. Much of the available work, however, fails to take into account the specifics of the object-oriented approach, in particular the "general relativity" principle which makes every operation dependent on a "current object" known only at run time and potentially different for every execution or evaluation.

The most critical obstacle, for the practice of verification, is that there is still no easily applicable approach to handle the manipulation of *references* (pointers), which plays a central role in the practice of O-O development. Separation logic, the method that has attracted the most attention, rests on an extensive model of the heap, requires extensive program annotations, and fails to take advantage of the abstraction mechanisms that define object technology. A typical example is Bornat's important work on "proving pointer programs" [1], which does not consider any object-oriented mechanisms—in fact not even routine calls, O-O or not—and focuses its discussion on modeling remote field assignments, $x.a := c$, a mechanism that no

B. Meyer
ITMO & Eiffel Software, ETH Zurich, Zürich, Switzerland
se.ethz.ch

K.K. Breitman, R.N. Horspool (eds.), *Patterns, Programming and Everything*,
DOI 10.1007/978-1-4471-2350-7_8,

careful object-oriented programmer would use. (The appropriate idiom, whether or not the language imposes it, is to go through a call to a setter procedure $x.set\_a(c)$, or a semantically equivalent variant such as a property setter in C#.)

The present discussion describes an approach to verifying object-oriented programs with particular emphasis on the handling of references as required for linked data structures. The techniques closely follow the way object-oriented programmers think about their programs; it uses standard annotations (contracts) of the form already present in Eiffel, Spec# or JML, with only small extensions to the concepts of axiomatic (Hoare-style) specification. It retains the possibility of evaluating assertions at run time, for testing purposes, in addition to using them for static verification. Although the present paper presents the concepts only, the integration into a state-of-the-art proof seems within reach.

The approach includes four components:

- *Compositional logic* (Sect. 3), which describes the semantics of program elements in terms of their effects on program values, generalizing the assertions of Hoare-Dijkstra semantics to expressions of arbitrary types.
- The notion of *negative variable* (Sect. 4), which provides a simple machinery to model the distinctive properties of object-oriented programming, making it possible in particular to reason on properties of the fundamental operation of object-oriented programming, the call $x.f(args)$.
- The *alias calculus*, an automatic approach (not relying on annotations) to determine that two given expressions in a program can never denote the same object. The alias calculus was presented in an earlier paper [15]; Sect. 5 summarizes its results and its application to the present work.
- The *calculus of object structures* (Sect. 6), a set of techniques for describing properties of run-time structures involving references. Reasoning effectively about object structures requires suitably abstract models; the calculus defines these abstractions, in particular through the integral operator $\int$, and the associated semantic rules.

The "Calculus of Object Programs" is the combination of these four techniques. It yields, as an example, a simple proof of a program known to be challenging for verification: linked list reversal. To enable the reader to understand right away how the techniques work, this proof appears in Sect. 2, where each step includes a forward reference to the formal rule that justifies it. Sections 3 to 6 detail these rules; Sect. 7 is a comparison with other approaches, Sect. 8 concludes, and Appendix provides some supplementary theoretical background.

Starting with the example should enable the reader to see the simplicity of the method, and encourage the study of the theory in the remainder of the paper.

The approach has limitations, detailed in Sect. 8; for example, it does not yet address inheritance. Also, the ideas have not yet been implemented; integrating them into a practical verification environment [30] will, we hope, show their practicability and scalability. Another possible criticism is that not much attention has been devoted so far to modular provability. In spite of these limitations, the Calculus of Object Programs presented here may hold some of the elements of a simple method for verifying programs that routinely manipulate sophisticated object structures.

2 A Proof: Linked List Reversal

The example proof addresses an important and typical problem involving somewhat intricate manipulations of references: the in-place reversal of a linked list.

As evidence that many people consider this problem tricky, we note that it is a staple interview question for programmers; dozens of Web pages, which one will readily find through a search for terms such as "list reversal algorithm", present variants of the solution, for the benefit of job candidates preparing such interviews. (A blog article [16] discusses some of these pages, noting that they typically fail to mention the loop invariant even though it is the key to understanding the algorithm.)

Although the steps are simple, we will perform the key part of the proof in almost full detail, in the way one would present a proof of Euclid's algorithm in an introductory course on axiomatic semantics. The intent is to demonstrate that the techniques presented here allow programmers to reason formally about programs manipulating linked data structures as simply and naturally as about traditional programs involving just integers and booleans.

Terminology note: an object is made of a number of elementary values known as *fields*. Of direct interest for the present discussion are fields of reference types (rather than of basic types such as integers). Every field in an object corresponds to an *attribute* of the associated class. Attributes are also called "member variables" (or "fields", although this term may cause confusion between the static and dynamic views).

2.1 Algorithm Idea

The goal is to reverse a list of cells (of type *LINKABLE*) linked to each other through fields labeled *right*; the first cell is accessed through the field *first* of the list class:

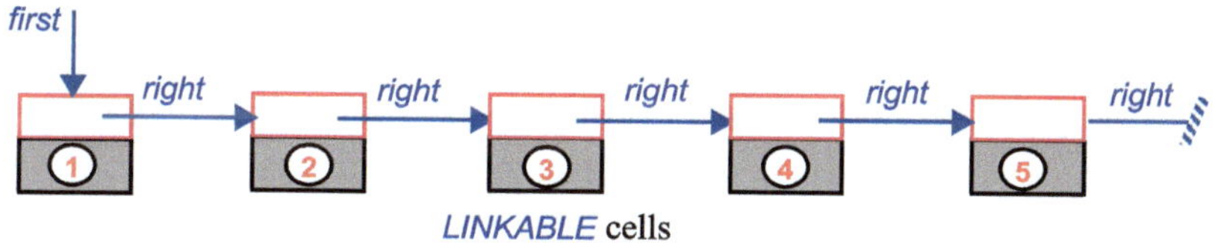

(The figures and part of the discussion are taken from an introductory programming textbook [14].) As illustrated, each cell contains both a *right* link and some other information, shown here as just an integer. We will assume that the structure induced by the *right* links is acyclic; this property, formalized below, must remain invariant throughout the algorithm. The desired final situation is:

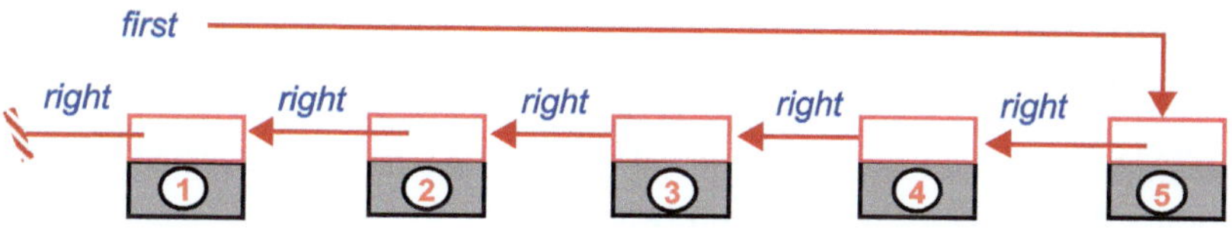

By convention, the algorithm reorders the cells by changing their *right* fields, but does not change the rest of the cell's contents (so that in this example each cell in the final picture is the same object as the one that had the same integer identifier in the original). Other variants are of course possible.

The best way to understand the basic idea of the algorithm, which relies on a loop, is to consider the state of the data structure after a typical iteration of the loop:

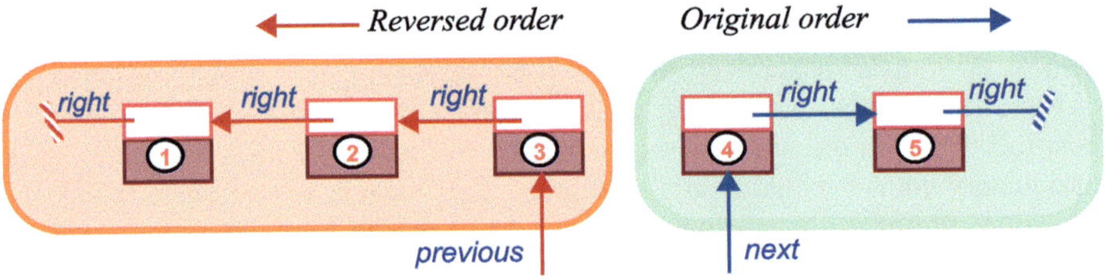

In this intermediate state, we actually have two lists, accessible through the local variables *previous* and *next*. The key property, as illustrated, is that the first list contains an initial subset of the original sequence, but now in reversed order, and the second list contains the remaining elements, in their original order. Then the task of the loop body is to preserve this property but move the boundary between the two lists by one position to the right:

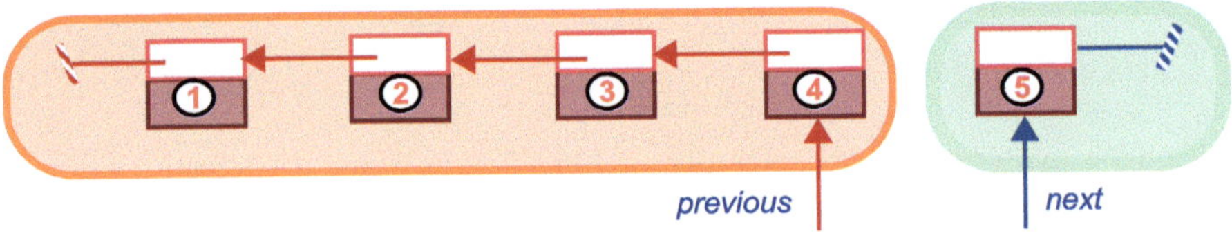

To achieve this change, the loop body will perform a short pointer ballet, which will be detailed below. Note in particular that it must change the *right* field of the first item to the right of the border (in the example, the one with value 4).

Repeating this process, we will eventually reach a state where *next* is void (null) and *previous* points to the last element of the original list, giving us the desired result if we then set *first* to *previous*. The process is easy to initialize: just set *previous* to void and *next* to *first*.

2.2 Algorithm Text

All common forms of linked list reversal use the scheme just described, with small variations. We will work with the following form:

```
reverse
        -- Rearrange cells into the reverse of their original order.
    local
        previous, next, temp: detachable LINKABLE
    do
        from
            previous := Void ; next := first
        until
            next = Void
        loop
            temp := previous                          -- i1
            previous := next                          -- i2
            next := next.right                        -- i3
            previous.set_right(temp)                  -- i4
        end
        first := previous
    end
```

The procedure *set_right* sets the *right* field of its target to the value of its argument. A Java or C# programmer might write the call *previous.set_right* (*temp*) as a remote assignment *previous.right* := *temp*, but we restrict ourselves to a proper form of O-O programming which rules out such violations of information hiding: the only way to set a field of another object is through a setter procedure such as *set_right*. The **detachable** declaration marks variables whose value might be void [18].

Some simplifications are possible: the initial assignment of **Void** to *previous* is not necessary thanks to default initialization rules; we can get rid of the variable *previous* altogether, and of the final assignment to *first*, by working directly with *first*. We omit these simplifications in the interest of clarity.

For ease of reference in the proof, the four instructions of the loop body have been given names, *i1* to *i4*.

2.3 Specification

The first step in verifying software is to specify what must be verified. Proper notations are essential: concise, clear, and applicable to a wide class of problems. We need to equip the routine *reverse* with a postcondition stating the property illustrated informally in the preceding figures: that the original list is the concatenation of the list starting at *previous*, reversed, and the list starting at *next*. We express this postcondition as:

$$first.\int right = -\,\mathbf{old}\ first.\int right \qquad (1)$$

The expression **old** e denotes, as usual, the value of e on entry to the routine. If s is a sequence (a mathematical object, not a list from programming), $-s$ is the reverse sequence. The "integral" operator $\int$ is a new notation: starting from the current object, $\int b$ denotes the sequence containing that object, then the objects attached to b, $b.b$, $b.b.b$ and so on, for as long as it makes sense (and stopping at any cycle, although here we are dealing with acyclic structures). The sequence $p.\int b$ similarly contains the objects attached to p, $p.b$, $p.b.b$ and so on. The integral notation allows us to express the goal of the routine as (1).

It similarly enables us to express the fundamental invariant property of the loop algorithm. Considered the typical intermediate step, which was illustrated as follows:

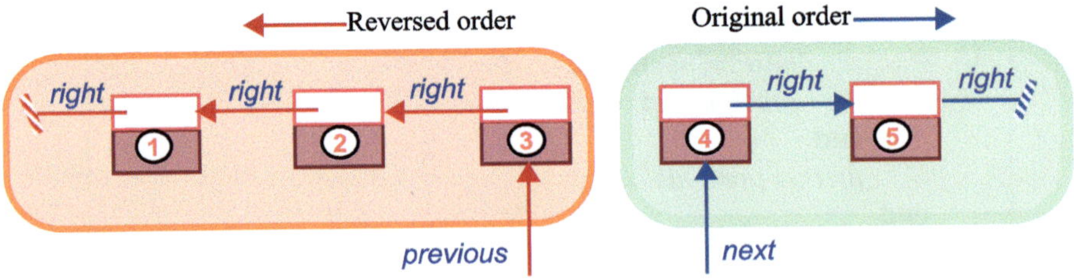

We may express the invariant property that this figure represents as:

$$-previous.\int right + next.\int right = \mathbf{old} \int first.\int right \qquad (2)$$

where "+" denotes sequence concatenation. Proving this property to be a loop invariant is the key step of proving the program. Once we establish this result, it remains only to prove that the invariant is ensured by the initialization ($previous := \mathbf{Void}$; $next := first$), and that when combined with the loop exit condition ($next = \mathbf{Void}$) and the property $previous = first$ it yields the desired postcondition (1). Both of these properties are obvious and any good proof machinery will discharge them easily; so the rest of this discussion limits itself to proving that the loop body (when $next /= \mathbf{Void}$) preserves (2) and that the loop terminates.

We can in fact simplify the proof further since compositional logic generalizes the notion of loop invariant from boolean expressions to expressions of arbitrary type. We say that an expression e is an invariant of a loop simply to mean that an execution of the loop body, performed when the loop exit condition does not hold, preserves its value. (In addition, an invariant of boolean type must have value true after the initialization, and hence will remain true, in keeping with the semantics of traditional invariants.) With this convention the property to prove is that the following expression, which we call *INV*

$$-previous.\int right + next.\int right \qquad (INV)$$

is an invariant of the loop; it no longer needs the **old** operator. (In Eiffel the loop itself would be written

from ... **until** ... **invariant**	–Other clauses as above
$-\mathit{previous}.\int \mathit{right} + \mathit{next}.\int \mathit{right}$	
loop ... **end**	

assuming a suitable extension of the language to accept arbitrary expression types in **invariant** clauses.)

A point of notation: in (1), (2) and all later assertions involving sequences, the "=" symbol represents mathematical equality, here between two sequences. In an O-O programming language, such assertions will have to use the notation for object equality ("~" in Eiffel, where "=", applied to references, represents reference equality).

2.4 Proof Approach

In compositional logic, the property expressing that *INV* is an invariant is

$(b\ ;\ \mathit{INV}) = \mathit{INV}$	–Where b is the loop body : *i1* ; *i2* ; *i3* ; *i4*

(under the assumption that the exit condition $\mathit{next} =$ **Void** does not hold). The notation $i\ ;\ e$, for an instruction i and an expression e, denotes the value of e after execution of i, stated as an expression in the state preceding that execution. Note that the semicolon is also used in its traditional role as separator of sequentially executed instructions, as in *i1* ; *i2*; the two uses reflect, as we will see, the same mathematical operator. If an expression is present, as *INV* here, it must be the last element. (We may think of programming languages such as Algol W and C where a block may end with an expression, following a sequence of instructions, and then evaluates to the value of the expression after execution of the instructions.)

INV is the sum (concatenation) $-\mathit{previous}.\int \mathit{right} + \mathit{next}.\int \mathit{right}$. Since the semicolon distributes over "+" as over most operators, the proof that $b\ ;\ \mathit{INV} = \mathit{INV}$ can be split into three parts:

- Computing $b\ ;\ \mathit{previous}.\int \mathit{right}$ (Sect. 2.5); call the result *bp*.
- Computing $b\ ;\ \mathit{next}.\int \mathit{right}$ (Sect. 2.6); call the result *bn*.
- Computing $-bp + bn$ and showing that it is equal to *INV* (Sect. 2.7).

In addition, Sect. 2.8 will prove loop termination.

The semicolon is right-associative: $(i\ ;\ j)\ ;\ e$ is $i\ ;\ (j\ ;\ e)$. As a consequence, since b is *i1* ; *i2* ; *i3* ; *i4*, the computation of b ; *e4* (where *e4* is $\mathit{previous}.\int \mathit{right}$ in 2.5 and $\mathit{next}.\int \mathit{right}$ in 2.6) will proceed as the computation of *e3* = (*i4* ; *e4*), then of *e2* = (*i3* ; *e3*), then of *e1* = (*i2* ; *e2*), then of the result as *i1* ; *e1*. The basic form

i ; e of compositional logic leads to this backward order, recalling how the Hoare assignment axiom leads to backward reasoning.

For ease of reference here is the loop body b again:

$temp := previous$	$-i1$
$previous := next$	$-i2$
$next := next.right$	$-i3$
$previous.set\_right(temp)$	$-i4$

One of the attractions of the style of proofs presented in this work is that it closely matches the intuitive semantics of object-oriented programs and the way programmers think about their execution. To take advantage of this property, the reader may find it useful to relate intermediate steps of the proofs to intermediate steps of the computation, as reflected in the illustration of the pointer ballet (on the next page). Going from the bottom up in the figure, the successively computed expressions *e4*, *e3*, *e2* and *e1* correspond to the states S4, S3, S2 and S1.

2.5 Handling the Previous Part

We first compute *i4* ; p where p is $previous.\int right$ and *i4* is a call to a setter procedure: $previous.put\_right(t)$. By coincidence this first step of the proof uses one of the most powerful rules to be seen below, ICX (34), which states that with a setting procedure *set_a* that sets the value of an attribute a in the target object x, then

$$x.set\_a(c)\,;\, x.\int a \quad = \quad \langle x\rangle + c.\int a$$

where $\langle x\rangle$ denotes the sequence consisting of the single element x. We get:

$$i4\,;\, p \qquad = \langle previous\rangle + temp.\int right \qquad \text{(p3)}$$

We can indeed see at the bottom of the figure how p from state S4, that is to say the sequence starting at *previous*, corresponds in state S3 to the element $\langle previous\rangle$ followed by the sequence starting at *temp*.

Next we compute *i3* ; *p3* where *i3* is $next := next.right$. (In this proof the label given for each new step, here (p3), will also denote the value of the expression obtained at that step.) We apply distributivity to compute the effect of the assignment on the two operands of the "+" expression. In both cases, the assignment affects none of the elements in the given expressions, and no cycles are involved; these conditions enable us to apply a theorem seen below, IAY (30), which indicates that both sides are untouched:

$$i3\,;\, p3 \qquad = p3 \qquad = \langle previous\rangle + temp.\int right \qquad \text{(p2)}$$

The figure indeed suggests that the assignment *i3* only affects the "*next*" part of the structure and that the "*previous*" and "*temp*" parts are unchanged between S2 and S3.

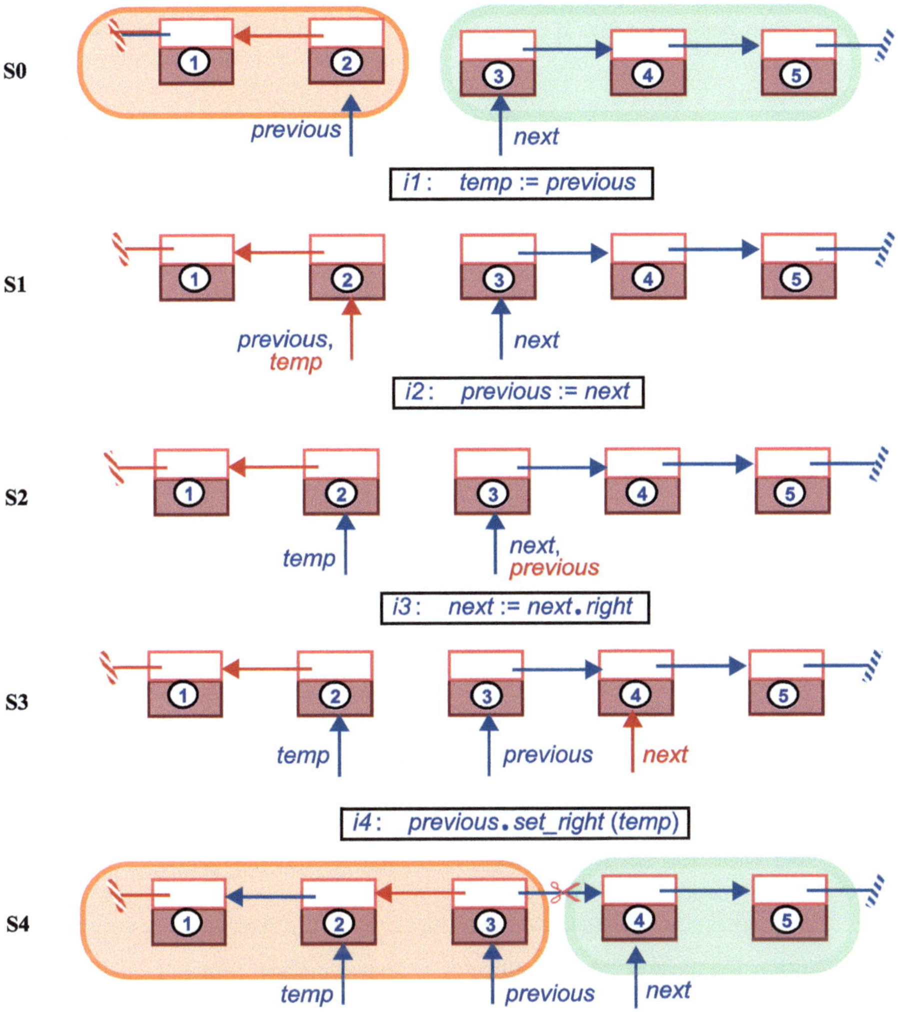

Continuing up the loop body *b*, we compute *i2* ; *p2* where *i2* is the assignment *previous* := *next*. We again consider the two operands separately. The assignment axiom of compositional logic tells us that:

- $((x := e)\ ;\ x) = e$; this will be rule AX (5). It applies here to the first operand since *previous* is the assignment's target.
- For a variable y other than x, $((x := e)\ ;\ y) = y$; this will be rule AY (6), which IAY (30) generalizes to expressions, under conditions of acyclicity satisfied here. It tells us that the assignment has no effect on the second operand.

As a consequence

$$i2\ ;\ p2 \qquad = \langle next \rangle + temp.\textstyle\int right \qquad \text{(p1)}$$

We may again perform a visual check on the figure: the sequence that starts with *previous* in state S4 was, in state S1, the concatenation of the *next* element and the sequence starting with *temp*.

In the last proof step, the instruction *i1* is the loop's initial assignment, *temp* := *previous*. Axiom AY (6) tells us that has no effect on the *next* operand, but axiom IAX (29) tells us that $(x := y)\ ;\ x.\int a$ is (in the absence of cycles) $y.\int a$. We get as a result the value of $b\ ;\ p$ on entry to the loop:

$$b\ ;\ (previous.\textstyle\int right) \qquad = \langle next \rangle + previous.\textstyle\int right \qquad \text{(bp)}$$

which can again be checked for reasonableness in the figure, by looking at the counterpart in state S0 of the sequence starting with *previous* in state S4. This completes the computation of the effect of *b* on the first operand of our conjectured invariant expression.

2.6 Handling the next Part

We now apply the same process to compute $b\ ;\ n$ where n is the second operand, $next.\int right$. The reader is invited to follow the intermediate steps in the figure as was done for the first part.

The frame theorem ICY (36) indicates that the final instruction *i4* of the loop, **call** *previous.put_right*(*t*), has no effect on $next.\int right$:

$$i4\ ;\ n \qquad = n \qquad \text{AX (1)}$$

– where *i4* is "**call** *previous.put_right*(*t*)"
– and *n* is "$next.\int right$".

The condition for the rule to be applicable is that *previous* must not be aliased to *next*; the alias calculus yields it here automatically (although we could also establish it through classical techniques).

For *i3*, the assignment *next* := *next.right*, theorem IAX (29) gives the next step:

$$i3\ ;\ n3 \qquad = next.right.\textstyle\int right \qquad \text{AX (2)}$$

The initial assignments, *i1* and *i2*, have *previous* and *right* as their respective targets. Rule IAY (30) tells us that they have no effect on the right side of the above: the next two steps $n1 = (i2\ ;\ n2)$ and $bn = (i1\ ;\ n1)$ give the same result as *n2*. As a consequence, we get the final answer for the second operand:

$$b\ ;\ (next\,\boldsymbol{.}\int right) \qquad = bn = next.right\,\boldsymbol{.}\int right \qquad \text{(bp)}$$

2.7 Combining the Results

The value we are computing (the value of the conjectured invariant in the initial state of the loop) is $-bp + bn$, or, from the preceding computations

$$-(\langle next\rangle + previous\,\boldsymbol{.}\int right) + next.right\,\boldsymbol{.}\int right$$

Three simple properties of mathematical sequences are that $-(s1 + s2)$ is $(-s2) + (-s1)$; that concatenation "+" is associative; and that a one-element sequence is its own inverse: $-\langle a\rangle = \langle a\rangle$ for any element a. We can use them to simplify the result into

$$-previous\,\boldsymbol{.}\int right + \langle next\rangle + next.right\,\boldsymbol{.}\int right \qquad \text{(bp1)}$$

Theorem SIE (25), which follows directly from the definition of the integral operator $\int$, states that for any attribute a

$$\int a \qquad = \langle a\rangle + a\,\boldsymbol{.}\int a$$

indicating that the last two terms in *bp1* combine into $next\,\boldsymbol{.}\int right$, and finally giving us, for the entire expression:

$$-previous\,\boldsymbol{.}\int right + next\,\boldsymbol{.}\int right$$

This is the original expression, completing the proof that the expression is a loop invariant.

2.8 Termination

So far the proof has not addressed termination. Informally: since the loop's exit condition is *next* = **Void**, we must make sure that the repeated applications of the loop body finitely reach a void link, thanks in particular to the instruction *i3*: *next* := *next.right*. This would not be the case with a cyclic structure; indeed, the routine needs a precondition and should be written as:

reverse
    – Reverse order of the cells.
  require
    $first\,\boldsymbol{.}\boxtimes right$
  . . . The rest as above . . .

where the property $\boxtimes a$, for an attribute a, states that the structure induced by a starting from the current object has no cycle; more generally, $p.\boxtimes a$ states that the structure induced by a starting from p has no cycle.

As a consequence of the precondition, the program will maintain the properties *previous*. $\boxtimes$ *right* and *next*. $\boxtimes$ *right*. In other words, the figures showing both the *previous* and *next* lists as acyclic do not lie. This property is proved automatically by application of the alias calculus to the program.

To prove termination formally we need, as usual, a loop variant. If $p.\boxtimes a$ holds, there is an integer n, the "depth of a after p", written $p.\downarrow a$, such that following the a links n times from p leads to an object whose own a link is **Void**. In the example *next*.$\downarrow$*right* is a variant for the loop, guaranteeing termination.

This step completes the example proof, which demonstrates the method developed in this article. We will now review the basis for the properties on which the proof has relied.

3 Compositional Logic

The first step is to define a proof framework appropriate for reasoning about complex programs. Compositional logic is a variation on the familiar forms of programming language semantics; its main advantage over axiomatic techniques—an advantage of style rather than substance—is that it does not rely on textual substitutions, except in the case of modeling argument passing.

3.1 Basics

Compositional logic works with formulae of the following form, for an instruction i and an expression e:

$$i\ ;\ e$$

denoting the value of e after the execution of i. For the various kinds of instruction and expression, the rules of compositional logic define $i\ ;\ e$ in terms of expressions evaluated in the state preceding that execution.

As an example, the following axiom applies to any instruction i if c is a constant:

$i\ ;\ c$	$= c$	– For any instruction i	CUR (3)

(For ease of reference, all rules appear in shaded boxes and are given both a name and a number.) If we extend this property of constants to arbitrary expressions, we get a generalized version of the concept of "*relative purity*" of an instruction i for an assertion P, defined in [31] as $\{P\}i\{P\}$: we may say that i is relatively pure for an expression e of any type if $(i \; ; \; e) = e$.

In object-oriented programming, a particularly important constant is **Current** (also called **this** or **self** in various O-O languages), denoting the current object. No construct can ever change the value of **Current**:

i ; **Current**	= **Current**	– For any instruction i	AX (4)

This rule is our first encounter with the O-O principle of general relativity: as an observer traveling in a spacecraft can change the contents of that vessel but not move to another spacecraft, the execution of an operation on an object can change the contents of that object but not make another object current. (Another analogy is that although you can change some of your own properties you cannot become someone else.)

The CUR property holds of all basic instructions and must be preserved by rules for composite instructions such as calls.

The next two axioms define assignment; for variables x and y and an arbitrary expression e:

$(x := e) \; ; \; x$	$= e$	AX (5)
$(x := e) \; ; \; y$	$= y$	AY (6)

Here, and elsewhere unless explicitly noted otherwise, different variable names in the axioms, such as x and y, denote different variables. (The *values* of the variables could, of course, be equal at run time.)

AX and AY replace the usual assignment axiom of axiomatic semantics. They apply to individual variables rather than arbitrary expressions; to determine the effect of an assignment on a composite expression, we need a distributivity theorem.

3.2 Distributivity and Associativity

The distributivity theorem

$i \; ; \; (e \; \S \; f)$	$= (i \; ; \; e) \; \S \; (i \; ; \; f)$	DIST (7)

is applicable to all ordinary operators § on basic types and references. An example proof using this property and some of the previous ones is:

$(x := e) \; ; \; (x + 1)$	$= ((x := e) \; ; \; x) + ((x := e) \; ; \; 1)$	– by DIST (7)
	$= ((x := e) \; ; \; x) + 1$	– by CUR (3)
	$= e + 1$	– by AX (5)

In words: the value of $x + 1$ after the assignment $x := e$ is the value that $e + 1$ had in the initial state.

An associativity rule applies, where the semicolon is also used in its traditional role as instruction sequencer:

$$(i\ ;\ j)\ ;\ e \qquad = i\ ;\ (j\ ;\ e)$$

– If e does not involve **old** (see next)
ASSOC (8)

3.3 *Rule for "old"*

The operator **old** makes it possible to refer to the original value of an expression. The corresponding axiom reflects this property:

$$i\ ;\ \textbf{old}\, e \qquad = e \qquad \text{OLD (9)}$$

This property holds of all basic instructions i and must be preserved by rules for composite instructions such as routine calls.

It must be clear what the scope of i is: as stated in the restriction to the ASSOC rule, associativity does not apply if **old** is involved. Compare:

$$(x := 0)\ ;\ (x := 1))\ ;\ \textbf{old}\, x \qquad = x \qquad \text{– by OLD}$$

– but:

$$(x := 0)\ ;\ ((x := 1)\ ;\ \textbf{old}\, x) \qquad = (x := 0)\ ;\ x \qquad \text{– by OLD}$$
$$= 0 \qquad \text{– by AX (5)}$$

As an example of a proof involving **old**, consider the following property:

$$(item := item + 1)\ ;\ (item = \textbf{old}\, item + 1)$$

which might appear in a class describing a integer counter, whose value is given by *item*. As the expression is to the right of the semicolon is of boolean type, this is the equivalent to proving the Hoare triple $\{\textbf{True}\}(item := item + 1)\{item = \textbf{old}\, item + 1\}$. Through DIST (7) applied to the equality operator "=", the property expands to

$$((item := item + 1)\ ;\ item) = ((item := item + 1)\ ;\ (\textbf{old}\, item + 1) \qquad \text{AX (10)}$$

The left side of this equality is $item + 1$ by the assignment axiom AX (5). The right side can be further expanded through DIST to

$$((item := item + 1)\ ;\ (\textbf{old}\, item)) + ((item := item + 1)\ ;\ 1)$$

The first term is *item* by OLD (9); the second term is 1 by CUR (3), yielding $item + 1$ for the right side of AX (10), and hence establishing AX (10).

Comparing this proof with its counterpart in Hoare or weakest-precondition semantics, we note that it avoids using substitution, relying instead on algebraic laws of distributivity and associativity. On the other hand it requires two assignment axioms, AX (5) and AY (6), instead of the single axiom of axiomatic semantics.

3.4 Calls

Consider a routine r. The body of r, a sequence of instructions, will be denoted by $\underline{r}$, and the list of formal arguments by $r^\bullet$. A call to the routine, with actual arguments l, will be written **call** $r(l)$. (Modern languages typically do not need the keyword **call**, but we keep it here for clarity.) The compositional logic rule is

$$(\textbf{call}\, r(l))\, ;\, e \qquad = (\underline{r}\, ;\, e)[r^\bullet : l] \qquad \text{UC (11)}$$

where $f[v : l]$ denotes the expression f with every occurrence of an element in the list of variables replaced by the corresponding element in the list of expressions l. This is the only place where compositional logic uses substitution, to represent actual-formal argument association. The rule's name stands for "Unqualified Call"; the version for qualified calls (**call** $x.r(l)$) will appear later as QC (21).

Since rule UC defines the semantics of calls in terms of the semantics of their constituent instructions, it preserves the AX (4) and OLD (9) properties.

3.5 Setters

A theorem applies to setter procedures of the form

```
set_a(...; f: T; ...)                                          AX (12)
        – Among other possible actions, set the value of a to f.
    do
        anything_else
        a := f
    ensure
        a = f              – There may be other postcondition clauses.
    end
```

where a is (in an object-oriented context) an attribute of the enclosing class. We say that a routine with a postcondition clause $a := f$, where a is an attribute and f an argument, is a **setter for** a. The theorem is:

$(\textbf{call}\, r(\ldots, c, \ldots))\ ;\ a$	$= c$ – If r is a setter for a	US (13)

("Unqualified Setter" rule). The position of c in the actual argument list is the position of the setting argument, f above, in the formal argument list.

The proof of US immediately from the previous rule UC (11), and associativity ASSOC (8) which enables us to ignore whatever *anything_else* does.

It is often important to deduce properties of routines of which we do not have the implementation but only a contract. UC is applicable whenever the routine has the postcondition $a = f$. An informal proof of this property simply notes that the semantics of such a routine does not change if we add the assignment $a := f$ at the end of its body (including if we do this in any order for distinct attributes a), so that the previous proof is still applicable.

3.6 Mathematical Basis

The ";" operator has a simple mathematical meaning. To see it, we start by looking at non-OO (such as Pascal- or C-style) programming, then move to an object-oriented context where the idea is the same but the functions' signature involves one more level.

Fundamentally, ";" is a variant of mathematical composition. Let us use the operator "$\circ$" to denote the composition of functions or relations; for functions f and g, their composition $h = f \circ g$ is such that $h(x) = g(f(x)$. (Frequent mathematical convention lists the functions in the reverse order, but for programming it makes more sense to write them in the order of application.)

Consider first a non-OO framework. $A \rightarrow B$ will denote the set of functions from A to B where A and B are arbitrary states. Let *State* be the set of states and *Value* the set of run-time values. An instruction is a function in *State* $\rightarrow$ *State*. (More precisely, it may be a partial function, to account for undefined computations, or a general binary relation, to account for non-deterministic programs; since these cases do not affect the discussion, we keep "$\rightarrow$" for simplicity.) An expression is a function in *State* $\rightarrow$ *Value*.

The ";" operator in this context is just function composition "$\circ$". This definition of the operator also explains why we can apply it both between instructions, as in $i\ ;\ j$, and between an instruction and an expression, as in the basic formula of computational logic, $i\ ;\ e$. Associativity ASSOC (8) applies, enabling us to write $i1\ ;\ i2; \ldots; i_n\ ;\ e$, as long as we use an expression only as the last element. The first n functions being composed are in *State* $\rightarrow$ *State*, yielding as their composition another function with the same signature; we then compose this result with e, of signature *State* $\rightarrow$ *Value*, giving as overall result another *State* $\rightarrow$ *Value* function representing an expression.

In object-oriented programming the signatures are different as a consequence of general relativity: every instruction and expression is relative to a current object, not specified in the class text (and not changeable by it, see AX (4)). With *Object* representing the set of objects, the signatures are now:

$Object \rightarrow State \rightarrow State$	– For an instruction
$Object \rightarrow State \rightarrow Value$	– For an expression

and the semicolon operator has the following definition, denoting a generalized form of composition where both operands are applied to the same object:

$$i\ ;\ f \qquad = \lambda x:\ Object \mid \lambda s:\ State \mid (i(x) \circ f(x))(\sigma)$$

(In other words, $(i\ ;\ f)(x)$, applied to a state σ, is the result of applying $f(x)$ to the result of applying $i(x)$ to σ.) As before, f can be either an instruction or an expression but the definition is the same, justifying the use of a single operator ";".

3.7 Comparison with Other Semantic Description Methods

We may assess the level of abstraction of compositional logic against other approaches to defining the semantics of programs and programming languages.

Denotational semantics specifies the programming language by explicitly defining, for every kind of instruction i, a function in *State* → *State*, and similarly a function in *State* → *Value* for every kind of expression. (For O-O languages, the signatures also involve *Object*.)

Axiomatic semantics works at a higher level of abstraction by defining the effect of instructions on boolean properties of the program state (or, for postconditions, of two states). The *weakest-precondition* variant attempts to turn such properties into a calculus whose rules yield the precondition from the construct and the postcondition.

Compositional logic is at a higher level of abstraction than denotational semantics since it does not explicitly manipulate the state, but only talks about the effect of computations on expressions of interest to the programmer. Unlike axiomatic semantics, however, it defines these properties for arbitrary expressions, not just boolean ones.

In the case of boolean expressions, compositional logic reduces to the weakest-precondition calculus: $i\ ;\ Q$ is $i\,\mathbf{wp}\,Q$ (the weakest precondition of the instruction i for the postcondition Q).

The correspondence with Hoare-style semantics is similar: the Hoare triple $\{P\}i\{Q\}$ expresses that P **implies**$(i\ ;\ Q)$, where **implies** is implication between assertions.

4 Negative Variables: Reasoning on Object-Oriented Calls

In the object-oriented style of programming, the basic operation is the "qualified call"

$$\textbf{call}\, x.r(l) \qquad \text{AX (14)}$$

which calls the routine r, with actual arguments l, on the object OX denoted in the current class text by x. For the duration of the call, OX will be the current object; the previously current object will become current again upon termination of the call, including any other calls that it may in turn have triggered.

The terms "client object" and "client class" will denote the caller side (the context that issues the above call); "supplier object" and "supplier class" refer to the target object OX and its class:

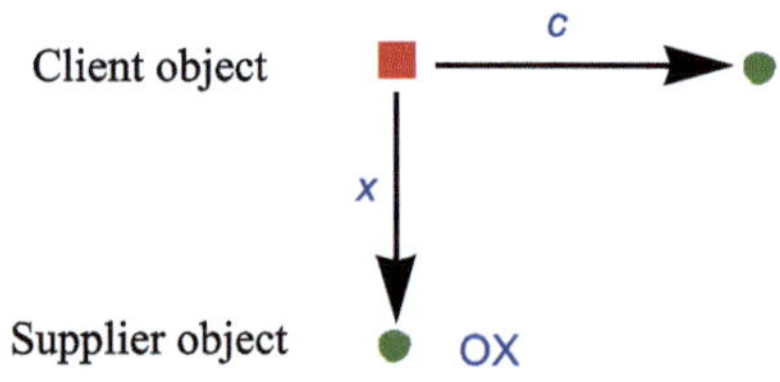

Client and supplier objects

The figure (using the precise conventions of "alias diagrams" introduced in [15] for presenting properties of object structures) also shows a field of the client object, corresponding to an attribute c, which can be used as an actual argument to the call (part of the list l).

The unqualified call rules, such as UC (11) above, or its equivalent in axiomatic semantics, which tells us that from $\{P\}\underline{r}\{Q\}$ we may deduce $\{P[r^\bullet : l]\}\, \textbf{call}\, r(l)\{Q[r^\bullet : l]\}$, do not directly apply because they fail to take into account the relativity of expressions in the different contexts of the caller object and the target object. If f is a formal argument of r (part of $r^\bullet$) and the corresponding actual argument in l is c, we cannot just substitute c for f in reasoning about the call, since the name c is meaningless for the supplier: it denotes a field of another object, and generally of a different class.

We need, however, to be able to use this field; for example the routine body could perform the instruction

$$y := f.item$$

where y is an attribute of the supplier class. In the execution of $\textbf{call}\, x.r(c)$, where the formal argument is f, we expect this instruction to assign to y the value of $c.item$:

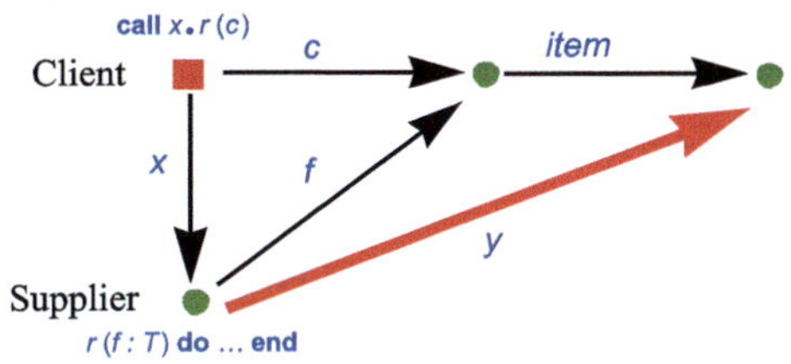

The supplier may need access to the client context

Note that *item* itself is a feature of the class of c. The thick red arrow in the figure illustrates the intended result of the assignment to y. The figure also shows that the formal argument f refers, in the supplier's context for this particular call, to the object known in the client's context as c.

One way to deal with these changes of context is to assume a preprocessing step in which all unqualified references to features of a class (including attributes, but not formal routine arguments) are prefixed by **Current** (or **this**), then to include in the call rule a substitution of the target, x in the example, for all occurrences of **Current**. This is the technique used in [20]. It implies, however, many textual manipulations. We will use instead an algebraic technique based on the notion of negative variable introduced in [15]. The idea is that in a call of target x the negated variable x', applicable to the supplier context, denotes a link back to the client object, making it possible in the supplier context to refer to any expression e stated in terms of the client context: simply use $x'.e$.

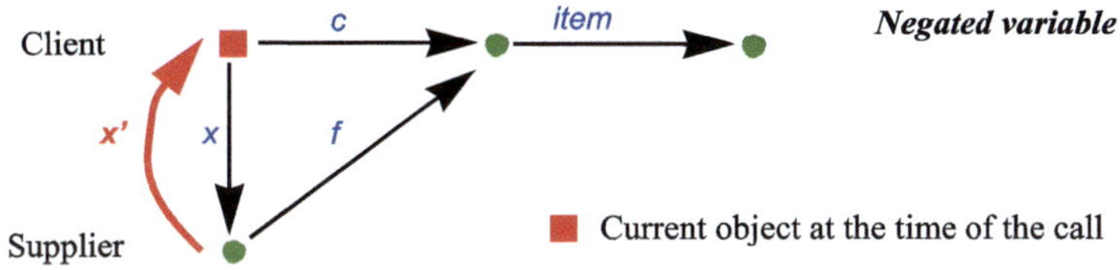

Negated variable

For example, passing c as the argument in **call** $x.r(c)$ means binding the corresponding formal f not to c (as in an unqualified call **call** $r(c)$) but to $x'.c$.

The following rules apply to negative variables and **Current**:

$x.x'$	=	**Current**	– For any variable x	NEG1 (15)
x'.**old** x	=	**Current**		NEG2 (16)
Current.e	=	e	– For any expression e	CUR1 (17)
e.**Current**	=	e		CUR2 (18)

(These rules come from [15], with NEG2 adjusted.) The presence of **old** in NEG2 is necessary to account for a "frame" issue: the possibility that a call $x.r(\ldots)$ might, through a callback, change the value of the x field of the current object. Then during the execution of r, evaluating $x'.x$ might lead to the object newly attached to x, labeled O′ in the next figure, rather than to the call's target OX:

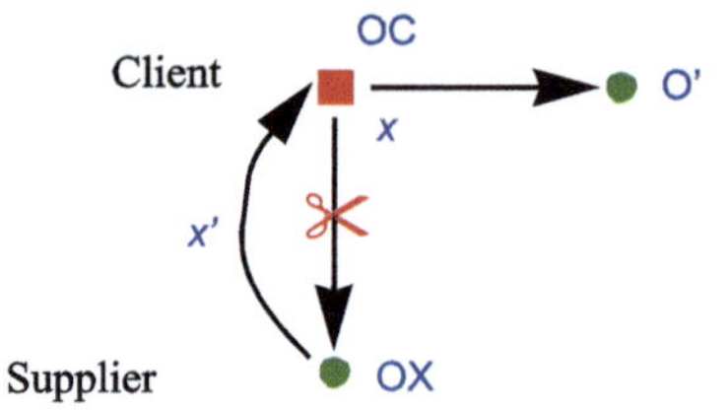

A callback with side effect can cause x'.x ***to be no longer*** **Current**

Object-oriented languages do permit this behavior, in which a routine call changes the field that served as the call's target; NEG2 handles them. Such schemes complicate verification, however, and break the symmetry between NEG1 and NEG2. It is preferable, as a matter of programming methodology, to avoid them by requiring routines to satisfy the following property:

Definition: nonprodigal routine

A routine is *nonprodigal* if for any call of target x it satisfies the postcondition

$x'.x =$ **Current** NP (19)

(The name suggests that the routine preserves its relation with its genitors.) No use of **old** is necessary in NEG1, since the expression $x.x'$ only makes sense if used from a client in relation to a call of target x, and then x' always refers back to the client.

The AX (4) rule stated that since the current object is given by the context of execution no instruction may ever change the value of **Current**. Similarly, you never get a chance to change the back-link to your client:

$i\ ;\ x' \quad = x' \quad$ – For any instruction i BL (20)

(Pursuing the earlier analogy: while your parents can disown you by designating someone else as their child, you cannot disown them, that is to say, become the child of someone else.)

Negated variables yield a simple semantic description for qualified calls $x.r(c)$, the central mechanism of object-oriented computation. Appendix gives the full semantic rules in both denotational and axiomatic styles. In compositional logic, the rule is

$(\textbf{call}\, x.r(l))\ ;\ e \quad = x.((\textbf{call}\, r(x'\,.\,l)\ ;\ (x'.e))$ QC (21)

where "**.**" denotes the dot operator "." distributed over a list (so that $x\,.\,\langle u, v, \ldots\rangle$ is $\langle x.u, x.v, \ldots\rangle$). The rule determines how to obtain the effect on e of calling $x.r(l)$:

- Transpose the arguments of the original call to the context of the supplier, by prefixing them with "x'.". The result of this transposition is **call** $r\,(x' \centerdot l)$.
- Find out the effect of this call on the expression $x'.e$, which represents e also transposed to the supplier context. The result is (**call** $r\,(x' \centerdot l)$; $x'.e$.
- Interpret this result back in the context of the client by prefixing it with "x.", giving QC.

This process of transposing the client information to the supplier side then transposing back to the client side reflects the unique nature of object-oriented computation with its reliance on the current object. A qualified call makes a new object (the target) current; when the call terminates, the previous current object resumes this role.

If e is **old** x, the general rule AX (4) governing **Current**, applied to the unqualified call, tells us that **call** $x.r(l))$; **Current** is **Current.Current** and hence (from CUR1 (17)) **Current**. It follows that the qualified call rule QC also conforms to CUR.

Similarly, (**call** $x.r(l)$) ; **old** $x) = x$ from QC, NEG2 (16) and CUR2 (18). It is not necessarily true, however, that (**call** $x.r(l)$) ; $x) = x$ because of the frame issue noted above: a callback in the execution of r might modify the client's x. field. We may only deduce (**call** $x.r(l)$) ; $x) = x$ if the routine is nonprodigal as defined above (19).

The QC rule relies on the effect of **call** $r\,(x' \centerdot l)$, the unqualified call. That effect is given by the rule for unqualified calls UC (11), which defines it as the effect of the body after argument substitution. By expanding that earlier rule we get a more detailed version of QC:

(**call** $x.r(l)$) ; e	$= x.((\underline{r}\ ;\ x'.e)[r^{\bullet} : (x' \centerdot l)]$	QC′ (22)

From the qualified call rule (in either form) we get a theorem on qualified calls to setter procedures. As before (Sect. 3.5), we assume that a is an attribute and *set_a*(f) has the postcondition $a = f$. Then:

(x.**call** *set_a*(c)) ; ((**old** x).a)	$= c$	QS (23)

("Qualified Setter" rule, compare with US (13).)

Although the definition of setter procedures such as *set_a* (3.5) allows any number of arguments, the rest of the discussion ignores, for brevity, any arguments other than the one used in a setting role.

The proof of QS is as follows:

$$
\begin{aligned}
(x.\mathbf{call}\, set\_a(c))\,;\,((\mathbf{old}\, x).a) &= x.((\mathbf{call}\, set\_a(x'.c)\,;\,(x'.\mathbf{old}\, x.a))) \\
&\qquad\qquad \text{– From QC (21)} \\
&= x.((\mathbf{call}\, set\_a(x'.c)\,;\,(\mathbf{Current}.a))) \\
&\qquad\qquad \text{– From NEG2 (16)} \\
&= x.((\mathbf{call}\, set\_a(x'.c)\,;\,a)) \\
&\qquad\qquad \text{– From CUR1 (17)} \\
&= x.(x'.c) \qquad \text{– From US (13)} \\
&= \mathbf{Current}.c \qquad \text{– From NEG1 (15)} \\
&= c \qquad \text{– From CUR1 (17)}
\end{aligned}
$$

Often we may prefer a property involving x rather than **old** x:

$$(x.\mathbf{call}\, set\_a(c))\,;\,x.a \quad = c \quad \text{– If } r \text{ is nonprodigal} \qquad \text{AX (24)}$$

This property only holds if the routine preserves the link back from its client, as expressed by the "nonprodigal" property NP (19).

5 The Alias Calculus

The third component of the approach is the alias calculus, developed in an earlier article [15]. For any expressions e and f denoting references, and any program location *pl*, the alias calculus yields the answer to the question: *can the values of e and f ever denote the same object when a program execution is at pl*? The theory is (barring any errors in [15]) *sound*, in the sense that if the answer is "no" it provides a guarantee that e and f will always denote different objects—precisely the guarantee we need for the applications discussed here. If the answer is "yes", it could still be the case that e and f never get aliased in practice. In other words, the alias relation that the calculus determines may be an over-approximation of the real aliasings. The possibility of over-approximation comes not from the calculus itself but from the simplification it applies to programming languages: it ignores the conditions in conditionals (defining the aliasings of **if** c **then** i **else** j **end** to be the union of those induced by i and j separately, regardless of c) and in loops. The over-approximation is generally harmless; when undesired, it can be corrected through the insertion of an assertion $e /= f$ (expressed in the calculus as the instruction **cut** e, f), which needs to be proved, often trivially, through techniques outside of the alias calculus.

The main advantage of the calculus is that its application is automatic. Computing the alias relations induced by a program requires no annotation (except for the occasional **cut**). The calculus yields an algorithm, whose implementation described in [15], although still experimental, covers the entire theory and has been applied to sophisticated examples.

The existence of the alias calculus allows the rest of this discussion to define rules of the form "Property P holds if e and f can never be aliased at the given program point". Such rules are sound—they cannot lead us wrongly to deduce that P holds if it does not—if the calculus is sound.

To express that at a particular program point the expressions e and f, of reference types, can never be aliased, we will write $e \not\equiv f$. (In Eiffel the usual inequality notation $e \neq f$ suffices, since when applied to references it denotes reference inequality.) This notation has two useful generalizations:

- If *S1* and *S2* are sets or sequences of expressions, $S1 \not\equiv S2$ states that $e \not\equiv f$ for every e in *S1* and every f in *S2*.
- We may also use $\vec{e} \not\equiv S1$ and $\overrightarrow{e - \{a, b, \ldots\}} \not\equiv S1$ where $\vec{e}$ denotes the set of objects reachable from EO (the object denoted by e) by following reference fields any number of times, and $\overrightarrow{e - \{a, b, \ldots\}}$ denotes its subset obtained by starting from fields of EO other than $a, b, \ldots$.

These notations are useful to reason about programs, but programmers need not know them as they will not appear in assertions or other program elements.

6 Reasoning on Data Structures

It remains to define appropriate concepts and notations to express properties of the kind of object structures, often complex, that routinely arise in object-oriented programming but still defy the reasoning techniques of the usual approaches to program verification.

6.1 Background: Model-Based Specifications

One of the reasons for the difficulties experienced by traditional approaches may be that they usually fail to equip themselves with the right abstractions. Typically, they work with elementary values and individual objects. To reason effectively about lists, trees and other sophisticated data structures, we need higher-level abstractions, such as sequences, and we must relate them to the program text; for example, we must be able to refer to the sequence of objects obtained by repeatedly following, from a given object, the successive references of a given type.

The notations defined below, in particular the integral operator, address this requirement. They follow the idea of **model-based specification**, pursued by the author and colleagues [23, 29] but already present in approaches such as JML [11]. This specification method defines the effect of programs in terms of high-level abstractions, representing mathematical concepts (sets, sequences, relations and so on) but closely integrated into the program text and expressed in the host O-O programming language.

In devising these abstractions, we retain one of the key practical properties of the Design by Contract specification method, its support for verification of both the static (proofs) and dynamic (tests) kind, by making sure that contract elements (assertions) not only have a clear mathematical specification but can also be evaluated, under the control of compiler options [6], during program execution.

6.2 Context

We assume a statically typed object-oriented language, so that any pointer expression $x.y$ can be considered type-wise valid: there is an attribute of name x in the current class, of some type T, and in the class defining T there is an attribute of name y.

References can be "void" (or "null"). We need not concern ourselves with "void calls" (or "null-pointer dereferencing"), even in the absence of a mechanism as Eiffel's Void Safety which removes this problem entirely at compile time [18], since the conventions defined below will ensure that no void reference is used in an unsafe way.

Object-oriented languages allow attributes from different classes to bear the same names; in fact the Eiffel style rules promote the systematic use of standard attribute names such as *item*. When citing attribute names, the present discussion assumes that they have been disambiguated first, so that each represents an attribute of a single class (and its descendants). Another way of stating this assumption is to assume that every attribute name is prefixed by the name of its class, as in *LINKABLE_item* and *LINKED_LIST_item*.

6.3 Paths

The first notion we need (already implicitly used in earlier discussions, with expressions such as $x'.x.c$) is that of a path. A path is a sequence of zero or more attribute names. If the path contains more than one attribute we separate them by periods, as in $a.b.c$.

We may without risk of confusion apply the dot operator to paths (such as p and q) as well as attributes (such as a, b, c, d, e), combining them freely as in $a.p$, $p.a$ and $p.q$, with associativity. For example if p is $a.b.c$ and q is $d.e$, then $p.q$ is $a.b.c.d.e$. This associativity was used in the proof of QS (23), when it obtained $x.(x'.c)$ and treated it as $(x.x').c$.

A path always denotes an *object*, defined (as the relativistic nature of object-oriented programming requires) in relation to the current object. Informally, we obtain the object denoted by a path p by starting from the current object and following, as long as possible, the references given by the fields corresponding to the elements of p, as in this example:

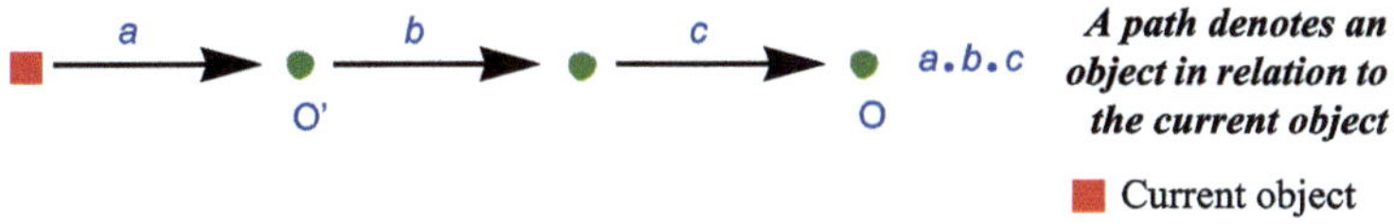

"As long as possible" means that the process stops if it encounters a void field, so if the c link in the above figure were void the value of $a.b.c$ would be the same as that of $a.b$. This convention of stopping at void links simplifies the discussion considerably; that it obviously does not reflect the semantics of **Void** or **null** in O-O languages does not matter, since the problem of void safety is not in the scope of the present discussion and should be addressed through separate techniques, such as the framework presented in [18].

To avoid any ambiguity we may define precisely the object $\bigcirc$ associated with a path p:

- If p is empty, $\bigcirc$ is the current object. In the remaining cases, let a be the first element and q the remainder of p (i.e. $p = a.q$, unless q is void in which case $p = \langle a \rangle$).
- If the a link from the current object is void, $\bigcirc$ is also the current object.
- Otherwise, let $\bigcirc'$ be the object to which the a field of the current object is attached. Then $\bigcirc$ is the object associated (recursively) with q if $\bigcirc'$ is used as current object.

As this definition unambiguously associates an object with every path, the rest of the discussion often allows itself to talk about "the object p" where p is a path.

The *length* $|p|$ of a path p is the number of attributes in its definition. The empty path has length 0 and $a.b.c$ has length 3. In the absence of void links, the length is the number of objects, other than the current object, involved in the path.

If a is an attribute, a^0 denotes the empty path, a^1 the path $\langle a \rangle$, and a^{n+1} for $n > 0$ the path $a^n.a$ (which is also $a.a^n$). In line with the general conventions noted above, using this notation assumes proper typing: the type of the attribute a must be the same as the type of the current object, or conform to it.

The notation $\boxtimes a$ expresses that a is **acyclic**, in the sense that from any current object the sequence a^n, for all $n \geq 0$, is acyclic. This property is defined as $a^n \not\doteq$ **Current** for all n, meaning, from the definition of "$\not\doteq$" in Sect. 5, that a^n can never become aliased to the current object (and hence, if the property is satisfied for all possible current objects, that there are no other cycles in the sequence either). One of the principal contributions of the alias calculus to the Calculus of Object Programs is that it tells us, through an automated procedure, that certain attributes are acyclic.

The notation generalizes to $p.\boxtimes a$, stating that there are no cycles after p in the sequence $p.a^n$.

One more notation is $p.\downarrow a$, the **depth** of a after p, defined as the largest n such that all $p.a^i$, for $0 \leq i \leq n$ are different objects. (For empty p, we talk of just "the depth of a" and write it $\downarrow a$.) This definition covers two cases; calling s the sequence of objects obtained by starting at p and following a links:

- If s is acyclic ($p.\boxtimes a$ holds), it must reach a void a link: otherwise it would have to be infinite, but our object structures are finite. Then $p.a^n$ is the first object O in the sequence whose a field is void.

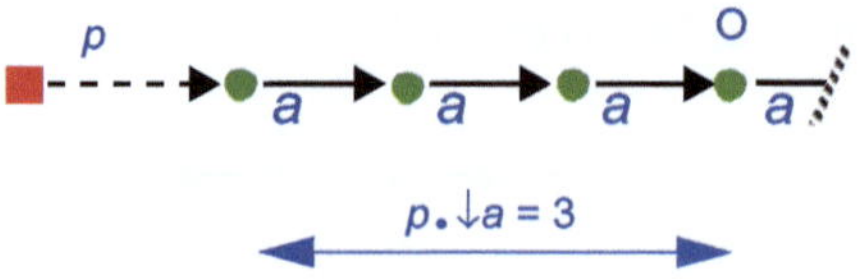

- If s is cyclic, then $p.a^n$ is the first object O in s whose a link leads to O itself or a previous element of s ($p.a^i$ for some i in $0..n$).

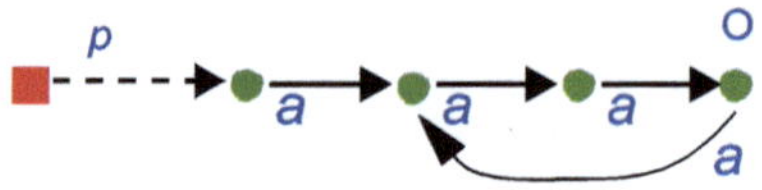

If we know that an attribute is acyclic, the first case applies and we can think of $p.\downarrow a$ as the "distance to **Void** through a". As a consequence, $x.\downarrow a$ can serve as the variant for a loop of exit condition $x = \textbf{Void}$, whose body executes $x := x.a$, as in Sect. 2.8 of the example proof.

6.4 Integrals

A path denotes a single object. We also need a notation for the *sequence* of objects encountered by repeatedly following the links corresponding to a certain attribute. The integral notation serves that purpose. If p is a path, the notation $p.\int a$ represents the finite sequence of objects $p.a^i$, for all i in $0..n$ where n is $p.\downarrow a$. In other words, it is the sequence of objects that starts with p and continues by following a links, up to the first object in which the a link either is void or leads to an object already in the sequence.

For empty p, we write just $\int a$ ("simple integral") denoting a sequence that starts with the current object and continues until the a link would give **Void** or a repetition.

In both cases, the sequence has the following properties:

- It is never empty, since $\int a$ always contains the current object, and $p.\int a$ contains the object associated with p (which always exists as discussed in 6.3).
- It is acyclic by construction.
- It contains objects all of the same type, or of types all conforming to a common ancestor type: the type of the object attached to the a field in the current object. (This property follows from the assumptions: a typed O-O language, and attribute names that have been disambiguated so that each denotes an attribute of just one class.) In the example, a denotes the same attribute for all objects in the sequence $\int a$ or $p.\int a$.

The notation is inspired by the integrals of classical analysis: as the integral $\int f$ in analysis accumulates the value of the function f, so our sequence $\int a$ accumulates the values of the attribute a. Our integrals can also be compared to regular expressions, but a regular expression denotes a set of sequences, whereas an integral denotes a single sequence.

It would also be possible to define expressions of the form $p.\int a.q$, or even to include several $\int$ terms, but we do not need such extensions in the present discussion.

Other properties of integrals are:

$\int a$	$=$	$\langle \textbf{Current} \rangle + a.\int a$	SIE (25)
$p.\int a$	$=$	$p + p.a.\int a$	NIE (26)

("Simple Integral Equation" and "Non-simple Integral Equation".) They follow directly from the definitions. Note that the second operand of the "+" is an empty sequence if the a link from (respectively) the current object or p is void.

A general theorem allows us to deduce properties of integrals from properties of paths:

Integral theorem

Let p be a path and a an attribute; let f a predicate on objects, which can be generalized to a predicate on sequences of objects (which holds if f holds of every element of the sequence). Then we may deduce $f(\int a)$ (resp. $f(p.\int a)$) from any of the following properties:

1. $f(a^n)$ (resp. $f(p.a^n)$) for any $n \geq 0$ such that a^n (resp. $p.a^n$) is acyclic.
2. $f(q)$ (resp. $f(p.q)$) for any path q such that q (resp. $p.q$) is acyclic.
3. Either of the previous two without the acyclicity restriction.

To use the theorem, it suffices to show that f holds in the most specific case represented by the first property; in some cases, however, it may be just as simple to establish f in the more general cases represented by the second property or even the third.

We may generalize the "may not be aliased" operator "$\not\equiv$" to integrals as follows: $\int a \not\equiv p$, for a path p, means that $a^i \not\equiv p$ for all i, and similarly for non-simple integrals. To derive such properties, we may as before apply the alias calculus, an automated process.

6.5 Compositional Semantics of Paths and Integrals: Assignment

It remains to define the effect of instructions on paths and integrals, generalizing the rules defining their effect on simple variables.

There is no simple rule governing the effect of an arbitrary instruction i on a path $p.q$ in the general case. In particular, $i\,;(p.q)$ is not necessarily the same as $(i\,;p).q$ as illustrated by the following example where i reattaches the b link of O1 from O2 to O3:

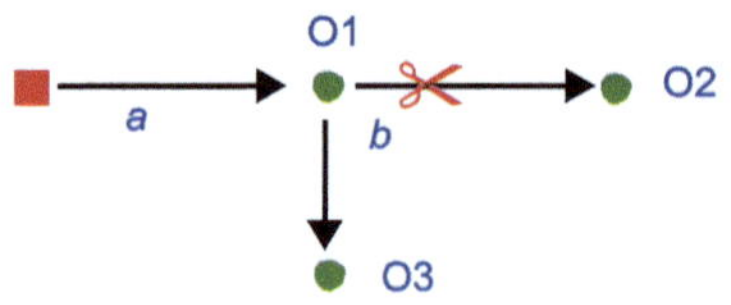

No associativity for the effect of instructions on paths

i ; $(a.b)$, is O3, but $(i$; $a)$ is still O1 so $(i$; $a).b$ is O2.

We can, however, generalize the assignment rule for single variables (AX (5) and AY (6)) to paths not involving cycles. The generalized assignment rule is as follows (as usual, y is assumed to denote an attribute other than x):

$(x := e)\ ;\ x.p$	$=$	$e.p$	– If $e.p$ is acyclic	PAX (27)
$(x := e)\ ;\ y.p$	$=$	$y.p$	– If $y.p$ is acyclic	PAY (28)
			– See less restrictive conditions below	

The basic assignment rules AX and AY (applicable to variables of any type, not just references) are special cases of PAX and PAY for an empty path p.

The reason we need an acyclicity restriction is that even though the assignment updates only one field of a single object (the x field of the current object), the p part of the path $e.p$ or $y.p$ could also be affected if it cycles back to that object. The following example shows how a cycle can invalidate PAX. We consider $(x := e)$; $x.z.x$ (so that p is $z.x$) under the following circumstances:

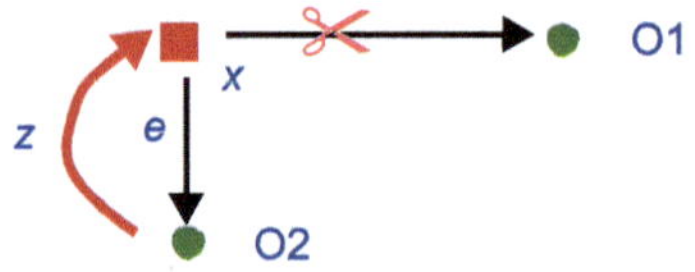

No associativity for the effect of instructions on paths

As illustrated, x denotes O1 before the assignment and O2 afterwards. The example assumes that z in O2 points back to the current object. So $(x := e)$; $x.z.x$ denotes O2. The value of $e.z.x$, however, is a reference to O1. Here PAX does not hold.

The rules PAX and PAY as stated above require the paths to be acyclic. This condition is stronger than needed since it precludes all cycles, including any that are harmless for the given instruction. A weaker condition suffices: that x (resp. y) be *cycle-free for e before p*. This means that no prefix of p is of the form $q.x$ where $e.q$ (resp. $y.q$) may be aliased to **Current**. Acyclic paths are a special case of this condition. Most cases encountered in practice involve paths that are acyclic by construction.

To ascertain acyclicity or cycle-freeness, one may apply the alias calculus.

PAX and PAY have counterparts for integrals:

$(x := e)\ ;\ x.p.\int a$	$=$	$e.p.\int a$	– If x is cycle-free – for e before p	IAX (29)
$(x := e)\ ;\ y.p.\int a$	$=$	$y.p.\int a$	– If y is cycle-free – for e before p	IAY (30)

These properties assume that x is not the attribute a. They follow from extending PAX and PAY through the integral theorem. Having x (resp. y) cycle-free for e before p—for example, acyclic—suffices, since the subsequent elements in the sequence, of the form $e.p.\int a$ (resp. $y.p.\int a$) result from following a links and cannot be modified by an assignment to an x field of an object.

For the case in which x and a are the same attribute, the following rules apply:

$(x := e)\ ;\ \int x$	$=$	$\langle \textbf{Current} \rangle + e.\int x$	– If $e.\int x \not\equiv \textbf{Current}$	IA (31)
$(x := e)\ ;\ x.\int x$	$=$	$e.\int x$	– If $e.\int x \not\equiv x$	IAP (32)

(Reminder: $p.\int a \not\equiv q$ means that $p.a^i$ cannot be aliased to q for any i.) These rules are theorems which follow from PAX; in particular the condition of IA, $e.\int x \not\equiv \textbf{Current}$, is a direct consequence of the condition in PAX: since $\int x$ is by construction acyclic, the only harmful cycles in $e.\int x$ could arise from $e.x^i$ being aliased to **Current**, and similarly for IAP.

The following counter-example shows that these conditions are indeed necessary:

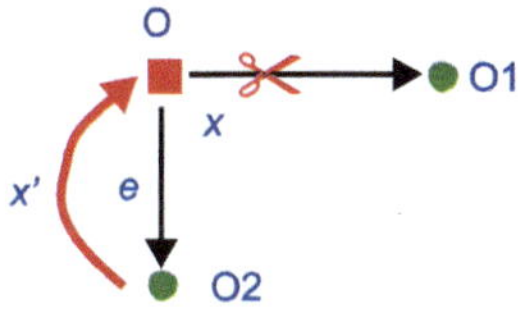

Cycles cause assignment surprises

Initially x (the x field of the current object, OS) is attached to O1, e to O2 and the x link of O2 back to O. After the assignment $x := e$, the value of $\int x$ will be the sequence $\langle$O, O2$\rangle$, stopping there because the next x link would cause a cycle. But $\langle \textbf{Current} \rangle + e.\int x$ in the initial state was $\langle$O, O2, O, O1$\rangle$. IA does not hold here; indeed its condition is not satisfied since $e.\int x$ was aliased to **Current**.

The six rules just seen enable us to reason about the effect of assignments on paths (for the first two of these rules, PAX and PAY) and integrals. It remains to see the rules defining the effect of calls.

6.6 Compositional Semantics of Paths and Integrals: Setter Calls

The final four rules govern the effect of qualified setter calls **call** x.*set_a*(c) on paths and integrals. Their application requires some conditions, whose definitions follow;

the definitions strive for generality, but any "simple setter" such as *set_right* used in the list reversal example, which just sets an attribute, trivially satisfies them.

The first two of these rules state the effect of a setter call on a path or sequence starting with the call's target:

$$(\mathbf{call}\, x.\mathit{set\_a}(c))\;;\;(\mathbf{old}\, x).p \quad = \langle x\rangle + c.p \qquad \text{PCX (33)}$$

– If *set_a* is a setter for a

– and does not indirectly affect a

$$(\mathbf{call}\, x.\mathit{set\_a}(c)\;;\;(\mathbf{old}\, x).\textstyle\int a \quad = \langle x\rangle + c.\textstyle\int a \qquad \text{ICX (34)}$$

– Same condition as previous rule

We may apply these rules to x rather than **old** x if *set_a* is nonprodigal (NP (19)).

The last two rules are **frame conditions** indicating that there is no effect on paths starting with an attribute other than the target:

$$(\mathbf{call}\, x.\mathit{set\_a}(c))\;;\;y.p \quad = y.p \qquad \text{PCY (35)}$$

– If *set_a* is a setter for a

– and does not indirectly affect a

$$(\mathbf{call}\, x.\mathit{set\_a}(c))\;;\;(y.\textstyle\int a) \quad = y.\textstyle\int a \qquad \text{ICY (36)}$$

– Same condition as previous rule

As before, the "P" versions are for paths and the "I" versions for integrals. The conditions are defined as follows, for a routine r and an attribute a:

- Reminder from 3.5: r is a *setter* for a if it satisfies the postcondition $a = f$, where f is one of the routine's arguments.
- The routine is *a simple setter* for a if its implementation entirely consists of assignments $f := a$, where f is a formal argument of r, and possibly of other such assignments of a formal argument to an attribute. The routine *set_right* of list reversal is an example. A simple setter for a is a setter for a.
- r directly affects a if it may change the value of a. A setter for a affects a.
- r *indirectly affects* a if it may change the value of $p.a$ for some non-empty path p, or includes a qualified call to a routine that (recursively) affects a.

A simple setter for a directly affects a, and affects no attribute (a or another) indirectly.

In the list reversal example, the conditions of the above rules are satisfied since *set_right* is a simple setter for *right*. In addition, a simple setter is nonprodigal, so we can drop the **old** in PCX and ICX. For more general cases, these conditions should be established from the setter's specification:

- The postcondition should express that the routine is a setter.
- It should also limit the scope of changes by expressing that the routine does not indirectly affect the relevant attributes, and possibly that it is nonprodigal; it is preferable, however, to avoid having to state such frame properties explicitly, and rely instead on simple language conventions [17] which imply them.

7 Comparison with Previous Work

The proper handling of references for a verification environment has occupied researchers for a long time. An early paper by Morris [19] defined important steps towards making the problem tractable. Further impetus to research on the topic was spurred by a paper by Hoare and He at ECOOP 99 [9], which took an object-oriented approach. None of the techniques proposed until recently, however, was anywhere close to allowing practical proofs of programs manipulating realistic object structures.

Separation logic [24] has enjoyed considerable attention and achieved verification successes. The basic idea is to allow modular reasoning about the heap thanks to the addition to Hoare logic of the $*$ operator, where $P * Q$ means that P and Q separately hold on disjoint parts of the heap. Bornat [1] has published a proof of list reversal using separation logic using C-like programs that manipulate heap addresses directly, quite far from the style of modern object-oriented programming. In recent years, there have been applications of separation logic to object-oriented languages, notably [21, 22] and [31], and the development of a proof system based on separation logic, jStar [4]. The main problem with separation logic is the extensive amount of additional annotation that it requires, expressing properties of the heap that are below the level of abstraction at which object-oriented programmers normally work. The corresponding issues are handled in the Calculus of Object Programs through the alias calculus, whose application is automatic. Because of the over-approximation that follows from ignoring conditional and loop conditions in the alias calculus, the results may not be strong enough to allow the desired proofs, in which case the proof engineer will have to add **cut** instructions (Sect. 5 and reference [15]); these instructions are the counterpart, in the Calculus of Object Programs, to the added annotations of separation logic. Their advantage, however, is that (as consistently suggested by experience so far) there will be far fewer of them, and they will only involve specific disjointness properties needed for a particular proof, rather than a complete specification of the heap's state. For example, establishing the alias properties of the proof of linked list reversal in this article required no **cut** instruction whatsoever. This is a good omen for the ease of applying the approach to other applications.

Another property that sets apart the present work from separation logic is its use of properties of object structures, expressed by paths and, through the integral operator, sequences. In separation logic the basic properties of references apply to a single pair of objects, in the form $x \mapsto y$ expressing that the reference in x points to y. One of the assumptions behind the present work is that proofs, and hence specifications, should rely on concepts at a level of abstraction corresponding to how programmers normally think about their programs; the high-level specification techniques that we have seen above pursue this goal, part of a general scheme of *model-based specification* [23, 28]. Recent work has started to apply separation logic in connection with such specifications. It might be possible to apply Separation logic and the present Calculus of Object Programs; the Calculus might for example benefit from the inclusion of some separation logic assertions when it encounters delicate cases. Conversely, the alias calculus may be able to infer or at least suggest separation logic assertions, relieving programmers from having to invent them from scratch.

Another approach that has provided significant advances in the search for techniques to prove object-oriented programs is *dynamic frames* [10] (see also [28] which applies the ideas to an object-oriented language). The theory of dynamic frames addresses the problem of specifying and verifying, in a modular way and in the presence of references, the properties that an operation will *not* modify. While the method is elegant and theoretically attractive, it again requires a significant annotation effort on the programmer's part, to specify frame properties. While it is legitimate, for software reliability, to require programmers to write down the functional specification of the program, it is harder to justify forcing them to state frame properties, since such properties are accessory to the program's real goals and many of them can in principle, if the program is decently written, be inferred automatically from the program text. In the Calculus of Object Programs, the alias calculus is responsible for performing this automatic inference, avoiding the extra specification effort required by dynamic frames. As was noted for separation logic, manual annotations, in the form of **cut** instructions, will only be required if the proof hits a snag; there should be few such cases.

As in the case of separation logic, there may be room for combining dynamic frames with the Calculus of Object Programs, for example by using the alias calculus to infer dynamic frame specifications automatically.

Unlike the previous approaches cited—but like the Calculus of Object Programs —*shape analysis* does not require an extensive annotation effort and is instead intended to be automatic. Its roots go back to a long history of work on compiler optimization, but more recent references [12, 25, 26] have developed it in new directions for the benefit of program verification. (The first two references cited use as an example the list reversal algorithm in a form very close to the version of the present article.) Such recent work uses abstract interpretation [3] to construct a Static Shape Graph (SSG) representing an idealized version of the concrete heap. It can then perform analyses of the SSG and relate them back to the actual store; an example, pursuing the same goal as the alias calculus, is a "may-alias" analysis, but the approach can also be applied to many other properties, including proofs, for which an experimental tool, TVLA [27], has been developed. The tool has been applied to a successful automatic proof of a difficult pointer algorithm, Deutsch-Schorre-Waite binary tree traversal [12]. A practical obstacle to using the method, however, is combinatorial explosion of the size of SSGs, resulting in a 9-hour computation time for the example in [12]. The Calculus of Object Programs does not perform any abstraction step but relies on high-level primitives such as the integral operator to capture relevant properties of object structures and reason directly on them in the standard framework of Hoare semantics. It could benefit from the insights of shape analysis; in particular, [26] uses a number of predicates describing high-level properties of object structures: reachability, reachability-from-x, sharing, cyclicity, reverse cyclicity. Integrating some of them into the calculus of object structures, in addition to paths and integrals, might increase the expressiveness of the calculus and facilitate proofs.

8 Conclusion

The work presented here suffers from several limitations:

- While the alias calculus has been implemented, the rest of the approach has not. It has been designed for integration into an automated proof environment, which should progress quickly.
- The techniques do not yet address inheritance. The main step in adding inheritance is to handle calls to routines that may have several redeclarations in descendant classes. The rules of the Calculus have been defined in reference to specifications of routines—more precisely, their postconditions—rather than their implementation; since these specifications are binding on routine redeclarations through the principles of Design by Contract [5, 13], which limit changes to precondition weakening and postcondition strengthening, their application in the presence of inheritance appears to be a natural extension.
- While the rules should be applicable in a modular way, no particular attention has been devoted to this point as yet.
- The list reversal example is the most significant covered so far. Many more should be tried, involving a variety of data structures.
- The Calculus of Object Structures may need some generalization, for example with a disjunction operator to allow path sets of the form *root*. $\int$(*left* | *right*) in a tree example. It has so far been kept as simple as possible.
- On the theoretical side, a proof of soundness is needed to justify the rules of this article.
- All these problems will have to be addressed. I believe, however, that in its present state the Calculus of Object Programs holds the promise of a comprehensive approach to proving full functional correctness of object-oriented programs involving possibly complex run-time object structures. The approach should live up to the claims made on its behalf through the preceding discussion:
- It closely fits the way programmers using modern object-oriented programming languages devise their programs and reason about them.
- The annotations it requires—as any approach addressing functional correctness must—are minimal (alias properties, in particular, are for the most part computed automatically); they express abstract properties of O-O structures, meaningful to the programmer, not low-level descriptions of the make-up of the heap. In fact the

notions of heap and stack do not appear, as they are inappropriate at the level of reasoning suitable for modern programming.
- The notations for expressing correctness properties are a small extension to usual Design by Contract mechanisms and remain amenable to run-time evaluation; the approach thereby retains support for both of the dual forms of verification: static (proofs) and dynamic (tests).

The continuing development of the Calculus will endeavor to make these benefits directly available to programmers building and verifying object-oriented programs.

Acknowledgements The software verification work of the Chair of Software Engineering at ETH Zurich has been supported by a generous grant from the Hasler Foundation as part of the MANCOM program, by several grants from the Swiss National Science Foundation (FNS/SNF), and by two internal research grants (TH-Gesuch, now ETHIIRA) from ETH Zurich. While not directly performed in response to any of these grants, the work reported here would not have been possible without them.

Part of the work was carried out in the Software Engineering Laboratory of ITMO State University in Saint Petersburg, which also provides an excellent environment.

Appendix: Using Negative Variables in Other Semantics

Here is the background for the rules involving negative variables. For the Calculus of Object Programs we only need the rule of compositional logic QC (21), allowing us to prove properties of programs involving qualified routine calls $\textbf{call}\, x.r(l)$, the central mechanism of object-oriented computation. That rule, however, is a consequence of a more fundamental property, giving the denotational definition of qualified calls:

$$\textbf{call}\, x.r(l) \qquad = x \bullet (\textbf{call}\, r(x'.l)) \qquad \text{DC (37)}$$

The two sides of the equality are functions in $Object \rightarrow State \rightarrow State$. The rule states that the effect of calling $x.r(l)$ is obtained by calling r on arguments transposed to the context of the supplier, as expressed by prefixing them by x', then interpreting the result transposed back to the context of the client, as expressed by prefixing it by x. In this result, no occurrences of x' will remain as they go away through the rules on negated variables (NEG1 (15) to NP (19)).

Some technical notes on this rule:

- The value of $\textbf{call}\, r(x'.l)$ is given by the formula for unqualified calls, which states that $\textbf{call}\, r(l))(\sigma)$ is $\underline{r}(\sigma[r^\bullet : l])$. This formula is the basis for the corresponding compositional logic rule UC (11).
- The rule uses "$\bullet$" to distribute "$.$" over a function, viewed as a list of pairs.
- For a generally applicable form of DC and its unqualified counterpart it is necessary to add to the right side a term that limits the scope of the resulting function to the domain of the original state, getting rid of any temporary associations (affecting for example local variables) that only make sense in the context of the called routine. This restriction is not important for the Calculus of Object Programs.

- DC is an equation rather than a definition, since in the presence of recursion the right-side expression could expand to an expression that includes an occurrence of the left-side expression. Such fixpoint equations are routine in denotational semantics and the theory handles them properly.
- The rule does not directly use substitution, although it relies on the semantics of the unqualified call **call** $r\,(x'.l)$ which can be defined as $\underline{r}[r^\bullet : l]$ (where, following notations introduced earlier, $\underline{r}$ is the semantics of the loop body, $r^\bullet$ denotes the formal arguments, and $e[x : y]$ denotes substitution of y for x in e).

From this denotational rule we can deduce the axiomatic semantic rule, the object-oriented variant of Hoare's procedure rule [8]:

$$\frac{\{P\}\mathbf{call}\, r\,(x'.l)\{Q\}}{\{x\,.\,P\}\mathbf{call}\, x.r\,(l)\{x\,.\,Q\}} \qquad \text{AC (38)}$$

where $x\,.\,e$, for a non-reference expression e (here e is P or Q, an assertion, treated as a boolean expression), applies "." distributively, for example $x\,.\,(a = b)$ means $x.a = x.b$. In the application of this rule, P and Q may contain occurrences of x'; for example the rule enables us to deduce $\{\mathbf{True}\}\mathbf{call}\, x.set\_a(c)\{x.a = c\}$ from $\{\mathbf{True}\}\mathbf{call}\, set\_a(c)\{a = x'.c\}$.

To establish this last property, and more generally the antecedent of any application of AC, we use the ordinary Hoare procedure rule for unqualified calls **call** $r\,(l)$. Expanding this rule (ignoring recursion) in AC gives us a directly applicable version of AC:

$$\frac{\{P\}\underline{r}(r^\bullet : x'\,.\,l)\{Q\}}{\{x\,.\,P\}\mathbf{call}\, x.r\,(l)\{x\,.\,Q\}} \qquad \text{AC}'\text{ (39)}$$

(where the first "." denotes "." distributed over the list l of actual arguments). Since the denotational rule DC (37) describes the nature of object-oriented calls at the most fundamental level, we may use it to express properties of such calls in any semantic framework. More generally, let Π be a property of program elements, such that the dot operator "." distributes over Π. Then we may use the general rule

$$\Pi(\mathbf{call}\, x.r\,(l)) \qquad = x\,.\,\Pi(\mathbf{call}\, r\,(x'.l)) \qquad \text{GC (40)}$$

AC, the axiomatic rule, is just one instance of GC. Another instance appears in the alias calculus article [15], which for the various kinds of instructions i and an arbitrary relation a (a set of pairs of expressions that might become aliased to each other) defines $a \gg i$, the alias relation resulting from executing i in a state where the alias relation was a. The rule for qualified calls (with "." here denoting "." distributed over a set of pairs) is

$$a \gg \mathbf{call}\, x.r\,(l) \qquad = \qquad x\,.\,((x'\,.\,a) \gg \mathbf{call}\, r\,(x'.l))$$

A final example of applying GC is the weakest precondition rule for qualified calls (using i **wp** Q to denote the weakest precondition guaranteeing that execution of the instruction i will ensure the postcondition Q):

$$(\mathbf{call}\, x.r(l))\,\mathbf{wp}\, x.Q \quad = x \centerdot ((\mathbf{call}\, r(x'.l))\,\mathbf{wp}\, Q) \qquad \text{WC (41)}$$

The simplicity of these rules appears to confirm the usefulness of negative variables as a tool for reasoning about object-oriented computations.

References

1. Bornat, R.: Proving pointer programs in Hoare logic. In: Backhouse, R., Oliviera, J. (eds.) MPC '00 (Mathematics of Program Construction). Lecture Notes in Computer Science, vol. 1837, pp. 102–126. Springer, Berlin (2000)
2. Clarke, D., Potter, J., Noble, J.: Ownership types for flexible alias protection. In: OOPSLA 1998. ACM SIGPLAN Notices, vol. 33, no. 10, pp. 48–64 (1998)
3. Cousot, P., Cousot, R.: Abstract interpretation: A unified lattice model for static analysis of programs by construction of approximations of fixed points. In: POPL 77 (ACM Symposium on Principles of Programming Languages), pp. 232–245 (1997)
4. Distefano, D., Parkinson, M.: jStar: Towards practical verication for Java. In: OOPSLA '08, Proceedings of the 23rd ACM SIGPLAN Conference on Object-Oriented Programming Systems, Languages and Applications, pp. 213–226 (2008)
5. ECMA International: Standard ECMA-367: Eiffel: Analysis, Design and Programming Language, 2nd edn. (June 2006), ed. B. Meyer; also International Standards Organization standard ISO/IEC 25436:2006. Text available online at www.ecma-international.org/publications/standards/Ecma-367.htm
6. Eiffel Software: EiffelStudio documentation (in particular on contract monitoring), at docs.eiffel.com
7. Hoare, C.A.R.: An axiomatic basis for computer programming. In: Communications of the ACM, vol. 12, no. 10, pp. 576–580 (1969)
8. Hoare, C.A.R.: Procedures and parameters: An axiomatic approach. In: Engeler, E. (ed.) Symposium on Semantics of Algorithmic Languages. Springer Lecture Notes in Mathematics, vol. 188, pp. 102–116 (1971)
9. Hoare, C.A.R., He, J.: A trace model for pointers and objects. In: Guerraoui, R. (ed.) ECOOP 1999 (13th European Conference on Object-Oriented Programming). Springer Lecture Notes in Computer Science, vol. 1628, pp. 1–17 (1999)
10. Kassios, I.: Dynamic frames: support for framing, dependencies and sharing without restrictions. In: Misra, J., Nipkow, T., Sekerinski, E. (eds.) Formal Methods 2006. Lecture Notes in Computer Science, vol. 4085, pp. 268–283. Springer, Berlin (2006)
11. Leavens, G.T., Baker, A.L., Ruby, C.: Preliminary design of JML: A behavioral interface specification language for Java. In: ACM SIGSOFT Software Engineering Notes, vol. 31, pp. 1–38 (2006), no. 3. Additional JML documentation at www.eecs.ucf.edu/~leavens/JML/
12. Loginov, A., Reps, T., Sagiv, M.: Automated verification of the Deutsch-Schorr-Waite tree-traversal algorithm. In: Static Analysis Symposium, pp. 261–269 (2006)
13. Meyer, B.: Object-Oriented Software Construction, 2nd edn. Prentice Hall, New York (1998)
14. Meyer, B.: Touch of Class: Learning to Program Well, Using Objects and Contracts. Springer, Berlin (2009)
15. Meyer, B.: Towards a theory and calculus of aliasing. Int. J. Softw. Inform. (July 2011, to appear). Slightly updated version available at se.ethz.ch/~meyer/publications/aliasing/alias-revised.pdf

16. Meyer, B.: Publish no loop without its invariant. Blog entry at bertrandmeyer.com/2011/05/12/publish-no-loop-without-its-invariant/, 12 May 2011
17. Meyer, B.: If I'm not pure, at least my functions are. Blog entry at bertrandmeyer.com/2011/07/04/if-im-not-pure-at-least-my-functions-are/, 4 July 2011 (intended as a first step to an actual article on language conventions to specify purity and, more generally, frame properties)
18. Meyer, B., Kogtenkov, A., Stapf, E.: Avoid a void: The eradication of null dereferencing. In: Jones, C.B., Roscoe, A.W., Wood, K.R. (eds.) Reflections on the Work of C.A.R. Hoare, pp. 189–211. Springer, Berlin (2010)
19. Morris, J.M.: A general axiom of assignment; Assignment and linked data structure; A proof of the Schorr-Waite algorithm (three articles). In: Broy, M., Schmidt, G. (eds.) Theoretical Foundations of Programming Methodology, Proceedings of the 1981 Marktoberdorf Summer School, pp. 25–61. Reidel, Dordrecht (1982)
20. Müller, P.: Modular Specification and Verification of Object-Oriented Programs. Springer, Berlin (2002)
21. Parkinson, M., Bierman, G.: Separation logic and abstraction. In: POPL '05 (ACM Symposium on Principles of Programming Languages), January, pp. 247–258 (2005)
22. Parkinson, M., Bierman, G.: Separation logic, abstraction and inheritance. In: POPL '08 (ACM Symposium on Principles of Programming Languages), January, pp. 75–86 (2008)
23. Polikarpova, N., Furia, C., Meyer, B.: Specifying reusable components. In: Verified Software: Theories, Tools, Experiments (VSTTE '10), Edinburgh, UK, 16–19 August 2010. Lecture Notes in Computer Science. Springer, Berlin (2010)
24. Reynolds, J.C.: Separation logic: A logic for shared mutable data structures. In: Logic in Computer Science, 17th Annual IEEE Symposium, pp. 55–74 (2002)
25. Sagiv, M., Reps, T., Wilhelm, R.: Solving shape-analysis problems in languages with destructive updating. ACM Trans. Program. Lang. Syst. **20**(1), 1–50 (1998)
26. Sagiv, M., Reps, T., Wilhelm, R.: Parametric shape analysis via 3-valued logic. ACM Trans. Program. Lang. Syst. **24**(3), 217–298 (2002)
27. Sagiv, M., et al.: TVLA home page, at www.math.tau.ac.il/~tvla/
28. Schoeller, B.: Making classes provable through contracts, models and frames. PhD thesis, ETH, Zurich (2007). se.inf.ethz.ch/old/people/schoeller/pdfs/schoeller-diss.pdf
29. Schoeller, B., Widmer, T., Meyer, B.: Making specifications complete through models. In: Reussner, R., Stafford, J., Szyperski, C. (eds.) Architecting Systems with Trustworthy Components. Lecture Notes in Computer Science. Springer, Berlin (2006)
30. Tschannen, J., Furia, C.A., Nordio, M., Meyer, B.: Verifying Eiffel programs with Boogie. In: Boogie 2011, First International Workshop on Intermediate Verification Languages, Wroclaw, August 2011 (to appear). See documentation about the EVE project at eve.origo.ethz.ch
31. van Staden, S., Calcagno, C., Meyer, B.: Verifying executable object-oriented specifications with separation logic. In: ECOOP 2010, 24th European Conference on Object-Oriented Programming, Maribor (Slovenia), 21–25 June 2010. Lecture Notes in Computer Science. Springer, Berlin (2010)

[illegible]

Formal Specification as High-Level Programming: The ASSL Approach

Emil Vassev and Mike Hinchey

Abstract Formal methods aim to build correct software by eliminating both requirements and design flaws. Still, specification languages have a somewhat bad reputation in the software engineering community for being too heavy and difficult to use. This is mainly due to the use of complex mathematical notations often requiring experts in the field. We rely on our experience to show that writing formal specifications can be easier if a specification language is used as a high-level programming language, where the distinction between a specification language and a programming language is somewhat blurred. The Autonomic System Specification Language (ASSL) is a declarative specification language for autonomic systems with well-defined semantics. It implements modern concepts and constructs such as inheritance, modularity, type system, and parameterization. Specifications written in ASSL present a view of the system under consideration, where specification and design are intertwined.

1 Introduction

Nowadays, we talk about "building" or "constructing" software rather than writing computer programs. This is mainly due to the complexity involved in modern software in all possible forms: complexity of the problem to be solved, complexity of the software to be built, and last, but not least, complexity of the process used to develop software. Modern software applications are intended to solve complex problems (e.g., controlling airplanes) and may be enormous in size. Such complex applications are built through the efforts of large teams of software engineers and programmers, following the rules of a well-defined software development process. The process of "building" a computer program goes through a few important phases (e.g., requirements, design, etc.) before getting to the real "writing" of the program

E. Vassev (✉) · M. Hinchey
Lero–the Irish Software Engineering Research Centre, University of Limerick, Limerick, Ireland
e-mail: emil.vassev@lero.ie

M. Hinchey
e-mail: mike.hinchey@lero.ie

K.K. Breitman, R.N. Horspool (eds.), *Patterns, Programming and Everything*,
DOI 10.1007/978-1-4471-2350-7_9,

in question. Different tools and techniques might be used in each phase to support the process of building software. Moreover, just like the construction of a building, modern software is often constructed by using reusable components. Programming languages still have their important role in software development, however today those languages are "modern" languages, i.e., providing modern programming constructs and embedded in special development environments accompanied by supporting tools and libraries of reusable components. Apart from requirements and design, programming is not anymore just about writing software code that is to be interpreted by a computer. Instead, modern programming languages such as Java and C# might be considered as high-level programming languages, where we are provided with embedded mechanisms (e.g., garbage collection), strong abstraction from specifics of the computer, and natural language elements and human logic. High-level programming makes the overall process of building software simpler and easy to cope with. Note that the level of abstraction determines how high-level a programming language is. In that sense, formal specification languages, often used to describe requirements and model software systems before starting with the implementation, might also be considered as high-level programming languages. This is especially valid for formal specification languages accompanied by a code generator that uses a high-level specification of a software system to generate the real implementation, e.g., in C++. The problem is that often the use of a formal specification language introduces more complexity to the development process [1], e.g., software engineers need to change their abstract way of thinking to cope successfully with the new mathematical models.

We show how ASSL (Autonomic System Specification Language) [2, 3], a modern domain-specific and formal specification language, might be used as a high-level programming language where the difference between specification and programming is somewhat blurred. Dedicated to autonomic computing [4], ASSL is equipped with modern programming constructs such as *inheritance* and *parameterization*, thus helping developers to use the language as a high-level programming language. Moreover, a powerful toolset helps ASSL specifications be verified and implementation code be generated, which helps for a smooth transition from ASSL code to implementation.

The rest of this entry is organized as follows: In Sect. 2, we briefly outline the basics of formal methods and those of code generation. In Sect. 3, we present the ASSL framework. Section 4 is a show case demonstrating how ASSL might be used as a high-level programming language. Finally, Sect. 5 provides brief concluding remarks.

2 Formal Methods and Code Generation

One of the most important aspects of successful software development is software reliability. Practice has shown that traditional development methods cannot guarantee software reliability and prevent software failures. In that context, software developed using formal methods has been demonstrated to be more reliable. Generally speaking, formal methods are a means of providing a computer-system development approach where both a formal notation and mature tool support are provided. The approach heavily relies on mathematics to provide precise techniques for specification, development and verification of computer systems [1]. However, it is exactly those mathematical models that make formal specifications difficult to understand, especially by people who are not mathematically inclined. This is a major reason why formal methods are not well accepted in mainstream software development practices. Hence, in order to be used as a high-level programming language, a formal language must expose constructs and syntax similar to those of the modern programming languages, i.e., it must be close to the natural language. Modern formal languages like ASSL [2, 3] have modern programming constructs and simple and natural-language-like syntax, which significantly improves readability of formal specifications. Moreover, in order to be a successful high-level programming language, a formal method needs to be equipped with a code generator. The formal specification helps us build more robust and more maintainable software, but it is practically useless without the real implementation, and a code generator (or a high-level compiler) helps to avoid double programming.

Code generation is based on a formal (or semi-formal) specification of a system, which requires both a formal specification language and supporting tools. Note that as a high-level program, a formal specification presents a compact abstract model of the system in question, i.e., it is easy to be understood by software engineers. However, to generate a meaningful implementation, that model should also be expressive enough. Code generation allows for an easy way of implementing different versions of a system, by changing its formal specification and then generating the corresponding implementation. Along with the advantages coming with code generation, there are a few important tradeoffs that should be considered when we conduct high-level programming with formal methods:

- Any code generator is optimized for both the specification language and the targeted implementation language, which narrows the possibility of using all the possible constructs of the implementation language, which is presumably more powerful. Note that a powerful specification language, equipped with modern constructs such as inheritance, parameterization, etc., will definitely lead to a more powerful generated implementation.
- A code generator follows specific templates determined by the operational semantics of both the specification language and the implementation language. Thus, all the generated code is similar, i.e., it is like a program being written by the same programmer—the same style, coding standards, comments, etc. This is not necessarily bad, but possibly the imposed programming style is not always the best possible.

3 ASSL

The Autonomic System Specification Language (ASSL) [2, 3] is an initiative for self-management of complex systems which approaches the problem of formal

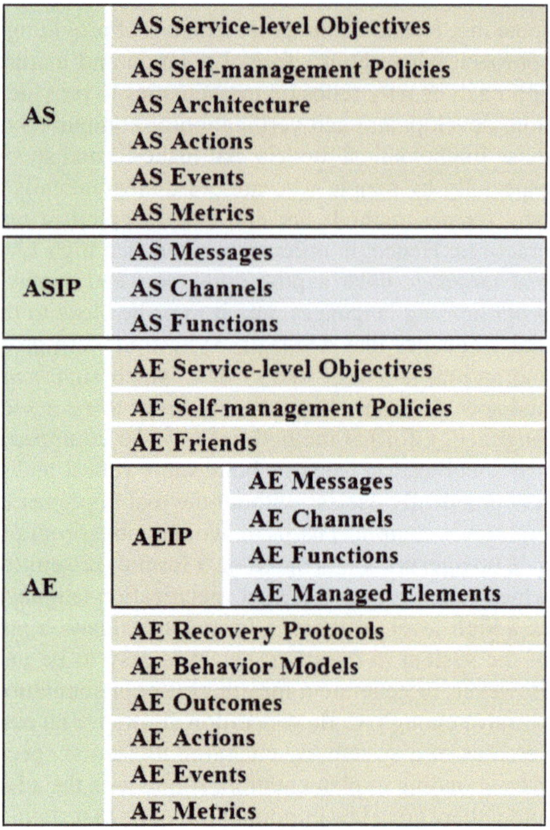

Fig. 1 ASSL multi-tier specification model

specification, validation, and code generation of autonomic systems (ASs) within a framework. Being dedicated to autonomic computing (AC) [4], ASSL helps AC researchers with problem formation, system design, system analysis and evaluation, and system implementation.

3.1 ASSL Programming Style and Specification Model

ASSL is a domain-specific specification language, i.e., it provides constructs and terms related to the AC domain. As such a language, it imposes a different specification style than the programming style of a general programming language such as Java. Thus, in ASSL we do have structures similar to Java classes and routines, but we also have unique domain-specific constructs. Moreover, the "programming style" of ASSL is different, but easy to cope with. The ASSL programming style is based on a specification model exposed over hierarchically organized formalization tiers (see Fig. 1) [2, 3]. This specification model provides both infrastructure elements and mechanisms needed by an AS. Each tier of the ASSL specification model is intended to describe different aspects of an AS, such as *service-level objectives*, *policies*, *interaction protocols*, *events*, *actions*, *autonomic elements*, etc. This allows us to specify an AS at different *levels of abstraction* (imposed by the ASSL tiers) where the AS in question is composed of special autonomic elements (AEs) interacting over interaction protocols (IPs).

As shown in Fig. 1, the ASSL specification model decomposes an AS in two directions: (1) into levels of functional abstraction; and (2) into functionally related sub-tiers. The first decomposition presents the system at three different tiers [2, 3]:

1. AS—*a general and global AS perspective*—defines general behavior rules, architecture topology, and global actions, events, and metrics applied in these rules;
2. ASIP—*an interaction protocol (IP) perspective*—defines a means of communication between AEs within an AS;
3. AE—*a unit-level perspective*—defines interacting sets of special computing elements (AEs) with their own autonomic behavior rules, actions, events, metrics, etc.

The second decomposition presents the major tiers as composed of functionally related sub-tiers, where new AS properties emerge at each sub-tier (see Fig. 1). The AS Tier specifies an AS in terms of *service-level objectives (AS SLOs)*, *self-management policies*, *architecture topology*, *actions*, *events*, and *metrics*. The AS SLOs are a high-level form of behavioral specification that helps developers establish system objectives, such as performance. The self-management policies are driven by events and trigger the execution of actions driving an AS in critical situations. The metrics constitute a set of parameters and observables controllable by an AS. With the ASIP Tier, the ASSL framework helps developers specify an *AS-level interaction protocol* as a public communication interface expressed with special *communication channels*, *communication functions*, and *communication messages*. At the AE Tier, the ASSL formal model exposes specification constructs for the specification of the *system's AEs*. Note that AEs are considered to be analogous to software agents able to manage their own behavior and their relationships with other AEs. An AE may also specify a private AE interaction protocol (AEIP) shared with special AE considered as "friends" (AE Friends tier).

3.1.1 ASSL Self-management Policies

It is important to mention that the ASSL tiers are intended to specify different aspects of an AS, but it is not necessary to employ all of them in order to develop an AS. Conceptually, it is sufficient to specify self-management policies only, because those provide self-management behavior at the level of AS (the AS tier) and at the level of AE (AE tier). These policies are specified within the AS/AE Self-management Policies sub-tier (ASSL construct: *AS[AE]SELF_MANAGEMENT*) with special ASSL constructs termed *fluents* and *mappings* [2, 3]. A fluent is a state where an AS enters with *fluent-activating events* and exits with *fluent-terminating*

```
ASSELF_MANAGEMENT {
 SELF_HEALING {
  FLUENT inLosingSpacecraft {
   INITIATED_BY {EVENTS.spaceCraftLost}
   TERMINATED_BY {EVENTS.earthNotified}}
  MAPPING { CONDITIONS {inLosingSpacecraft} DO_ACTIONS {ACTIONS.notifyEarth}}}
} // ASSELF_MANAGEMENT
```

Fig. 2 Self-healing policy

events. A mapping connects fluents with particular actions to be undertaken. Usually, an ASSL specification is programmed around one or more self-management policies, which makes that specification AS-driven. Self-management policies are driven by events and actions determined *deterministically*. The ASSL code shown in Fig. 2 presents a sample specification of a *self-healing policy*. As shown, fluents are expressed with *fluent-activating* and *fluent-terminating* events. In order to express mappings, conditions and actions are considered, where the former determine the latter in a deterministic manner. The example above also helps the reader grasp a bit of the ASSL syntax explained in the next subsection.

3.1.2 ASSL Events

ASSL aims at event-driven autonomic behavior. Hence, to specify self-management policies, we need to specify appropriate events. Here, we rely on the reach set of event types exposed by ASSL [2, 3]. To specify ASSL events, one may use logical expressions over SLOs, or may relate events with metrics (see Sect. 3.1.3), other events, actions, time, and messages. Moreover, ASSL allows for the specification of special conditions that must be met before an event is prompted.

3.1.3 ASSL Metrics

For an AS, one of the most important success factors is the ability to sense the environment and react to sensed events. Here, together with the rich set of events, ASSL imposes metrics that help to determine dynamic information about external and internal points of interest. Although four different types of metrics are allowed [2, 3], the most important type is the so-called *resource metrics*, which is intended to gather information about special *managed element*'s quantities.

3.1.4 Managed Elements

An AE typically controls *managed elements*. In an ASSL-developed AS, a managed element is specified with a set of special *interface functions* intended to provide control functionality over that managed element. Note that ASSL can specify and generate interfaces controlling a managed element (generated as a stub), but not the real implementation of these interfaces. This is just fine for prototyping, however when deploying an AS prototype the generated interfaces must be manually programmed to deal with the controlled system (or sub-system).

3.1.5 Interaction Protocols

ASSL interaction protocols provide a means of *communication interface* expressed with *messages* that can be exchanged among AEs via *communication channels* and *communication functions*. Thus, by specifying an ASSL interaction protocol we develop an embedded messaging system needed to connect the AEs of an AS. In a basic communication process ongoing in such a system, an AE relies on a communication function to receive a message over an incoming communication channel, changes its internal state and sends some new messages over an outgoing channel [2, 3].

3.2 ASSL Syntax

The following is a generic meta-grammar in Extended Backus-Naur Form (BNF) [5] presenting the syntax rules for specifying ASSL tiers.

```
GroupTier --> FINAL? ASSLGroupTierId { Tier+ }
Tier --> FINAL? ASSLTierId TierName? { Data* TierClause+ }
TierClause --> FINAL? ASSLClauseId ClauseName? { Data* }
Data --> TypeDecl* | VarDecl* | CllctnDecl* | Statement*
TypeDecl --> CustTypeIdentifier
VarDecl --> Type VarIdentifier
CllcntDecl --> Type CustCllctnIdentifier
Type --> CustType | PredefType
Statement --> Assign-Stmnt | Loop | If-Then-Else | Cllctn-Stmnt
Loop --> Foreach-Stmnt | DoWhile-Stmnt | WhileDo-Stmnt
```

Note that this meta-grammar is an abstraction of the ASSL grammar, which cannot be presented here due to the complex structure of the ASSL specification model (see Sect. 3.1), where each tier has its own syntax and semantic rules. The interested reader is advised to refer to [2] or [3] for the complete ASSL grammar expressed in BNF and for the semantics of the language.

As shown in the grammar above, an ASSL tier is syntactically specified with an ASSL tier identifier, an optional tier name and a content block bordered by curly braces "{ }". Moreover, we distinguish two syntactical types of tier: *single tiers* (*Tier*) and *group tiers* (*GroupTier*) where the latter comprise a set of single tiers. Each single tier has an *optional name* (*TierName*) and comprises a set of special *tier clauses* (*TierClause*) and *optional data* (*Data*). The latter is a set of *data declarations* and *statements*. Data declarations could be: (1) type declarations; (2) variable declarations; and (3) collection declarations. Statements could be: (1) loop statements; (2) assignment statements; (3) if-then-else statements; and (4) collection statements. Statements can comprise *Boolean* and *numeric expressions*. In addition, although not shown in the grammar above, note that identifiers participating in ASSL expressions are either simple, consisting of a *single identifier*, or *qualified*, consisting of a sequence of identifiers separated by "." tokens. From a programming language perspective, the ASSL *single tiers* can be regarded as C++ structures or classes. The ASSL *actions* (special single tiers) can be regarded as C++ functions, i.e., they can be called for execution, can accept parameters and return results.

3.3 ASSL Formalism

ASSL is a *declarative specification language* with well-defined semantics. It implements modern programming language concepts and constructs like *inheritance*, *modularity*, a *type system*, and highly *abstract expressiveness*. Specifications written in ASSL present a view of the system under consideration where specification and design are intertwined. Conceptually, ASSL is defined through formalization tiers (see Sect. 3.1), which together with the ASSL formalism determine the "programming style" of the language. ASSL can be classified as both *model-oriented* and *property-oriented* [6] specification language. The model-oriented style is typically associated with the use of *definitions*, whereas the property-oriented style is generally associated with the use of *axioms*. ASSL benefits from both styles by using a *property-oriented axiomatisation* as a top-level specification style and introducing a suitable number of specification layers with increasingly detailed *model-oriented descriptions*.

3.4 High-Level Programming Features of ASSL

In addition to the simple syntax, there are a few important features that make ASSL suitable for high-level programming.

3.4.1 Abstraction

In general, all computer programming languages can be considered as a "metaphor", because "they bridge the gap between something the computer can understand (binary) and something that humans can understand, and are capable of crafting programs with" [7]. In that sense, all programming languages (including ASSL) are an abstraction. However, ASSL goes even further, by imposing additional abstraction mechanisms, as part of the language. Just as Java and C# are high-level programming languages, in the sense that they are typed and structured, ASSL is a high-level language for modeling ASs in the sense that it is structured and domain-specific. The latter means that the language provides high-level structures to emphasize on the self-management properties of the system in question.

Abstraction has been well recognized as one of the best means for driving out complexity. Before going further in discussion, let us define the notion of abstraction. As stated by James Rumbaugh in [8], "Abstraction is the selective examination of certain aspects of a problem. The goal of abstraction is to isolate those aspects that are important for some purpose and suppress those aspects that are unimportant." Therefore, by emphasizing different elements, we can have many different abstractions of the same complex system. In fact, this is the main abstraction concept in ASSL. As designed, ASSL imposes different abstraction views of the system under consideration through isolation of the self-management properties into comprehensible sub-domains, those being the ASSL tiers and sub-tiers (see Fig. 1). Therefore, the ASSL concept of abstraction reduces complexity by emphasizing different important elements in different ASSL tiers and hiding the less important ones. Moreover, with its multi-tier specification model, ASSL provides an *abstraction hierarchy*. The ASSL abstraction hierarchy is derived from the single ASSL tiers, which form *hierarchically organized levels of abstraction* which highly positioned in the ASSL framework tiers (see Fig. 1) provide a higher level of abstraction.

Figure 3 depicts an abstraction hierarchy exposed by the ASSL framework. The abstraction views are presented as abstract classes, each comprising a set of more comprehensible sub-tiers. As shown, the *AS* tier forms the highest level of abstraction. It relies on the abstractions exposed by both the *ASIP* tier and the *AE* tier. In addition, the *AE* tier can be additionally abstracted by the *AEClass* tier through generalization. In general, all the abstractions (*AS*, *ASIP*, *AE*, and *AEClass*) rely on each other for specifying their sub-tiers. In addition, they can be reused among different ASSL specifications, i.e., an *ASIP* abstraction can be used in the specification of many ASs, thus reducing the complexity in programming with ASSL through reusability.

As a formal language, ASSL defines an implementation-independent presentation for computer systems. The ASSL specifications are free from any implementation specifics, i.e., we specify important aspects of a system and generate implementation.

3.4.2 Generalization and Aggregation

Generalization and aggregation are fundamentally important in ASSL, because they both reduce complexity in programming ASs. In ASSL, generalization refers to a set of similar AEs presented as a single *AEClass* abstraction. The AE classes are considered abstract AEs used to embody commonalities among the AEs in an AS through generalization. The ASSL code shown in Fig. 4 demonstrates the use of ASSL classes.

As shown in Fig. 3, the *AEClass* tier does not participate in the formation of the AS tier, but it generalizes the AE tier. AE classes define AE properties like SLO (service-level objectives), policies, behavior models, actions, etc., inherited by concrete AEs constituting the AS in question. Figure 3 also depicts the AS abstraction, as an aggregation of many constituent AEs and one constituent ASIP. Thus, the AS

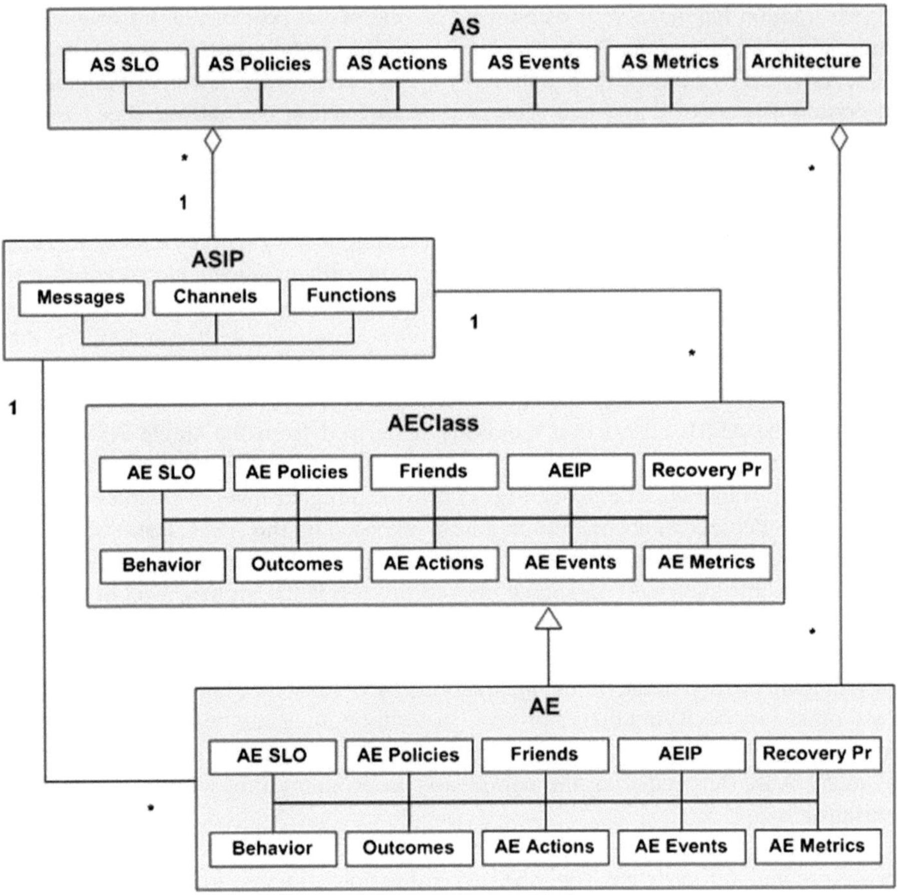

Fig. 3 ASSL abstraction hierarchy

```
AECLASSSES {
 AECLASS worker { .... }
}
AES {
 AE xWorker EXTENDS AECLASSSES.worker { }
 AE yWorker EXTENDS AECLASSSES.worker {
  AESLO { SLO lowRiskLevel { .... } }
  ACTIONS { ACTION normalizeRiskLevel { .... } }
 }
}
```

Fig. 4 AE classes

in question is treated as a unit in many operations, although physically it is made of several lesser objects.

3.4.3 Decomposition and Modularity

Modeling an AS with ASSL is to determine the AEs constituting that system and to determine the communication protocols (ASIP and AEIPs), which provide a means of communication among the AEs. Hence, modeling with ASSL can be seen as a decomposition of the AS in question into AEs and communication protocols. In ASSL, decomposition is an abstraction technique where we start with a high-level description of the system and create low-level implementations of the latter where features and functions fit together. Note that both high-level and low-level abstractions are defined explicitly by the ASSL framework:

- The high-level abstractions form high-level modules in terms of ASSL tiers—AS tier, ASIP tier, and AE tier.
- The low-level implementations are defined as comprehensible sub-domains (sub-tiers), forming low-level system modules.

This kind of modularity is based on explicitly-assigned functions to components, thus reducing the programming effort and complexity.

3.4.4 Granularity

Granularity is a sort of high-level organization technique for complex systems. As Martin states in [9], "the class, while a very convenient unit for organizing small applications, is too finely grained to be used as an organizational unit for large applications". Hence, something larger and more abstract than a class is needed to organize ASs as these are considered large and intrinsically very complex [4].

In ASSL, AEs are the highest form of granularity. Both AEs and AE Classes embody all the properties of a "mini" AS. Thus, an AE has its own SLO (service-level objectives), self-management policies, behavior models, actions, events, metrics, and even a private communication protocol (see Fig. 1). Considering implementation, the AEs are generated by the framework as Java packages, i.e., as logical groups of Java classes. This provides an abstraction at implementation level and allows us to reason about the high-level program and draw parallels between implementation and specification.

3.4.5 Separation of Concerns

ASSL helps to design and generate AC *self-management wrappers* in the form of ASs that embed the components of regular systems. The latter are considered as *managed elements* (managed resource), controlled by the AS in question. In general, a managed element is a separate software system performing services. ASSL emphasizes the self-managing functionality and the architecture of the self-management wrapper, but not the managed element functionality and architecture. Thus, it specifies only a special interface needed to control a managed element.

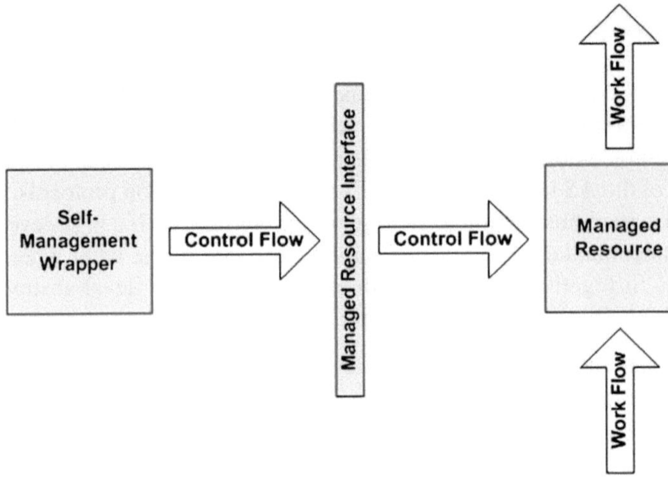

Fig. 5 Self-managing control process

```
MANAGED_ELEMENTS {
 MANAGED_ELEMENT STAGE_ME {
  INTERFACE_FUNCTION countFailedNodes {
   RETURNS { INTEGER }
  }
  ....
  INTERFACE_FUNCTION runNodeReplica { PARAMETERS { DMARFNode node }
   ONERR_TRIGGERS { EVENTS.nodeReplicaFailed }
  }
 }
}
```

Fig. 6 Managed element specification

Here, ASSL provides an *abstraction* of the managed elements via a special interface (see Fig. 5).

Figure 6 presents a partial specification of the managed resource interface for a managed element called *STAGE_ME*. Note that the *runNodeReplica* interface function triggers an erroneous event in case the managed element failed on this function's execution.

Here, as it is demonstrated by the example above, the *separation-of-concern* technique allows for modeling the self-management part of an AS without being concerned of the design and implementation of the system-service part (managed element). The latter could be built separately by implementing the *managed resource interface*, or an already existing system can be adapted to that interface and turned into a managed element for the self-management wrapper. By using interface abstraction, we also can take advantage of *polymorphism*. There can be many managed elements implementing differently the same interface, i.e., we can use the same interface to control many systems, thus reducing the development effort

Table 1 Code generation statistics

Lines of ASSL Code	Lines of Java Code	Efficiency Ratio
44	3737	85
201	5853	29
293	8159	28
1192	18709	17

and complexity. In addition, this technique also provides an abstraction of the self-management wrapper to the architects of the managed element. Here, both the self-management wrapper and the managed element use each other as a "black box", with no concerns about internal details. Least but not last, the clear distinction between the self-managing and non-self-managing parts of a system allows for much better perception and understanding of the system's features and consecutively handling the same.

3.5 Code Generation

Once a specification is complete, it can be validated with the ASSL built-in verification mechanisms [10] and a functional application skeleton can be generated automatically. The application skeletons generated with the ASSL framework are fully-operational multithreaded event-driven applications with embedded messaging. Once completed and consistent, an ASSL specification (high-level program) is translated into Java code that forms the skeleton of the AS under consideration. The advantage is that the generated code implicitly inherits the specification models and reduces the amount of code that must be implemented by the developers. ASSL provides for a *synthetic* (versus *analytic*) approach to code implementation. There are many possible ways to implement an ASSL specification. However, while most of these possible implementations are redundant or differ slightly in unimportant ways, the analytic approach can capture any one of them, thus risking the capture of one with higher complexity. On the other hand, the synthetic approach aims at reasonable and smaller, and thus less complex, implementations. Moreover, code generation ensures that the implementation meets its specification. This is due to the mathematical approach to code generation, where the underlying ASSL formal semantics determine an unambiguous interpretation of the ASSL specifications. Note that the ASSL code generator generates relatively simple and efficient implementations, thus reducing significantly the complexity associated with the development of ASs. Table 1 presents some code generation statistics [11].

We may consider three levels of complexity in ASSL specifications:

- *low complexity*—specifications with up to 200 lines of ASSL code;
- *moderate complexity*—specifications with 201–600 lines of ASSL code;
- *high complexity*—specifications involving over 600 lines of ASSL code.

The efficiency ratio (Java generated code versus ASSL specification code) shown in Table 1 demonstrates an impressive degree of complexity reduction, due mainly to the ASSL's multi-tier specification model and code generation mechanism.

4 Case Study: Programming ANTS Missions with ASSL

4.1 ANTS

The Autonomous Nano-Technology Swarm (ANTS) concept sub-mission PAM (Prospecting Asteroids Mission) is a novel approach to asteroid belt resource exploration that provides for extremely high autonomy, minimal communication requirements with Earth, and a set of very small explorers with a few consumables [12]. These explorers forming the swarm are pico-class, low-power, and low-weight spacecraft, yet capable of operating as fully autonomous and adaptable units. The units in a swarm are able to interact with each other, thus helping them to self-organize based on the emergent behavior of the simple interactions. Each spacecraft is equipped with a solar sail for power; thus it relies primarily on power from the sun, using only tiny thrusters to navigate independently. Moreover, each spacecraft also has onboard computation, artificial intelligence, and heuristics systems for control at the individual and team levels. There are three classes of spacecraft—*rulers*, *messengers*, and *workers*. Sub-swarms are formed to explore particular asteroids. In general, a swarm consists of several sub-swarms where every sub-swarm has a group leader (ruler), one or more messengers, and a number of workers carrying a specialized instrument. The messengers are needed to connect the team members when they cannot connect directly, due to a long distance or a barrier.

4.2 Programming Self-healing Behavior for ANTS

In this exercise we programmed with ASSL a self-healing behavior for ANTS [13]. This behavior was programmed by specifying self-management policies using ASSL tiers and clauses as follows:

- self-management policies—define the self-management behavior of the system through a finite set of *fluents* and *mappings*;
- actions—a finite set of actions that can be undertaken by ANTS in response to conditions, and according to the self-management policies;
- events—a set of events that initiate fluents and are prompted by the actions according to the policies;
- metrics—a set of metrics needed by the events and actions.

The following code (see Fig. 7) presents the ASSL high-level program for self-healing in ANTS. Note that the specification presented here is partial, due to space

```
AE ANT_Worker {
 AESELF_MANAGEMENT {
  SELF_HEALING {
   FLUENT inCollision {
    INITIATED_BY {EVENTS.collisionHappen} TERMINATED_BY {EVENTS.instrumentChecked}}
   FLUENT inInstrumentBroken {
    INITIATED_BY { EVENTS.instrumentBroken }
     TERMINATED_BY { EVENTS.isMsgInstrumentBrokenSent } }
   FLUENT inHeartbeatNotification {
    INITIATED_BY { EVENTS.timeToSendHeartbeatMsg }
    TERMINATED_BY { EVENTS.isMsgHeartbeatSent } }
   MAPPING { // if collision then check if the instrument is still operational
    CONDITIONS { inCollision } DO_ACTIONS {ACTIONS.checkANTInstrument } }
   MAPPING { // if the instrument is broken then notify the group leader
    CONDITIONS {inInstrumentBroken} DO_ACTIONS {ACTIONS.notifyForBrokenInstrument}}
   MAPPING { // time to send a heartbeat message has come
    CONDITIONS {inHeartbeatNotification} DO_ACTIONS {ACTIONS.notifyForHeartbeat}}
 }
}
....
ACTIONS {
 ACTION IMPL checkInstrument {
  RETURNS { BOOLEAN }
  TRIGGERS { EVENTS.instrumentChecked } }
 ACTION checkANTInstrument {
  GUARDS { AESELF_MANAGEMENT.SELF_HEALING.inCollision }
  ENSURES { EVENTS.instrumentChecked }
  VARS { BOOLEAN canOperate }
  DOES { canOperate = CALL ACTIONS.checkInstrument }
  TRIGGERS { IF (not canOperate) THEN EVENTS.instrumentBroken END }
  ONERR_TRIGGERS { IF (not canOperate) THEN EVENTS.instrumentBroken END }
 }
....
}
....
EVENTS {
 EVENT collisionHappen {
  GUARDS { not METRICS.distanceToNearestObject }
  ACTIVATION { CHANGED { METRICS.distanceToNearestObject } } }
 EVENT timeToSendHeartbeatMsg { ACTIVATION { PERIOD { 1 min } } }
}
....
METRICS {
 METRIC distanceToNearestObject {
  METRIC_TYPE { RESOURCE }
  METRIC_SOURCE {AEIP.MANAGED_ELEMENTS.worker.getDistanceToNearestObject}
  THRESHOLD_CLASS { DECIMAL [0.001 ~ ) } }
 } // METRICS
} // ANT_Worker
```

Fig. 7 ASSL specification for self-healing in ANTS

limitations. In our approach, we assume that each worker sends, on a regular basis, heartbeat messages to the ruler [13]. The latter uses these messages to determine when a worker is not able to continue its operation, due to a crash or malfunction in its communication device or instrument. The specification shows only fluents and mappings forming the specification for the self-healing policy for an ANTS Worker. Here, the key features are:

- an *inCollision* fluent that takes place when the worker crashes into an asteroid or into another spacecraft, but it is still able to perform self-checking operations;

- an *inInstrumentBroken* fluent that takes place when the self-checking operation reports that the instrument is not operational anymore;
- an *inHeartbeatNotification* fluent that is initiated on a regular basis by a timed event to send the heartbeat message to the ruler;
- a *checkANTInstrument* action that performs operational checking on the carried instrument.
- a *distanceToNearestObject* metric that measures the distance to the nearest object in space (not presented here).
- a *collisionHappened* event prompted by the distanceToNearestObject metric when the latter changes its value and the same does not satisfy the metric's threshold class.

The high-level program shown above is an abstract view of the special self-healing behavior expressed with ASSL constructs. As can be seen, to program with ASSL, one does not need to write standard classes and methods, e.g., the *main*() method in Java. Instead, the ASSL program is built around the *AESELF_MANAGEMENT* construct, which ideally can be regarded as a starting point of the program, i.e., something similar to the Java's *main*() method. Moreover, just like in object-oriented programming, an ASSL program is divided into class-like structures. In our example, we can regard as high-level classes the *ANT_WorkerAE*, the actions *checkInstrument* and *checkANTInstrument*, the *collisionHappen* event and the *distanceToNearestObject* metric. As specified, *ANT_Worker* is a sort of a "main" high-level class nesting the other high-level classes. The ACTION classes can be regarded as specification of high-level functions, i.e., they declare parameters, variables, executable statements and a sort of error-handling mechanism through events.

Obviously, an ASSL program does not look like a regular OOP program, but it is rather an abstraction of such written in ASSL. The ASSL code generator translates this abstraction into a concrete Java program that inherits names and features from the ASSL program and can be run on a Java Virtual Machine.

5 Summary

High-level programming is a promising approach to the future software development. The approach helps us deal with the challenge of building contemporary software systems, which are inherently complex and often contain millions of lines of code and a complex multi-component structure. Abstraction and simple natural language syntax drive out the complexity and help developers better perceive and maintain their programs. The question is how "high" should be the level of abstraction in order not to lose the precision needed to correctly program system's behavior.

We have demonstrated that formal specification languages might be used to do high-level programming. However, appropriate specification languages need to: (1) impose an "easy- to-cope-with" syntax, close to the natural language; and (2) provide developers with an appropriate code-generation mechanism that will generate the implementation of a system from the formal specification of the same.

ASSL (Autonomic System Specification Language) is such a formal language that successfully might be used for high-level programming. ASSL is dedicated to autonomic computing and it establishes a development environment emphasizing future self-managing features of the system in question and abstracting away the unnecessary details. An ASSL specification is abstract and platform independent. The language is formal but provides developers with modern programming-language constructs and mechanisms such as inheritance, parameterization, a type system, modularity and user-friendly syntax. Although, a high-level program written in ASSL does not look like a regular OOP program, it can be easily understood by developers. A powerful code generator, accompanied by software-verification mechanisms, helps such high-level programs be translated into fully operational, multithreading Java applications.

Overall, practice has shown that formal methods, when applied properly, can have a significant impact on the software development lifecycle in terms of cost and time reduction. Moreover, modern formal languages might lay the basis for a new approach to software programming, where specification and implementation are intertwined.

Acknowledgements This work was supported by Science Foundation Ireland grant 10/CE/I1855 to Lero–the Irish Software Engineering Research Centre.

References

1. Hinchey, M., Bowen, J.P., Vassev, E.: Formal methods. In: Encyclopedia of Software Engineering, pp. 308–320. Taylor & Francis, London (2010)
2. Vassev, E.: Towards a framework for specification and code generation of autonomic systems. PhD Thesis, Computer Science and Software Engineering Department, Concordia University, Quebec, Canada (2008)
3. Vassev, E.: ASSL: Autonomic System Specification Language—A Framework for Specification and Code Generation of Autonomic Systems. LAP Lambert Academic Publishing, Saarbrücken (2009)
4. Murch, R.: Autonomic Computing: On Demand Series. IBM Press, Indianapolis (2004)
5. Knuth, D.E.: Backus normal form vs. Backus Naur form. Commun. ACM **7**(12), 735–773 (1964)
6. Srivas, M., Miller, S.: Formal verification of the AAMP5 microprocessor: A case study in the industrial use of formal methods. In: Proceedings of the Workshop on Industrial-Strength Formal Specification Techniques (WIFT '95), pp. 2–16. IEEE Computer Society, Washington (1995)
7. Foord, M.: The future of programming: How high level can we get? The website, technical blog and projects of Michael Foord (2009). http://www.voidspace.org.uk/python/articles/object_shaped_future.shtml. Cited 30 Jan 2012
8. Blaha, M., Rumbaugh, J.: Object-Oriented Modeling and Design with UML, 2nd edn. Pearson, Prentice Hall, New York (2005)
9. Martin, R.C.: Granularity. C++ Rep. **8**(10), 57–62 (1996)
10. Vassev, E., Hinchey, M.: Software verification of autonomic systems developed with ASSL. In: Proceedings of the 16th Monterey Workshop on Modeling, Development and Verification of Adaptive Computer Systems: The Grand Challenge for Robotic Software (Monterey2010), Microsoft Research Center, Redmond, USA, pp. 1–16. Springer, Berlin (2010).

11. Vassev, E.: Code generation for autonomic systems with ASSL. In: Software Engineering Research, Management and Applications—Management and Applications. Studies in Computational Intelligence, vol. 296, pp. 1–15. Springer, Berlin (2010)
12. Truszkowski, W., Hinchey, M., Rash, J., Rouff, C.: NASA's swarm missions: The challenge of building autonomous software. IT Prof. **6**(5), 47–52 (2004)
13. Vassev, E., Hinchey, M.: ASSL specification and code generation of self-healing behavior for NASA swarm-based systems. In: Proceedings of the 6th IEEE International Workshop on Engineering of Autonomic and Autonomous Systems (EASe'09), pp. 77–86. IEEE Computer Society, Washington (2009)

Atomicity in Real-Time Computing

Jan Vitek

Abstract Writing safe and correct concurrent programs is a notoriously error-prone and difficult task. In real-time computing, the difficulties are aggravated by stringent responsiveness requirements. This paper reports on three experimental language features that aim to provide atomicity while bounding latency. The context for our experiments is the real-time extension of the Java programming language.

1 Introduction

Adding concurrency to any software system is challenging. It entails a paradigm shift away from sequential reasoning. Programmers must reason in terms of the possible interleavings of operations performed by the different threads of their program. This shift affects all aspects of the software lifecycle. During development, synchronization commands must be added to prevent data races. During verification and analysis, more powerful techniques must deployed to validate code. During testing, code coverage metrics must be revisited. Lastly, debugging becomes more complex as bugs become harder to reproduce. Aiming to simplify the task of writing correct concurrent algorithms, Herlihy and Moss proposed the idea of *transactional memory*, an alternative to lock-based mutual exclusion [8] that ensures *atomicity* and *isolation*. Atomicity means that either all of a given transaction's updates will be visible or none will. Isolation means that a transaction's data will not be observed in an intermediate state. While transactional memory has been studied extensively for general purpose computing, real-time systems have their own set of constraints. In particular, providing bounds on the execution time of any code fragment is key to being to ensure that a real-time task will meet its deadline and that a set of tasks is schedulable.

The tension between concurrency and real-time has been studied extensively. Practitioners are trained to keep critical sections short and to enforce strict programming protocols to avoid timing hazards. This requires a thorough understanding of the program's control flow. Unfortunately, the global view of the program required

J. Vitek (✉)
Computer Science Faculty, Purdue University, West Lafayette, USA

K.K. Breitman, R.N. Horspool (eds.), *Patterns, Programming and Everything*, DOI 10.1007/978-1-4471-2350-7_10, © Springer-Verlag London 2012 by these approaches does not mesh with modern software engineering practices which emphasize component-based systems and code reuse. The data abstraction and information hiding principles that are key to reusability in object-oriented programming tend to obscure the control flow of programs. Consider the Java code fragment:

```
synchronized ( obj ) {    obj.f = tgt.get();    }
```

Ensuring that the critical section is short requires non-local knowledge. The programmer must be able to tell which method is invoked in the call to `get()`, this in turn depends on the class of the object referenced by variable `tgt`. The question whether acquiring a lock on `obj` is sufficient is tricky too. It depends on which shared memory location are accessed by `get()`. Real-time scheduling theory refers to the time spent in a critical section as *blocking time*. This is the time a, possibly higher-priority, thread may have to wait until it can acquire the lock on `obj` and execute. For predictability the blocking time has to be bounded (and preferably small). A transactional memory equivalent of the above code, with appropriate language support, would be:

```
atomic {    obj.f = tgt.get();    }
```

The difference with the lock-based code is that it is not necessary for the programmer to specify a lock. Instead, it is up to the implementation to ensure atomicity and isolation of all of the operations performed by the critical section. Much like in a database, if two atomic sections attempt to perform conflicting changes to the memory, one of them will be aborted, its changes undone, and rescheduled for execution. The software engineering benefits of transactional memory are striking, especially in an object-oriented setting where it is often difficult to know which locks should be acquired to protect a particular sequence of memory operations and method invocations. The main disadvantage lies in the need to reexcute aborted transactions which entails maintaining a log of memory updates. Unless one can provide a hard bound on the number of aborts and on all of the implementation overheads, the approach may not be of use in a real-time context.

The notion of adding transactional facilities to a programming can be traced back all the way to Lomet [13]. As mentioned above, Herlihy and Moss introduced the concept of software transactional memory [8, 19], and were among the many to provide implementations for Java and other languages [7, 9]. Bershad worked on short atomic sections [3, 4] for performing compare-and-swaps without hardware support. Anderson et al. [1] described lock free objects for real-time systems, but did not explore compiler support. Welc et al. investigated the interaction of preemption and transactions on a multi-processor [22], but did not provide any real-time guarantees. Finally, Rigneburg and Grossman have used similar techniques to the ones developed here to add transactions to the Caml language on uniprocessors [16].

2 Preemptible Atomic Regions for Uniprocessor Systems

The first concurrency control abstraction we will review is the *preemptible atomic region* (PAR) introduced by Manson, Baker, Cunei, Jagannathan, Prochazka, Xin and Vitek in [14]. This work was done within the Ovm [2] project that implemented the first open source virtual machine for the Real-Time Specification for Java (RTSJ) [5].

PARs are a restricted form of software transactional memory that provide an alternative to mutual exclusion monitors for uniprocessor priority-preemptive real-time systems. A PAR consists of a sequence of instructions guaranteed to execute atomically. If a task is executing in a PAR and a higher-priority task is released by the scheduler, then the higher-priority task will get to execute right away. It will preempt the lower priority task and in the process, abort all memory operations performed within the atomic region. Once the lower-priority task is scheduled again, the PAR is transparently re-executed. The advantage of this approach is that high-priority tasks get to execute quickly, no special priority inversion avoidance protocol is needed, while atomicity and isolation of atomic regions is enforced.

Preemptible atomic regions differ from most transactional memory implementations in that tasks are aborted eagerly. This has the advantage forgoing conflict detection, but, on the other hand, results in more roll-backs than strictly necessary. Conflict detection is work that has to be performed on every read or write, while preemption happens relatively unfrequently. We believe that this was the right tradeoff.

We contrast lock-based code and PARs with an example, simplified code taken from the Zen real-time ORB [11]. Figure 1(a) makes extensive use of synchronization. Method `exec()` is synchronized to protect `ThreadPoolLane` instances against concurrent access. The lock on line 3 protects the shared `queue`. The `Queue` object relies on a private lock (line 6 and 8) to protect itself from mis-

```
   class ThreadPoolLane {
1.  synchronized void exec(Req t){
      if (borrow(t)) {
3.      synchronized(queue) {
4.        queue.enqueue(t);
5.        buffered++;
        }
      ...

   class Queue {
6.  final Object sync=new Object();
7.  void enqueue(Object d) {
      QueueNode n=getNode();
      n.value=d;
8.    synchronized(sync) {
9.      // enqueue the object
      ...
```

(a) With Monitors.

```
    class ThreadPoolLane {
10.   @PAR void exec(Req t){
11.     if (borrow(t)) {
12.       queue.enqueue(t);
13.       buffered++;
        }
      ...

    class Queue {
14.   @PAR void enqueue(Object d) {
15.     QueueNode n=getNode();
16.     n.value=d;
17.     // enqueue the object
      ...
```

(b) With Preemptible Atomic Regions.

Fig. 1 Example: a `ThreadPoolLane` from the Zen ORB. (Simplified) suse by client code. Atomic regions are declared by annotating a method as `@PAR`; they are active for the dynamic scope of the method, so all methods invoked by a method declared `@PAR` are transitively atomic. In Fig. 1(b), we use two atomic sections: one for the `exec()` method (10) and another for the `enqueue()` method (14). The first PAR is sufficient to prevent all data races within `exec()`; it is therefore unnecessary to obtain a lock on the queue. If `enqueue()` were only called from `exec()`, it would not need to be declared atomic (but declaring atomic does not hurt, as nested PARs are treated as a single atomic region). This solution is simpler to understand, as it does not rely on multiple locking granularities. A single PAR will protect all objects accessed within the dynamic extent of the annotated method. Contrast this with the lock-based solution, where all potentially exposed objects must be locked. Furthermore, the order of lock acquisition is critical to prevent deadlocks. On the other hand, PARs cannot deadlock: they do not block waiting for each other to finish.

The PAR-based mechanism avoids costs found in typical locking protocols. When a contended lock is acquired, one or more allocations may need to be performed. Additionally, whenever a lock is acquired or released, several locking queues need to be maintained; these determine who is "next in line" for the lock. In contrast, a PAR entrance only needs to store a book-keeping pointer to the current thread. When a PAR exits, the only overhead is the reset of the log; this consists of a single change to a pointer. Lock-based implementations also tend to have greater context-switching overhead. Consider the code in Fig. 1(a) with three threads: `t1`, `t2` and a higher-priority thread `t3`. Thread `t1` can acquire the lock on `sync` and be preempted by Thread `t2`, which then synchronizes on `queue`. Now, assume that Thread `t3` attempts to execute `exec()`. This scenario can result in five context switches. The first one occurs when `t3` preempts `t2`. The second and third occur when the system switches back to `t2` so that it can release the lock on `queue`. Finally, the fourth and fifth switches occur when the system schedules `t1` so that it can release the lock on `sync`. Under the same conditions, the use of PARs only requires one context switch. If `t2` preempts `t1` while it is in an atomic section, then `t1` will be aborted, and any changes it might have made will be undone. When `t3` is scheduled, it needs only undo the changes performed by `t2` to make progress. This does not require a context switch, as `t3` has access to the log. It is worth pointing out that roll-backs are never preempted.

PAR-based mechanisms incur two major costs that lock-based implementations do not. First, all writes to memory involve a log operation that records the current contents of the location being written. Second, if another thread preempts a thread that is executing a PAR, all changes performed by that thread will have to be undone; the heap will be restored based on the values stored in the log. Therefore, whenever writes are sparse, the overheads for a lock-based solution will be higher than those of the PAR-based solution. In our experience, aborts are cheap, because critical sections typically perform few writes.

2.1 Real-Time Guarantees

To ensure that a set of real-time tasks meet their deadlines, one must conduct a response time analysis. The theory for dealing with mutual exclusion has been developed and is well understood. We now consider how to plug in PARs into schedulability equations. Assume a set of n periodic tasks scheduled according to the *rate monotonic scheme* [6], which is widely used scheduling technique for fixed priority preemptive real-time systems. Tasks share a set of locks $\ell_1 \ldots \ell_k$. At most one task can be executing at any instant. Each task τ_i performs a job J_i. A job has period p_i such that $\forall i < n,\ p_i < p_{i+1}$. There is one critical section per job, and the critical section always ends before the job finishes. For each job, W_i is the maximal execution time spent in a critical section and U_i is the maximal time needed to perform an undo. R_i is the worst case response time of a job J_i. C_i is the worst-case execution time of job J_i. Tasks with higher priority π than τ_i are $hp(i) = \{j \mid \pi_j > \pi_i\}$, and ones with lower priority are $lp(i) = \{j \mid \pi_j < \pi_i\}$. Given that a task τ_i suffers *interference* from higher priority tasks and *blocking* from lower priority tasks, the response time is computed as $R_i = C_i + B_i + I_i$, where I_i is the maximum *interference time* and B_i the maximum *blocking factor* that J_i can experience [10]. The schedulability theorem is the following.

Theorem 1 *A set of n periodic tasks $\tau_i, 0 \le i < n$ is schedulable in RM, iff*

$$\forall i \le n, \exists R_i : R_i \le p_i$$

$$R_i = C_i + \max_{j \in lp(i)} U_j + \sum_{j \in hp(i)} \left\lceil \frac{R_i}{p_j} \right\rceil (C_j + U_i + W_i)$$

The intuition behind Theorem 1 is as follows. The expression $\max_{j \in lp(i)} U_j$ represents the worst case delay caused by rolling back a critical section executed by any task with priority lower than τ_i. The worst case interference of J_i with higher priority tasks, plus extra execution time needed to reexecute some critical sections, are computed as follows. Given that $\lceil \frac{R_i}{p_j} \rceil$ is the maximal number of releases of a higher priority task τ_j that can interfere with a task τ_i, we can compute the number of releases of τ_j in J_i as $\sum_{j \in hp(i)} \lceil \frac{R_i}{p_j} \rceil$. The most pessimistic approximation of how many rollbacks can occur is to assume that every interference implies a rollback of a critical section in J_i. Hence, every time a higher priority task τ_j preempts J_i, C_j is the worst case execution time of τ_j during which J_i is preempted and thus not progressing, and $U_i + W_i$ is the worst case time necessary to undo and reexecute the critical section of J_i preempted. As a critical section is undone by the higher priority task, $\sum_{j \in hp(i)} \lceil \frac{R_i}{p_j} \rceil U_i$ is a part of J_i's interference with higher priority tasks, while $\sum_{j \in hp(i)} \lceil \frac{R_i}{p_j} \rceil W_i$ is an extra execution time. The worst case for undo times is $U_i = W_i$; this occurs if all operations within a PAR are memory writes.

Let us compare PAR with the original priority inheritance protocol (PIP) by Sha et al. [18].

Theorem 2 (PIP Schedulability) *A set of n periodic tasks $\tau_i, 0 \leq i < n$ is schedulable in RM, iff*

$$\forall i \leq n, \exists R_i : R_i \leq p_i$$

$$R_i = C_i + m_i \max_{j \in lp(i)} W_j + \sum_{j \in hp(i)} \left\lceil \frac{R_i}{p_j} \right\rceil C_j$$

where m_i is the number of critical sections in J_i.

In PIP, the worst case delay of a job J_i caused by lower priority tasks sharing locks with J_i is proportional to the number of critical sections in J_i. Moreover, the worst case delay to enter to a single critical section is bounded by the worst case execution time of the conflicting critical section. In PAR, the worst case delay to enter a single critical section is bounded by the number of updates to be undone. In addition, the overall delay of J_i caused by lower priority tasks is not dependent on the number of critical sections in J_i. The cost of PAR is that the overall throughput is reduced due to the cost of undoing and reexecuting lower priority threads. While in all the priority inheritance schemes the cost of sharing locks degrades response times of higher priority threads through their blocking factor, in PAR the cost is paid by the lower priority threads in their higher execution time and interference.

In Java the number of threads (n) tends to be small, on the other hand the number of critical sections (m) is typically large. Assuming $U_i < W_i$, the trade-off between the PIP and PAR formulas is a question of comparing $m_i W_j$ with $2 \sum_{j \in hp(i)} \lceil \frac{R_i}{p_j} \rceil W_i$.

2.2 Implementation Sketch

As seen in Fig. 1, PARs can be declared by annotating a method `@PAR`. In our implementation, atomic methods are aborted every time a higher priority thread is released. This approach reduces blocking time, when a high-priority thread is released it only blocks for as long as it takes to abort one atomic region, and we only need to maintain a single undo log. Atomic regions introduce several costs. A single system wide log is preallocated with a user defined size (default of 10 KB). When control enters a PAR, it is necessary to store a reference to the current thread. Within the PAR, each time the application writes to memory, two additional writes are issued to the log: the original value of the location, and the location itself. The commit cost is limited to resetting the pointer into the log. The cost of undoing consists of traversing the log in reverse, which has the effect of undoing all writes performed within the critical section, and then throwing an internal exception to rewind the stack. For example, consider a program with two zero-initialized variables. If the instructions `x=1;y=1;x=2` were executed, the log would contain `(addressOf(x):0, addressOf(y):0, addressOf(x):1)`. If an abort took place, there would be

```
void f() {
   RETRY: try {
      try { PAR.start(); f$(); }
      finally { PAR.commit(); }
   } catch (AbortedFault_) { goto RETRY; }
}
```

Fig. 2 Code transformation for a method `@PAR void f`. The body of the original method is moved into a new synthetic method named `f$`

a write of 1 to `x`, then a write of 0 to `y`, and finally a write of 0 to `x`; both variables would then contain their initial values. The runtime cost of an abort is thus $O(n)$, where n is the number of writes performed by the transaction.

In traditional transactional systems, a conflict manager is required to deal with issues such as deadlock and starvation prevention. PARs are not subject to these limitations. Conflict detection is only required when a thread is ready to be released by the scheduler. Assume the scheduler is invoked to switch from the currently executing thread `t1` to a new higher priority thread `t2`. First, the scheduler checks the status of `t1`. If it is in an atomic region, the scheduler releases `t2`, which then executes the `abort` operation. If `t1` is in an atomic region that is already in the process of aborting, the abort must complete before thread `t2` is released. In either case, the pending `AbortedFault` will be thrown when thread `t1` is scheduled again.

The implementation proceeds by bytecode rewriting. We transform any method `f()` with the PAR annotation into a new method named `f$()`. A new `f()` method, as seen in Fig. 2, is added to the class; all of the original calls to `f()` will invoke this method instead of the original method. A transaction starts with an invocation of `start()`; this method enters a PAR and begins the logging process. The logged version of the original method is then executed. Upon successful completion, `commit()` resets the log. This method is enclosed in a `finally` clause to ensure that the transaction commits even if the method throws a Java exception. To deal with the consequences of an abort, we provide the class `AbortedFault`. When an abort occurs, the `AbortedFault` is thrown by the virtual machine. This exception class is treated specially by the virtual machine in that it can not be caught by normal catch clauses and sidesteps user defined `finally` clauses.

Rewriting extends down into the virtual machine; when a call is made that requires VM assistance, the invoked virtual machine code is rewritten as a PAR. Some calls can be rolled back. There are, effectively, four different types of code that can be encountered in the Ovm runtime: (a) Calls to Java methods that can be easily rolled back. This includes calls to allocators and garbage collectors. (b) Calls to Native methods that cannot be rolled back. This includes calls to system timers or to I/O methods. (c) Calls to Native methods that can easily be replaced with Java implementations. The `System.arraycopy` method, for example, calls the C function `memcpy`. `memcpy` is a native call, and so cannot be logged; however, it is trivial to write a Java implementation of this method. (d) Calls to Native methods that do not mutate system state. These methods can be handled individually, as well. Operations that must not be undone are called *non-retractable* operations. These include calls to I/O methods, as well as calls to user level data structures that are not specific to the thread currently running (such as timers or event counters), which must not be reset, as they are logically unrelated to the transaction. When encountered in a PAR, calls to such methods cause a compiler warning and are transformed to unconditionally throw an exceptions.

2.3 Experimental Evaluation

We evaluated the response times of high-priority threads with a program that executes a low and a high priority thread which access the same data structure, a `HashMap` from the `java.util` package. The low priority thread continually executes critical sections that perform a fixed number of read, insert and delete operations on the `HashMap`. Periodically, the high-priority thread executes a similar number of operations. In one configuration, the accesses are protected by the default RTSJ priority inheritance lock implementation. In the other, the accesses are protected by a PAR. For a PAR-based `HashMap`, this produced a high likelihood of aborts. In fact, an abort occurred every time a high-priority thread is scheduled. These measurements were obtained with Ovm running on a 300 MHz Embedded Planet PowerPC 8260 board with 256 MB SDRAM, 32 MB Flash, and Embedded Linux. Figure 3 shows the results of the test. Two points are noteworthy. First, the latency for the PAR-based HashMap is lower; this indicates that undoing the low priority thread's writes was faster than context switching to the other thread, finishing its critical section, and context switching back. Second, the response time of the PAR-based HashMap was more predictable; this is because it was not necessary to execute a indeterminately long critical section before executing the high-priority thread's PAR.

3 Obstruction-Free Communication with Atomic Methods

The second abstraction we have experimented with is *Atomic Methods* in the Reflex programming model [20] (this work was done with Jesper Honig Spring, Filip Pizlo, Jean Privat and Rachid Guerraoui). Atomic methods were introduced in the *Reflex* programming model for mixing highly-responsive tasks with timing-oblivious Java programs. A Reflex program consists of a graph of Reflex tasks connected according to some topology through a number of unidirectional communication channels. This relates directly to graph-based modeling systems, such as Simulink and Ptolemy [12], that are used to design real-time control systems, and to stream-based programming languages like StreamIt [21]. A Reflex graph is constructed as a Java program, following standard Java programming conventions. Reflex can run in isolation or as part of a larger Java application. To communicate with ordinary Java

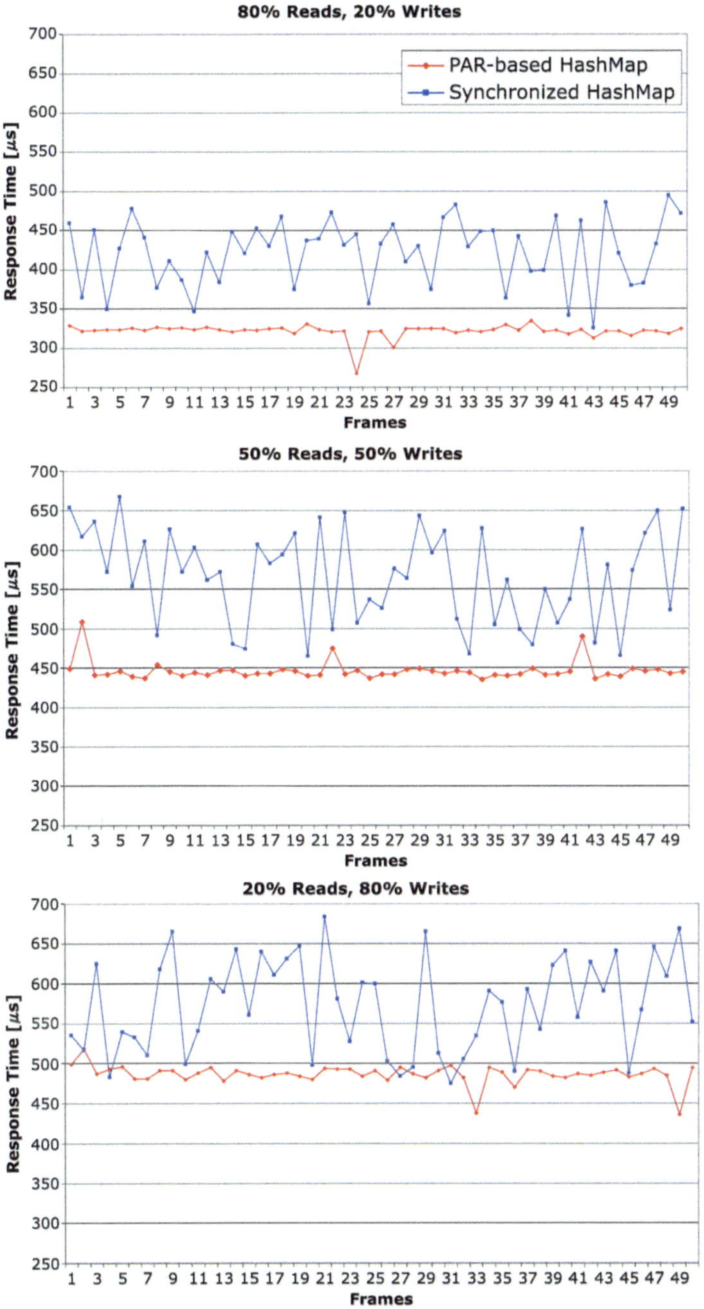

Fig. 3 Response time of a high-priority thread in the HashMap Microbenchmark. The x-axis indicates the number of periods (or frames) that have elapsed, and the y-axis indicates the response time of the high-priority thread (in microseconds)

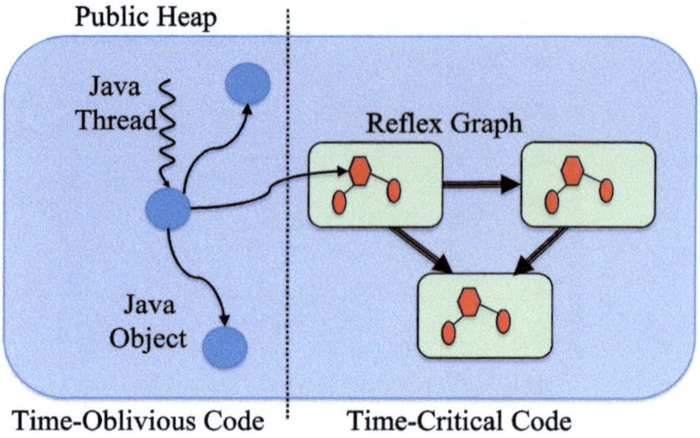

Fig. 4 Illustration of a Java application consisting of time-oblivious code (*blue*) and a time-critical Reflex graph with three connected tasks

threads, Reflex provides special methods which will ensure that real-time activities do not block for normal Java threads and ensures atomicity of changes performed by plain Java. Figure 4 illustrates a Reflex program.

A Reflex acts as the basic computational unit in the graph, consisting of user-defined persistent data structures, typed input and output channels for communication between Reflex, and user-specific logic implementing the functional behavior of the task. In order to ensure low latency, each Reflex lives in a partition of the virtual machine's memory outside of the control of the garbage collector. Furthermore, Reflex are executed with a priority higher than ordinary Java threads. This allows the Reflex scheduler to safely preempt any Java thread, including the garbage collector. Memory partitioning also prevents synchronization hazards, such as a task blocking on a lock held by an ordinary Java thread, which in turn can be blocked by the garbage collector. In the Reflex programming model, Reflex have access to disjoint memory partitions and developers can choose between a real-time garabage collector and region-based allocation for memory management within Reflex.

3.1 Atomic Methods

Reflex prevent synchronous operations by replacing lock-based synchronization with an obstruction-free communication. The principle behind atomic methods is to let an ordinary Java thread invoke certain methods on the time-critical task. Once inside the atomic method, the ordinary Java thread can access the data it shares with the Reflex. These methods ensure that any memory mutations made by the ordinary Java thread to objects allocated within a Reflex's stable memory will only be visible if the atomic method runs to completion. Again, given the default allocation context, any transient objects allocated during the invocation of the atomic method will be reclaimed when the method returns. If the ordinary Java thread is preempted by the Reflex scheduler, all of the changes will be discarded and the atomic method will be scheduled for re-execution. The semantics ensures that time-critical tasks can run obstruction-free without blocking.

```java
public class PacketReader extends ReflexTask {
    ...
    @atomic public void write(byte[] b) {...}
}
```

Fig. 5 Example of declaration of method on `ReflexTask` class to be invoked with transactional semantics by ordinary Java threads

Atomic methods to be invoked by ordinary Java threads are required to be declared on a subclass of the `ReflexTask` and must be annotated `@atomic` as demonstrated with the `write()` method in Fig. 5. Methods annotated with `@atomic` are implicitly synchronized, preventing concurrent invocation of the method by multiple ordinary Java threads.

For reasons of type-safety, parameters of atomic methods are limited to types allowed in capsules (capsules are the special message objects that can be sent across channels between Reflex), i.e. primitives and primitive array types. Return types are even more restricted, atomic method may only return primitives. This further restriction is necessary to prevent returning a transient object, which would lead to a dangling pointer, or a stable object, which would breach isolation. If an atomic methods need to return more than a single a primitive, it can only do it by side-effecting an argument (i.e. an array).

3.2 Example

Figure 6 shows the `PacketReader` class that creates capsules representing network packets from a raw stream of bytes. This class is part of a network intrusion detection application written as a Reflex graph. For our experiments, we simulate the network with the `Synthesizer` class. The synthesizer runs as an ordinary Java thread, and feeds the `PacketReader` task instance with a raw stream of bytes to be analyzed. Communication between the synthesizer and the `PacketReader` is done by invoking the `write` method on the `PacketReader`. This method takes a reference to a buffer of data (primitive byte array) allocated on the heap and parses it to create packets. The `write` method is annotated `@atomic` to give it transactional semantics, thereby ensuring that the task can safely preempt the synthesizer thread at any time.

3.3 Implementation Sketch

To implement atomic methods, we exploit the preemptible atomic regions facility of the Ovm virtual machine as presented in Sect. 2. Any method annotated `@atomic`

```
public class PacketReader extends ReflexTask {
  private Buffer buffer = new Buffer(16384);

  @atomic public void write(byte[] b) {
    buffer.write(b);
  }

  private int readPacket(TCP_Hdr p) {
    try {
      buffer.startRead();
      for (int i=0; i<Ether_Hdr.ETH_LEN; i++)
        p.e_dst[i] = buffer.read_8();
      ...
      return buffer.commitRead();
    } catch (UnderrunEx e) { buffer.abortRead(); ... }
  }
}
```

Fig. 6 An excerpt of the `PacketReader` task that reads packets received from the ordinary Java thread and pushes them down in the graph. The `write` method, invoked by the ordinary Java thread, is declared to have transactional semantics. The `readPacket` method is invoked from the Reflex `excute` method

is treated specially by the Ovm compiler. More specifically, the compiler will privatize the call-graph of a transactional method, i.e., recursively generate a transactional variant of each method reachable from the transactional method. This transactionalized variant of the call-graph is invoked by the ordinary Java thread, whereas the non-transactional variant is kept around as the Reflex task might itself invoke (from the `execute()` method which is invoked periodically by the Reflex framework) some of the methods, and those should not be invoked with transactional semantics. We have applied a subtle modification to the preemptible atomic region implementation. Rather than having a single global transaction log, a transactional log is created per `ReflexTask` instance in the graph, assuming that it declares atomic methods. This change ensures the encapsulation of each `ReflexTask` instance, and enables concurrent invocation of different atomic methods on different `ReflexTask` instances. The preemptible atomic regions use a roll-back approach in which for each field write performed by an ordinary Java thread on a stable object within the transactional method, the virtual machine inserts an entry in the transaction log and records the original value and address of field. With this approach, a transaction abort boils down to replaying the entries in the transaction log in reverse order. Running on a uni-processor virtual machine, no conflict detection is needed. Rather, the transaction aborts are simply performed eagerly at context switches. Specifically, the transaction log is rolled back by the high-priority thread before it invokes the `execute` method of the schedulable Reflex.

The Ovm garbage collector supports pinning for objects such that the objects are not moved or removed during a collection, and will therefore always be in a consistent state when observed by referent objects from other memory areas, including a Reflex task. Arguments to atomic methods are heap-allocated objects and must be pinned when the ordinary Java thread invokes a transactional method and unpinned again when the invocation exits. We have modified the bytecode rewriter of the Ovm compiler to instrument the method bodies of the atomic methods to pin any reference type objects passed in upon entry and unpin again upon exit.

3.3.1 Multicore Implementation

One of the limitations of the Ovm implementation is that the virtual machine is optimized for uni-processor systems. In order to validate applicability of our approach we ported much of the functionality of Reflex to the IBM WebSphere Real-Time VM, a virtual machine with multi-processor support and a RTSJ-implementation. The implementation of atomic methods in a multiprocessor setting is significantly different. We use a roll-forward approach in which an atomic method defers all memory mutations to a local log until commit time. Having reached commit time, it is mandatory to check if the state of the Reflex has changed during the method invocation, and if so abort the atomic method. The entries in the log can safely be discarded, in constant time, as the mutations will not be applied. If the task state did not change, the atomic method is permitted to commit its changes with the Reflex scheduler briefly locked out for a time corresponding to $\mathcal{O}(n)$, where n is the number of stable memory locations updated by the atomic method. We rely on a combination of program transformations and minimal native extensions to the VM to achieve this.

3.4 Real-Time Guarantees

The real-time guarantees for atomic methods are slightly different then those of preemptible atomic regions. To start, there is a single real-time thread per Reflex which can interact with possibly multiple plain Java threads. So, the blocking time of the real-time thread is at most the time required to abort the atomic method (i.e. time proportional to the log size). On the other hand, no progress guarantee is given to the plain Java threads trying to communicate with a Reflex. The programming model allows for unbounded aborts in the worst case, though this has not occurred in our experiments.

3.5 Experimental Evaluation

We evaluate the impact of atomic methods on predictability using a synthetic benchmark on an IBM blade server with 4 dual-core AMD Opteron 64 2.4 GHz processors

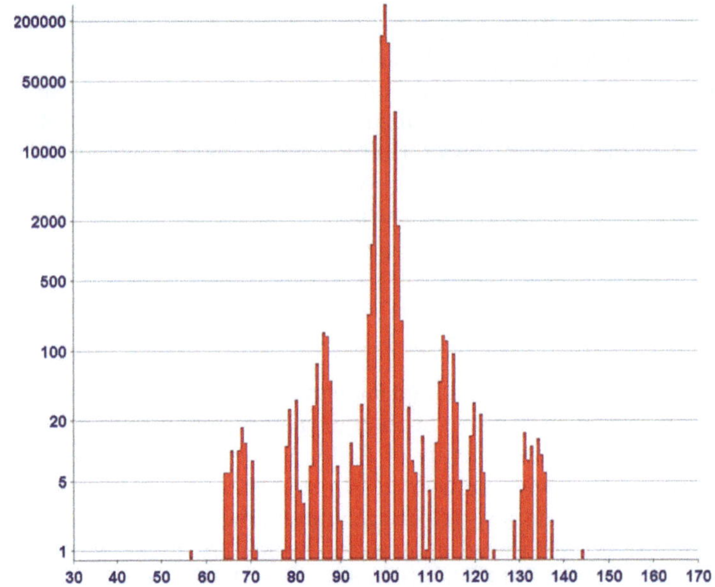

Fig. 7 Frequencies of inter-arrival times of a single Reflex task with a period of 100 μs continuously interrupted by an ordinary Java thread invoking an atomic method. The x-axis gives inter-arrival times in microseconds, the y-axis a logarithm of the frequency. The graph shows few departures from the ideal 100 μs inter-arrival times

and 12 GB of physical memory running Linux 2.6.21.4. A Reflex task is scheduled at a period of 100 μs, and when scheduled reads the data available on its input buffer in circular fashion into its stable state. An ordinary Java thread runs continuously and feeds the task with data by invoking an atomic method on the task every 20 ms. To evaluate the influence of computational noise and garbage collection, another ordinary Java thread runs concurrently, continuously allocating at the rate of 2 MB per second.

Figure 7 shows a histogram of the frequencies of inter-arrival times of the Reflex. The figure contains observations covering almost 600,000 periodic executions. Out of 3,000 invocations of the atomic method, 516 of them aborted, indicating that atomic methods were exercised. As can be seen, all observations of the inter-arrival time are centered around the scheduled period of 100 μs. Overall, there are only a few microseconds of jitter. The inter-arrival times range from 57 to 144 μs.

4 Atomicity with Micro-Transactions

The third real-time concurrency abstraction we have studied in [15, 17] is a hardware realization of transactional memory called RTTM for Real-Time Transactional Memory (work done with Schoeberl, Brandner, Meawad, Iyer). The main design goals for the RTTM were: (a) simple programming model and (b) analyzable timing properties. Therefore, all design and architecture decisions were driven by their impact on real-time guarantees. In contrast to other transactional memory proposals RTTM does not aim for a high average case throughput, but for time-predictability. RTTM supports small atomic sections with a few read and write operations. Therefore, it is more an extension of the CAS instruction to simplify the implementation of non-blocking communication algorithms.

In our proposal each core is equipped with a small, fully associative buffer to cache the changed data during the transaction. All writes go only into the buffer. Read addresses are marked in a read set—a simplification that uses only tag memories. The write buffer and tag memory for the read set are organized for single word access. This organization ensures that no false positive conflicts are detected. For the same reason the transaction buffer has to be a fully associative cache with a FIFO replacement strategy. Fully associative caches are expensive and therefore the size is limited. We assume that real-time systems programmers are aware of the high cost of synchronization and will use small atomic sections where a few words are read and written. On a commit the buffer is written to the shared memory. During the write burst on commit all other cores listen to the write addresses and compare those with their own read set. If one of the write addresses matches a read address the transaction is marked to be aborted. The atomicity of the commit itself is enforced by a single global lock—the commit token. The commit token can also be used on a buffer overflow. When a transaction overflows the write buffer or the tag memory for the read set the commit token is grabbed and the transaction continues. The atomicity is now enforced by the commit token. Grabbing the commit token before commit is intended as a backup solution on buffer overflow. It effectively serializes the atomic sections. The same mechanism can also be used to protect I/O operations that usually cannot be rolled back. On an I/O operation within a transaction the core also grabs the commit token. Conflict detection happens only during a commit when all $n - 1$ (on a n core multiprocessor) cores listen to the core that commits the transaction and not during local read/writes thus saving valuable CPU cycles. When a conflict is detected the transaction is aborted and restarted.

4.1 Example

We have implemented dynamically growing singly linked wait-free queues using different synchronization techniques. In our implementations, we use the Java synchronized and the annotation @atomic for micro-transactions. The implementation involves a 'head' node to keep track of the queue-empty condition. Both the head and the tail pointers point to the 'head' node at the beginning and when the queue is empty.

```
class SLQ {
  final static class Node {
```

```
    final Object value;
    volatile Node next;
  }

  volatile Node head = new Node(), tail = head;

  void insert(Node n) {
    tail.next = n; tail = n;
  }

  Object remove() {
     if (head.next == null) return null;
     head = head.next;
     return head.value;
  }
}
```

In the remove method, the removed node is retained as the special 'head' node until the next node is removed. This does not affect the number of retries.

4.2 Real-Time Guarantees

The real-time behavior of such transactions is established by bounding the number of retries r to $n-1$ on a n core multiprocessor. Assuming periodic threads, non-overlapping periods and execution deadline not exceeding the period, the worst case execution time (WCET) of any thread t is given by the equation

$$t = t_{na} + (r+1)t_{amax} \tag{1.1}$$

where t is the worst case execution time, t_{na} is the execution time of the non-atomic section of the thread and t_{amax} is the maximum of the execution times of the atomic sections of all the n threads in the system. Since r is bounded, the WCET of any thread is bounded.

5 Experimental Evaluation

The experimentation environment is an FPGA programmed with a symmetric shared-memory multi-processor hardware system with four JOP cores. As hardware platform we us an Altera DE2-70 Development board consisting of a Cyclone II EP2C70 FPGA. The Altera board contains 64 MB SDRAM, 2 MB SSRAM and an 8 MB Flash Memory and I/O interfaces such as USB 2.0, RS232, and a Byte-BlasterMV port. Each JOP core has a core local 4 KB instruction cache and 1 KB

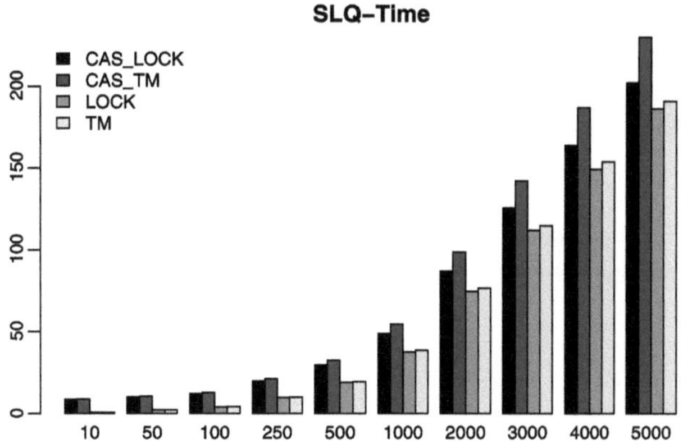

Fig. 8 SLQ Time. The x-axis gives number of nodes and the y-axis gives the execution time in milli-seconds

stack cache. The Cyclone FPGA was programmed to simulate the afore-mentioned symmetric shared-memory multi-processor environment.

Figure 8 plots the execution time to insert, move and remove a specified number of nodes from the singly linked queues. The x-axis indicates the number of nodes used in the experiment, we chose a sample of the small number of nodes followed by a linear increment starting from 1000. The bars indicate the time taken to complete the experiment when different synchronization methods are used. Time is measured from the instance when the insertion of the first node is started till the removal of the last node is completed. It can be noted that, as the number of nodes processed increase the average execution time increases almost linearly due to an increase in the number of locks, transactions and retries. The CAS numbers are simulation of hardware compare and swap as the architecture does not support such instructions. Execution times in the case of TM is 17 % lower compared to the CAS cases, it is 2.5 % higher than the LOCK case. The higher execution times of the TM implementation relative to that of LOCK can be attributed to the small sizes of the read/write sets and shorter atomic sections in singly linked queues. For example, in a singly linked list, an insert operation involves the modification only of a pointer and the queue tail. As a result, locks are held for a short period reducing overall waiting time. However, in the case of TM, retries, conflict detection and other transactional memory overhead is high as compared to the time lost in waiting for locks.

6 Conclusion

Correct and efficient design and implementation of concurrent programs is absolutely vital, but tremendously difficult to achieve. In this paper, we have reported on our experience with three concurrency control abstractions that leverage transactional memory ideas to provide time predictable performance. For uniprocessor systems, preemptible atomic regions provide a very good compromise between performance and responsiveness. They are fast and have simple semantics. They are arguably preferable to locks in most cases. If a restricted programming model is acceptable, then the atomic methods that are part of the Reflex programming model are a nice match that preserves most of the benefits of PARs but can be used in a multi-processor setting. Lastly, on a multi-core real-time system, a hardware implementation such as the one we have proposed with RTTM can provide the appropriate timing guarantee, but unfortunately our preliminary results suggest that there is a decrease in throughput due to the complexity of the hardware. Overall, we believe that transactional abstractions show promise to provide viable alternatives to lock based synchronization in the context of real-time systems.

References

1. Anderson, J., Ramamurthy, S., Moir, M., Jeffay, K.: Lock-free transactions for real-time systems. In: real-Time Database Systems: Issues and Applications. Kluwer Academic, Norwell (1997)
2. Armbuster, A., Baker, J., Cunei, A., Holmes, D., Flack, C., Pizlo, F., Pla, E., Prochazka, M., Vitek, J.: A Real-time Java virtual machine with applications in avionics. ACM Trans. Embed. Comput. Syst. **7**(1), 1–49 (2007)
3. Bershad, B.N.: Practical considerations for non-blocking concurrent objects. In: Proceedings of the 13th International Conference on Distributed Computing Systems, May, pp. 264–273 (1993)
4. Bershad, B.N., Redell, D.D., Ellis, J.R.: Fast mutual exclusion for uniprocessors. In: Fifth International Conference on Architectural Support for Programming Languages and Operating Systems (ASPLOS), pp. 223–233 (1992)
5. Bollella, G., Gosling, J., Brosgol, B., Dibble, P., Furr, S., Turnbull, M.: The Real-Time Specification for Java. Addison-Wesley, Reading (2000)
6. Ding, Y., Lehoczky, J.P., Sha, L.: The rate monotonic scheduling algorithm: exact characterization and average case behaviour. In: Proceedings of the 10th IEEE Real-Time Systems Symposium (1989)
7. Harris, T., Fraser, K.: Language support for lightweight transactions. In: Conference on Object-Oriented Programming, Systems, Languages, and Applications (OOPSLA'03), Seattle, Washington, November, pp. 388–402 (2003)
8. Herlihy, M., Moss, J.E.B.: Transactional memory: architectural support for lock-free data structures. In: ISCA'93: Proceedings of the 20th Annual International Symposium on Computer Architecture, pp. 289–300. ACM Press, New York (1993)
9. Herlihy, M., Luchangco, V., Moir, M., Scherer, W.: Software transactional memory for dynamic-sized data structures. In: ACM Conference on Principles of Distributed Computing, pp. 92–101 (2003)
10. Joseph, M., Pandya, P.: Finding response times in a real-time system. Comput. J. **29**(5), 390–395 (1986)
11. Krishna, A.S., Schmidt, D.C., Klefstad, R.: Enhancing real-time CORBA via real-time Java features. In: 24th International Conference on Distributed Computing Systems (ICDCS 2004), Hachioji Tokyo, Japan, March, pp. 66–73 (2004)
12. Lee, E.A.: Overview of the Ptolemy project. Technical report UCB/ERL M03/25, EECS Department, University of California, Berkeley (2003)
13. Lomet, D.B.: Process structuring, synchronisation and recovery using atomic actions. Proc. ACM Conf. Lang. Des. Reliab. Softw. **12**(3), 128–137 (1977)
14. Manson, J., Baker, J., Cunei, A., Jagannathan, S., Prochazka, M., Xin, B., Vitek, J.: Preemptible atomic regions for real-time Java. In: Proceedings of the 26th IEEE Real-Time Systems Symposium (RTSS), December (2005)

15. Meawad, F., Iyer, K., Schoeberl, M., Vitek, J.: Real-time wait-free queues using micro-transactions. In: International Workshop on Java Technologies for Real-Time and Embedded Systems (JTRES), October (2011)
16. Ringenburg, M.F., Grossman, D.: AtomCaml: First-class atomicity via rollback. In: Tenth ACM International Conference on Functional Programming, Tallinn, Estonia, September (2005)
17. Schoeberl, M., Brandner, F., Vitek, J.: Rttm: real-time transactional memory. In: Symposium on Applied Computing (SAC), pp. 326–333 (2010)
18. Sha, L., Rajkumar, R., Lehoczky, J.P.: Priority inheritance protocols: an approach to real-time synchronization. IEEE Trans. Comput. **39**(9), 1175–1185 (1990)
19. Shavit, N., Touitou, D.: Software transactional memory. In: Proceedings of the 14th Annual ACM Symposium on Principles of Distributed Computing (PODC'95), August, pp. 204–213 (1995)
20. Spring, J.H., Pizlo, F., Privat, J., Guerraoui, R., Vitek, J.: Reflexes: Abstractions for integrating highly responsive tasks into Java applications. ACM Trans. Embed. Comput. Syst. (2009)
21. Thies, W., Karczmarek, M., Amarasinghe, S.: Streamit: a language for streaming applications. In: Proceedings of the 11th International Conference on Compiler Construction (CC), April (2002)
22. Welc, A., Hosking, A.L., Jagannathan, S.: Preemption-based avoidance of priority inversion for Java. In: 33rd International Conference on Parallel Processing (ICPP 2004), Montreal, Canada, August, pp. 529–538 (2004)

Tuning Keyword Pattern Matching

Bruce W. Watson

Abstract I introduce two performance improvements to the Commentz-Walter family of multiple-keyword (exact) pattern matching algorithms. These algorithms (which are in the Boyer-Moore-Horspool style of keyword pattern matchers) consist of two nested loops: the outer one to process the input text and the inner one processing possible keyword matches. The guard of each loop is improved, thereby leading to non-trivial speedup, which could reach 20 % in practice, depending up on the input text and keywords.

1 Introduction

In this chapter, I introduce two improvements to the Commentz-Walter family of multiple-keyword (exact) pattern matching algorithms. These algorithms were derived by Commentz-Walter in [3, 4] and represent the multiple-keyword matching analogues of the well-known Boyer-Moore-Horspool style of single-keyword algorithms (see [5–7, 9, 10] for introductions to those algorithms). This *family* of algorithms shares a common algorithm skeleton, differing only in the tables used to skip portions of the input text in which no match can possibly occur. Benchmarking data in [10] shows that these algorithms significantly outperform the better-known Aho-Corasick [1] algorithms on both natural language and genomic inputs. It follows that any further improvements to the skeleton can have practical consequences.

Detailed derivations of the Commentz-Walter algorithms can also be found in [2, 10–12]. These algorithms are notoriously difficult to derive correctly, and most of the improvements arise from a correctness-by-construction approach to algorithmics.

I assume the reader is broadly familiar with the field of keyword pattern matching. For more details, see [9] or any other stringology book. Briefly, given an input string S and a finite set of keywords P (over the same alphabet), find *all occurrences* (including overlapping ones) of a keyword in S.

B.W. Watson (✉)
FASTAR Research Group, Center for Knowledge Dynamics and Decision-Making, Stellenbosch University, Stellenbosch, Republic of South Africa
e-mail: bruce@fastar.org

K.K. Breitman, R.N. Horspool (eds.), *Patterns, Programming and Everything*, 167
DOI 10.1007/978-1-4471-2350-7_11, © Springer-Verlag London 2012

2 Basic Algorithmic Skeleton

The skeleton is

```
1: i ← 0
2: while i < |S| do
3:    {attempt match of P from right-to-left at S_{0...i}}
4:    j ← i
5:    while j ≥ 0 and S_{j...i} is still a viable match in P do
6:       j ← j − 1
7:    end while
8:    if S_{j+1...i} ∈ P then
9:       print match found
10:   end if
11:   i ← i + distance based on knowledge of S_{j...i}
12: end while
```

The algorithm consists of an outer loop proceeding from left to right through S, attempting a match at every point. The match attempt proceeds from *right-to-left*. After each match attempt, we could naïvely move one position to the right in S, however, the information gathered during a match attempt can be used to shift further to the right (than just one position)—giving this family of algorithms its performance advantage. The match attempt is specifically right-to-left to allow for larger shifts. The shifts are implemented using tables precomputed from P.

In the two following sections, we tune the two loops.

3 Tuning the Outer Loop

The guard of the outer loop (see line 2 above) detects overruns on the right end of S, when $i \geq |S|$. The guard can be changed to **true** using the 'sentinel' technique of concatenating one of the keywords on the right of S; the loop can be terminated when the sentinel match is detected in:

```
i ← 0
S ← S · p (for some p ∈ P)
while true do
   {attempt match of P from right-to-left at S_{0...i}}
   j ← i
   while j ≥ 0 and S_{j...i} is still a viable match in P do
      j ← j − 1
   end while
   if S_{j+1...i} ∈ P then
      if sentinel is being matched then
         return
      end if
      print match found
```

14: **end if**
15: $i \leftarrow i +$ distance based on knowledge of $S_{j...i}$
16: **end while**

On most present-day architectures,[1] the new guard test (an empty test, as the guard is true) saves at least one instruction (and therefore one clock-cycle in a typical implementation) in an implementation of the outer loop. The outer loop executes between $|S|$ and

$$\frac{|S|}{|\text{the longest keyword in } P|}$$

times, depending on the properties of S and P. (The former case applies when shifts to the right of only one position are possible, whereas the latter applies when the longest shifts are possible.)

4 Tuning the Inner Loop

We can similarly tune the guard of the inner loop, appearing on line 6 in Sect. 3. The second conjunct ensures that the algorithm is still tracking a viable match, and is usually implemented using a reverse trie (a type of automaton) for keyword set P and the if-statement's guard. Little improvement can be made to that conjunct, other than using a different type of automaton. The first conjunct, $j \geq 0$, prevents j from running off the left of S. It can also be eliminated using a sentinel technique—attaching a special symbol $\perp$ on the left of S (and starting i at position 1), ensuring that no viable match is possible in:

1: $i \leftarrow 1$
2: $S \leftarrow \perp \cdot S \cdot p$ (for some $p \in P$)
3: **while true do**
4: {attempt match of P from right-to-left at $S_{0...i}$}
5: $j \leftarrow i$
6: **while** $S_{j...i}$ is still a viable match in P **do**
7: $j \leftarrow j - 1$
8: **end while**
9: **if** $S_{j+1...i} \in P$ **then**
10: **if** sentinel is being matched **then**
11: **return**
12: **end if**
13: **print** `match found`
14: **end if**
15: $i \leftarrow i +$ distance based on knowledge of $S_{j...i}$
16: **end while**

[1]For example on Knuth's MMIX [8], which is broadly representative.

The new guard also saves at least one instruction (and likely one clock-cycle) in a real implementation of the inner loop, which is executed between

$$\frac{|S|}{|\text{the longest keyword in } P|}$$

and

$$|S| \times |\text{the longest keyword in } P|$$

times. The remainder of the body of the inner loop can be implemented in as little as 4 clock cycles, indicating a maximum 20 % performance increase.

Readers familiar with the Boyer-Moore algorithms for single-keyword pattern matching might expect that the inner loop guard could also have been simplified by beginning i at position k, where k corresponds to the length of one of the keywords. Unfortunately, this *does not* lead to a correct algorithm. To see why not, consider $k = |\text{shortest keyword in } P|$. In this case, running off the left of S remains a possibility while pursuing a match of a longer keyword in P. The alternative $k = |\text{longest keyword in } P|$ leads to us potentially missing a match starting left of k of a shorter keyword in P.

5 Conclusions

I have introduced two straightforward optimizations of the Commentz-Walter family of algorithms. The practical performance improvements depend heavily on the characteristics of S and P, but could reach 20 % with efficient data-layouts of the trie (thereby minimizing the instructions required for the remaining loop guard). Interestingly, these optimizations (including the relatively trivial sentinel) have not previously been applied to this family of algorithms.

Acknowledgements This chapter is dedicated to Judith Bishop—good friend and colleague, and an outstanding computer scientist. In the 1990's, I was invited by Judith to present a colloquium on keyword pattern matching algorithms, then at the University of Pretoria. This research work grew directly out of the discussions surrounding the colloquium and research visit.

References

1. Aho, A.V., Corasick, M.J.: Efficient string matching: an aid to bibliographic search. Commun. ACM **18**(6), 333–340 (1975)
2. Cleophas, L., Watson, B.W., Zwaan, G.: A new taxonomy of sublinear right-to-left scanning keyword pattern matching algorithms. Sci. Comput. Program. **75**, 1095–1112 (2010). doi:10.1016/j.scico.2010.04.012
3. Commentz-Walter, B.: A string matching algorithm fast on the average. In: Maurer, H. (ed.) Proceedings of the Sixth International Colloquium on Automata, Languages and Programming, pp. 118–131. Springer, Berlin (1979)

4. Commentz-Walter, B.: A string matching algorithm fast on the average. Tech. Rep. 79.09.007, IBM Heidelberg Scientific Center (1979)
5. Crochemore, M.A., Rytter, W.: Text Algorithms. Oxford University Press, Oxford (1994)
6. Crochemore, M.A., Rytter, W.: Jewels of Stringology. World Scientific, Singapore (2003)
7. Hume, A., Sunday, D.: Fast string searching. Softw. Pract. Exp. **21**(11), 1221–1248 (1991)
8. Knuth, D.E.: MMIX—A RISC Computer for the New Millennium, vol. 1, fascicle 1. Addison-Wesley, Reading (2005)
9. Smyth, W.F.: Computing Patterns in Strings. Addison-Wesley, Reading (2003)
10. Watson, B.W.: Taxonomies and toolkits of regular language algorithms. Ph.D. thesis, Faculty of Computing Science, Eindhoven University of Technology, the Netherlands (1995)
11. Watson, B.W.: A new family and structure for Commentz-Walter-style multiple-keyword pattern matching algorithms. South Afr. Comput. J. **30**, 29–33 (2003)
12. Watson, B.W., Zwaan, G.: A taxonomy of sublinear multiple keyword pattern matching algorithms. Sci. Comput. Program. **27**(2), 85–118 (1996)

An Afterword for Judith: The Next Phase of Her Career

Tony Hey

I first met Judith in the 1970's when we were both at Southampton. I was a lecturer in theoretical physics in the Physics Department and Judith was a Ph.D. student in the very new Computer Studies Department. We met at a party hosted by a mutual friend and I remember that we had a common interest in wine. At that time, I was doing research on particle physics and more interested in quarks than computer architecture, of which I had only the vaguest notion. By the 1980's things had changed full circle and my research interests were now in computer architecture—specifically in building and using parallel computers. It was then I moved to the newly formed Department of Electronics and Computer Science at Southampton in which Judith was now a lecturer. Judith assisted my transition from physicist to computer scientist and was generous in re-educating me into the broad field of computer science. In research, my group was experimenting with parallel systems using occam and transputers and collaborating with David May at Inmos. As one of her research interests, Judith looked at implementations of Ada on our multi-transputer machines. It was therefore a great loss for me—and for the Department—when Judith decided to return to South Africa.

Over the years we kept in touch and I have followed Judith's career with interest. Her books were always useful and educational—from Pascal to Ada, through Java to C#. From 2001 to 2005, I was director of the UK eScience Core Program and concerned with funding multidisciplinary collaborations between scientists and computer scientists. Rather than go back to a university, I joined Microsoft in 2005 to set up a similar eScience program and entered the vibrant world of Microsoft Research. After a couple of years at Microsoft, my job was enlarged to include research collaborations not only with scientists but also with the computer science community. I now found myself needing someone to help construct and direct an exciting and impactful computer science research program and I immediately thought of Judith. I laid my plans with care and began by inviting her to attend our Faculty

T. Hey (✉)
Microsoft Research Connections, One Microsoft Way, Redmond, WA 98052-6399, USA
e-mail: tony.hey@microsoft.com

K.K. Breitman, R.N. Horspool (eds.), *Patterns, Programming and Everything*,
DOI 10.1007/978-1-4471-2350-7, © Springer-Verlag London 2012

Summit, held annually in July in Redmond, Microsoft's main campus near Seattle. After the summit, I raised the idea of Judith joining me in Microsoft Research and building up our collaborative research program with the global computer science community. During the next year, the General Manager, Daron Green, in my group, had a long series of international phone calls with Judith which culminated in her coming to Redmond to interview for the position. I was pleased that she accepted this new challenge.

Since arriving in Microsoft Research, Judith has set about her new task with characteristic vision and energy. Having long ago mastered the art of navigating the complexities of departments and faculties in a university, she has now had to learn a whole new set of skills in navigating the complexities of Microsoft. Not only are there the powerful Business Groups—such as Windows, Office and Xbox—but there are also many other groups in Microsoft who interact with universities in one way or another, with confusing names such as EdPG, DPE, DevDiv and WWPS. It was therefore with some amusement that I went with Judith to her first Company Meeting, held each September at Safeco Field, the home of the Seattle Mariners baseball team. The meeting is a cross between a religious revivalist meeting and rock concert and the contrast with an academic meeting could not be greater. Judith must have wondered what she was getting into!

One of the great things for researchers in Microsoft Research is the possibility of seeing their research end up in a product that is used by millions. However, achieving a successful technology transfer is still something of a black art, even in Microsoft. In the short time that Judith has been at Microsoft Research, her program has managed to achieve this as well as many other positive outcomes. She has visited our Research Labs in Europe, China and India and established great partnerships with many of our research groups. She is still writing of course, and recently contributed to a Microsoft book on parallel programming. With the multicore revolution now upon us, parallel computing is now a necessity and not an option. And, as you would expect, Judith has maintained her connections with the computer science research community outside of Microsoft Research. Besides initiating a new Microsoft Research conference on computer science in Europe, she has been actively involved in chairing and organizing other major computer science conferences. For Judith, coming to Microsoft Research is not just an 'afterword' to her career but a new stage on which she will continue to flourish.

Author Index

K.K. Breitman, R.N. Horspool (eds.), *Patterns, Programming and Everything*,
DOI 10.1007/978-1-4471-2350-7, © Springer-Verlag London 2012

MIX
Papier aus verantwortungsvollen Quellen
Paper from responsible sources
FSC® C105338

If you have any concerns about our products,
you can contact us on
ProductSafety@springernature.com

In case Publisher is established outside the EU,
the EU authorized representative is:
Springer Nature Customer Service Center GmbH
Europaplatz 3, 69115 Heidelberg, Germany

Printed by Libri Plureos GmbH
in Hamburg, Germany